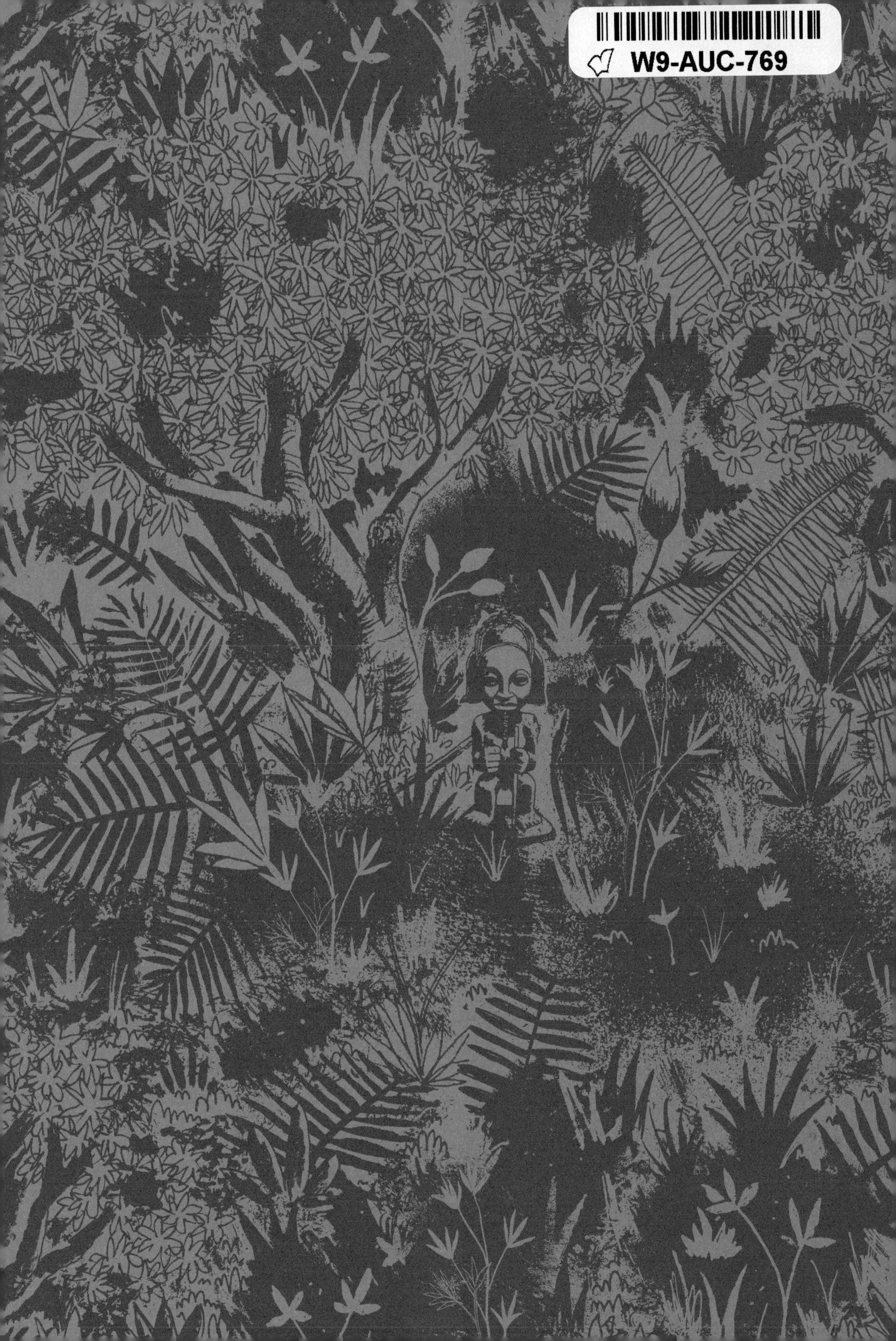

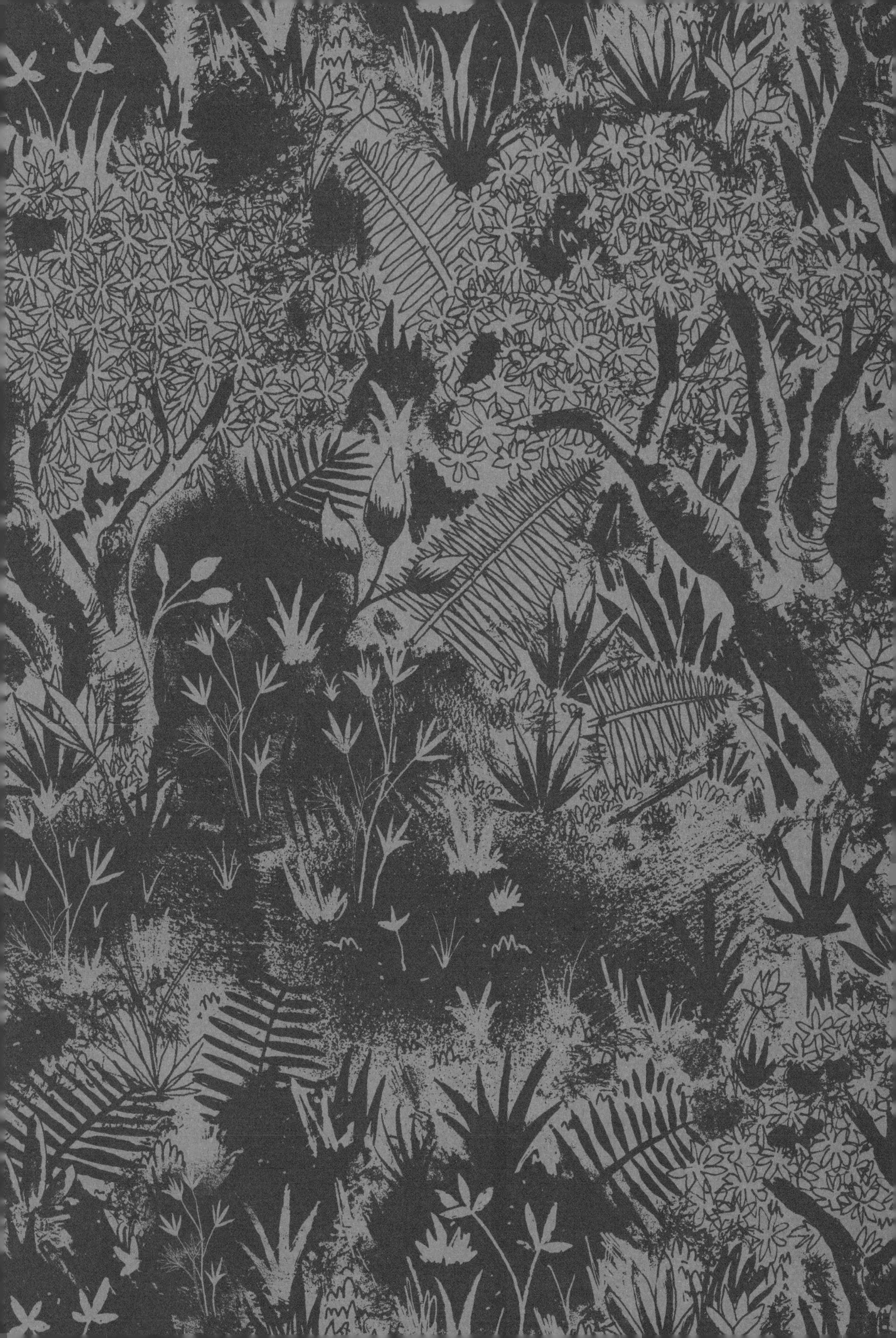

RUN FOR IT

——

STORIES OF SLAVES WHO FOUGHT
FOR THEIR FREEDOM

——

Marcelo D´Salete

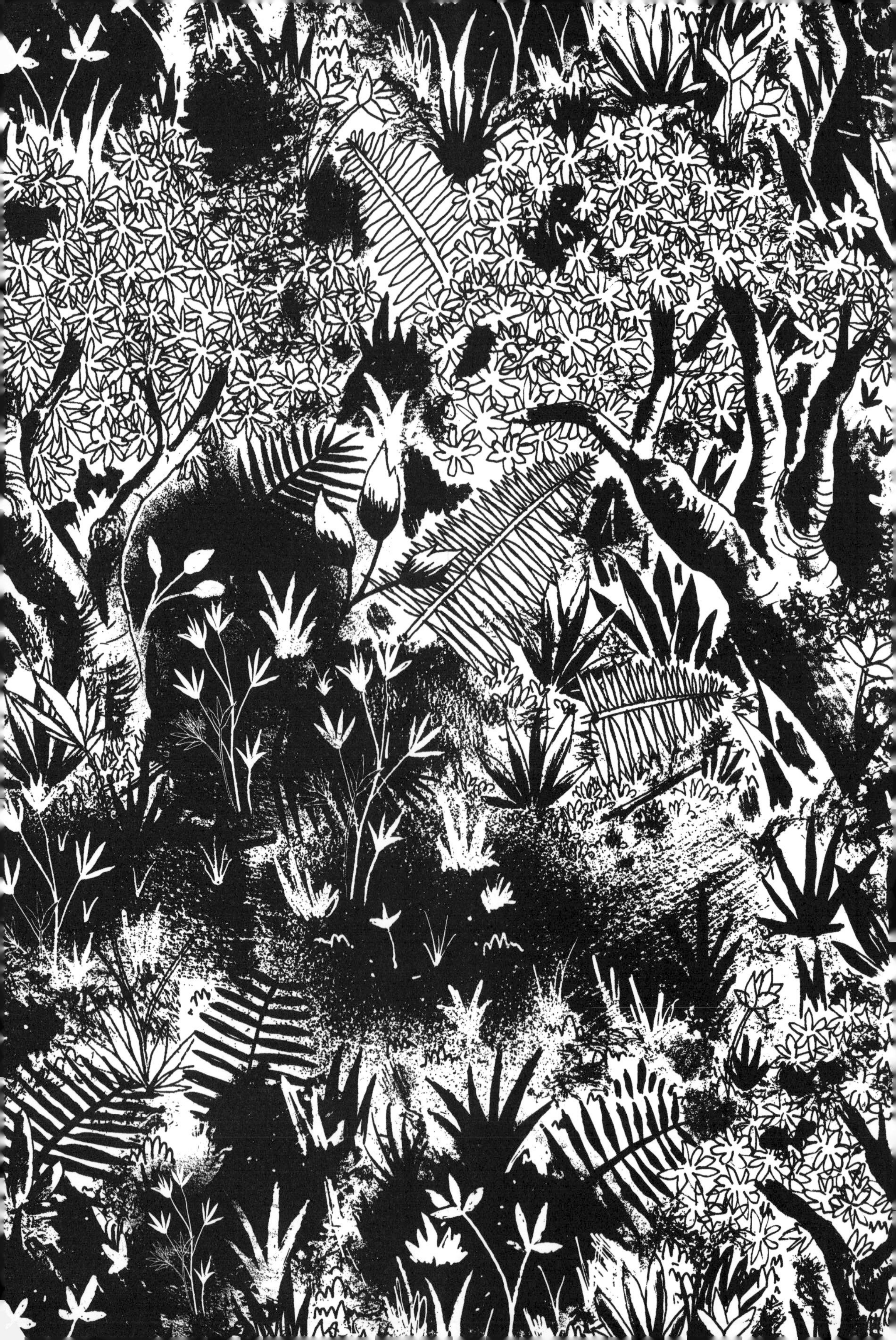

RUN FOR IT

MARCELO D´SALETE

Translator: Andrea Rosenberg
Editor: Kristy Valenti
Designer: Sean David Williams
Supervising Editor: Gary Groth
Production: Paul Baresh
Editorial Assistants: RJ Casey, Mackenzie Pitcock, Heidi Swenson
Associate Publisher: Eric Reynolds
Publisher: Gary Groth

 Fantagraphics Books, Inc. 7563 Lake City Way NE, Seattle, WA 98115 (800) 657-1100 www.fantagraphics.com. Follow us on Twitter @fantagraphics and on Facebook.com/Fantagraphics.

The author thanks Brisa Batista, Alaide, Allan da Rosa, and Matheus Gato.

ISBN: 978-1-68396-049-2
Library of Congress Control Number: 2017938231

First Printing: October 2017
Printed In China

CONTENTS

INTRODUCTION

RUN FOR IT (*Cumbe*) tells stories of black resistance to Brazilian slavery (1500s–1800s). Many Africans and their descendants rebelled; both directly, by running away to escapee settlements known as mocambos, and indirectly, in the small acts of everyday insurrection on the plantations—which demonstrate the tensions inherent in a society shaped by violence. These stories, some of which are inspired by historical documents, offer an opportunity to reflect on that world.

The word *cumbe* is a term used in some Latin American countries to refer to settlements on the Brazilian hinterlands inhabited by people of African descent, primarily runaway slaves. According to singer and historian Nei Lopes, it comes from the Kimbundu word *kumbi*, which is related to the Umbundu *ekumbi*, "sun." In the Congo-Angola languages, it also means day, fire, the force inherent in kings' power, and the way to trace and understand life and history.

THE SUN RISES ON BRAZILIAN BANTU CULTURE

IN THE PERIOD OF SLAVERY, millions of Bantus were forcibly transported to Brazil, especially from regions that are today part of Congo and Angola. The Bantu influence abounds in Brazilian life, whether in the religious or ritual realm; the aesthetic realm of music and the dramatic, literary, and visual arts; or the everyday realm of the gestures, uses, functions, and meanings given to countless objects, at home or on the streets, and in the ethics and values of much of the Brazilian population (which, by the way, is also the case in a number of other countries in the Americas).

The Bantu presence was constantly echoed in everyday interactions with free, poor comrades; in open conflicts between hostile players; and in the resistance to the shackles placed around people's necks, wrists, chests, and minds. Whether maintaining its African characteristics or interacting according to principles and paths dictated by Judeo-Christian norms, Bantu culture structured societies in Palmares and many other escaped slave settlements in a number of remote areas of Brazil, far from contemporary urban milieux. It shaped the black community's dances, courting, and martial arts. They strove to maintain their own ways of living and to fight the racism undergirding every relationship—economic and institutional alike—at a federal or municipal level, in neighborhoods, and even in the bed and in the yard.

The stories in this book trace visual marks that are significant in the Bantu universe, such as the circle and the crossroads, which is both a place and between places, a point of power. There are patterns that evoke the mysteries and the pedagogies of Africanness, such as the enigmatic images of animals with symbolic power and the references to majestic statues in warrior poses. The dramas that play out in the panels of Marcelo D'Salete's stories introduce characters and contexts that slide across or dive into the bilge of madness, pain, passion, masculinist obsession, and the contradictions associated with emotional and sexual involvement with whites; people dancing to the beat of their own moral drum inside the discord of slavery, tripping on the threads of revolt, and standing upright atop the pillar of vengeance. In that web of stories thrums a growing, collective political movement that has a vital role in organizing shelters and engaging in armed combat against the forces of slavery, a movement intertwined with the precarious stability and joy of minuscule, marginal resistance, with personal relationships simmered in the waters of exhausted dreams.

—Allan da Rosa, Angolan writer and teacher

Kalunga

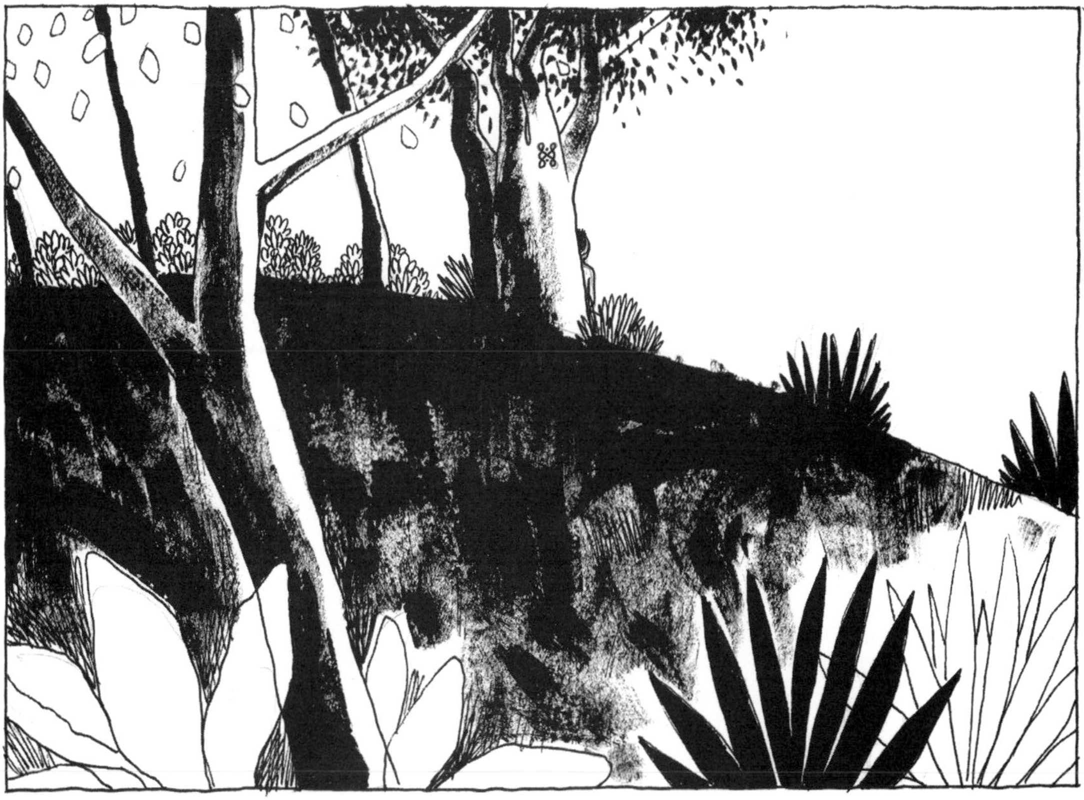

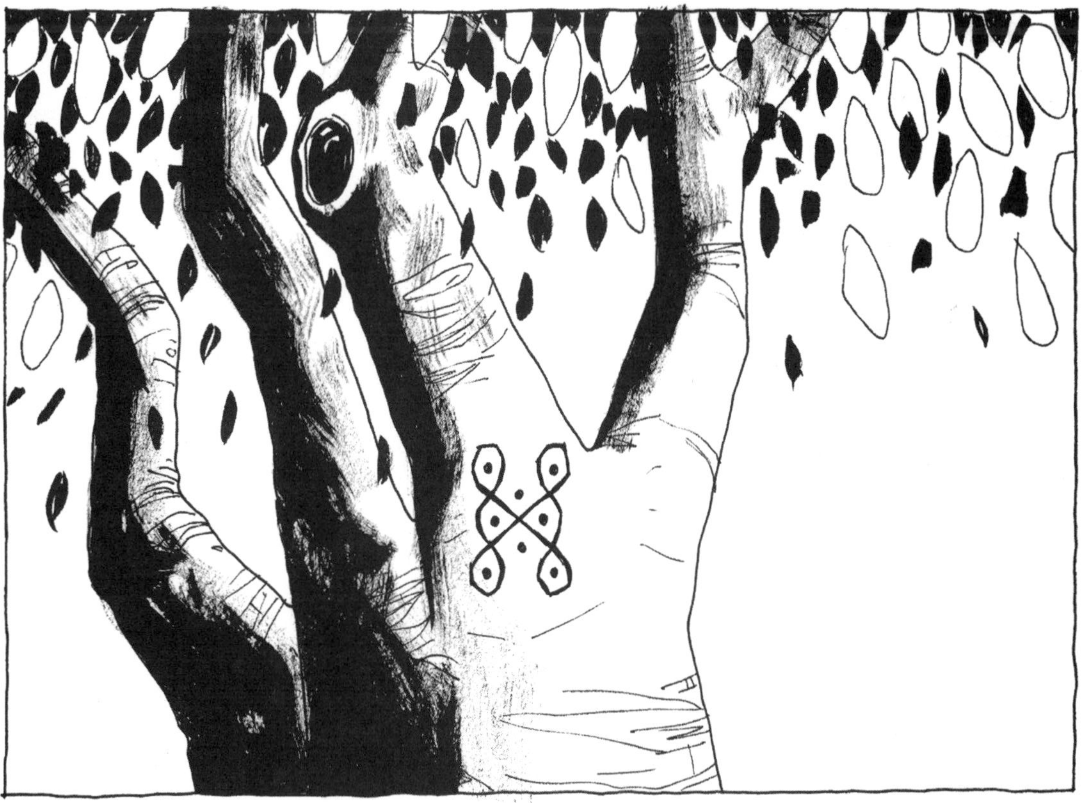

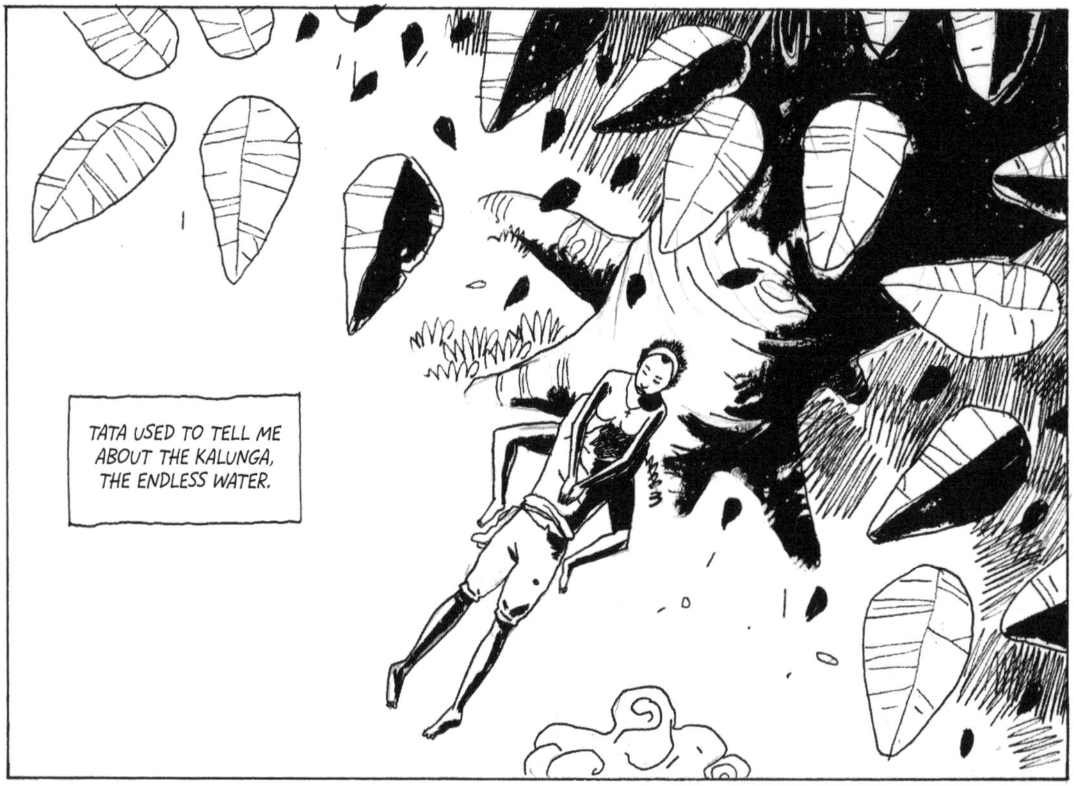
TATA USED TO TELL ME ABOUT THE KALUNGA, THE ENDLESS WATER.

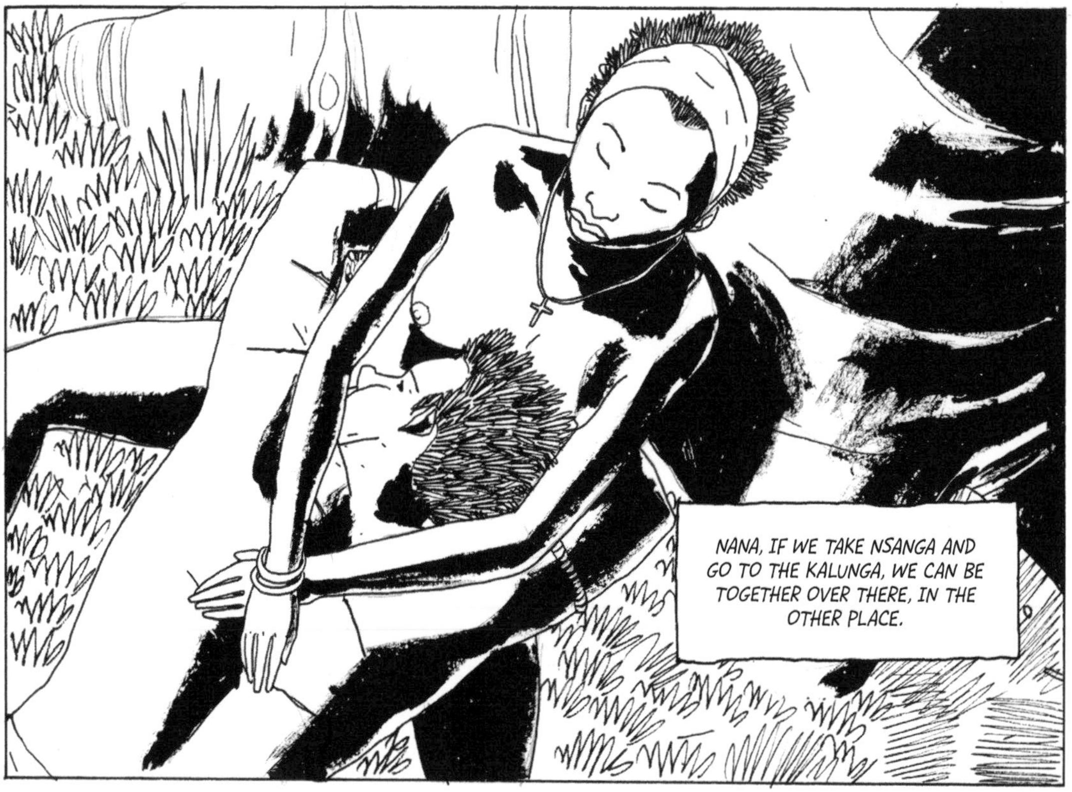
NANA, IF WE TAKE NSANGA AND GO TO THE KALUNGA, WE CAN BE TOGETHER OVER THERE, IN THE OTHER PLACE.

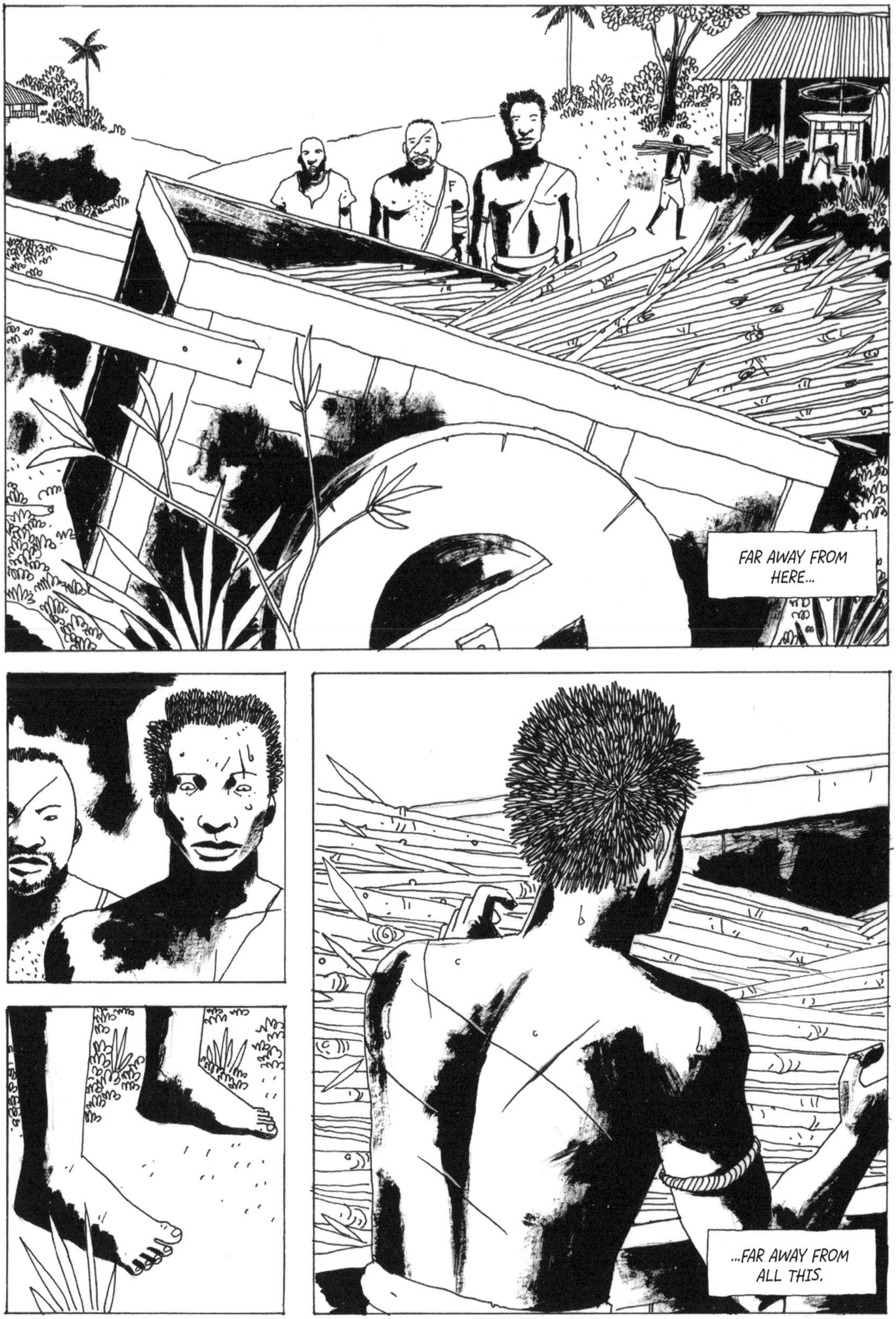
FAR AWAY FROM HERE...
...FAR AWAY FROM ALL THIS.

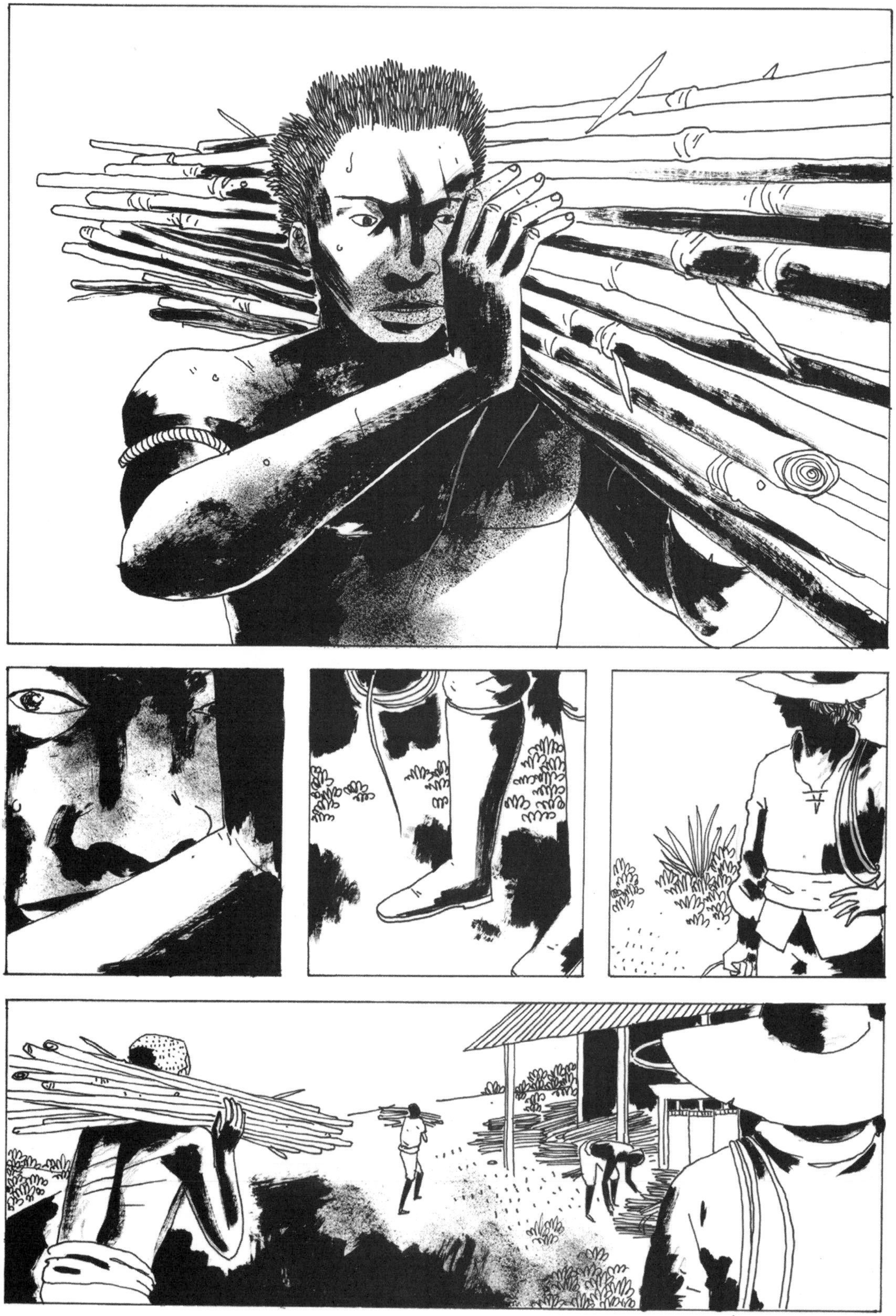

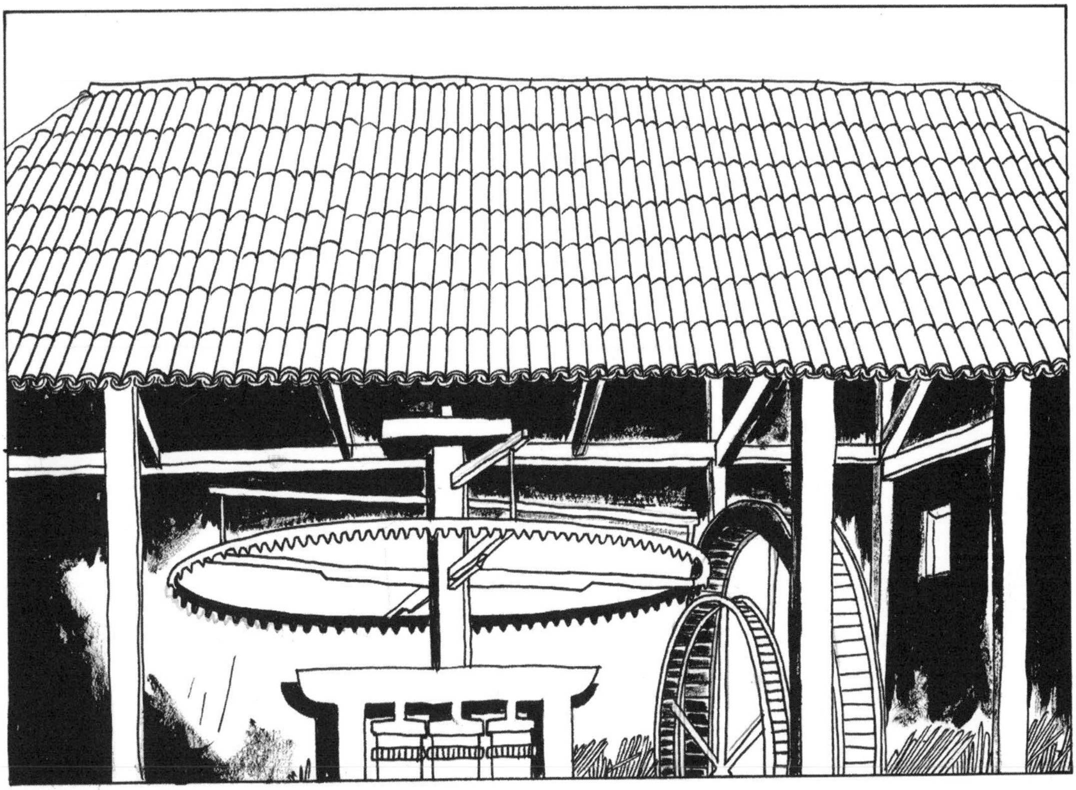

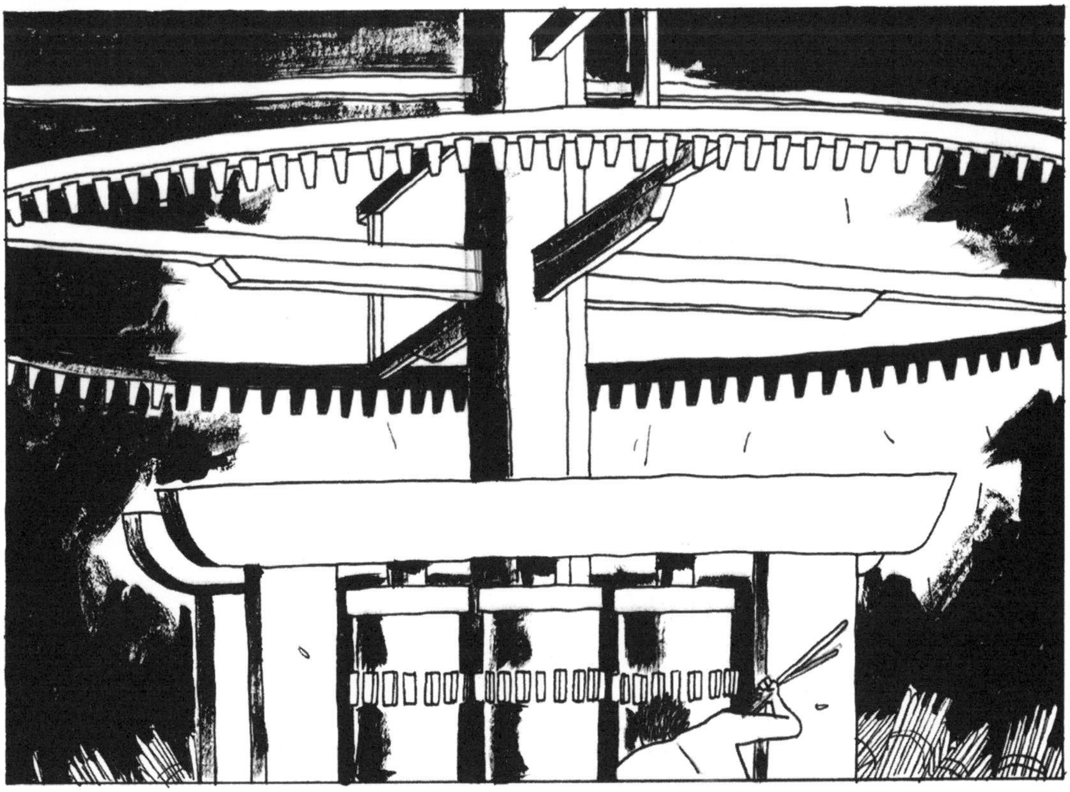

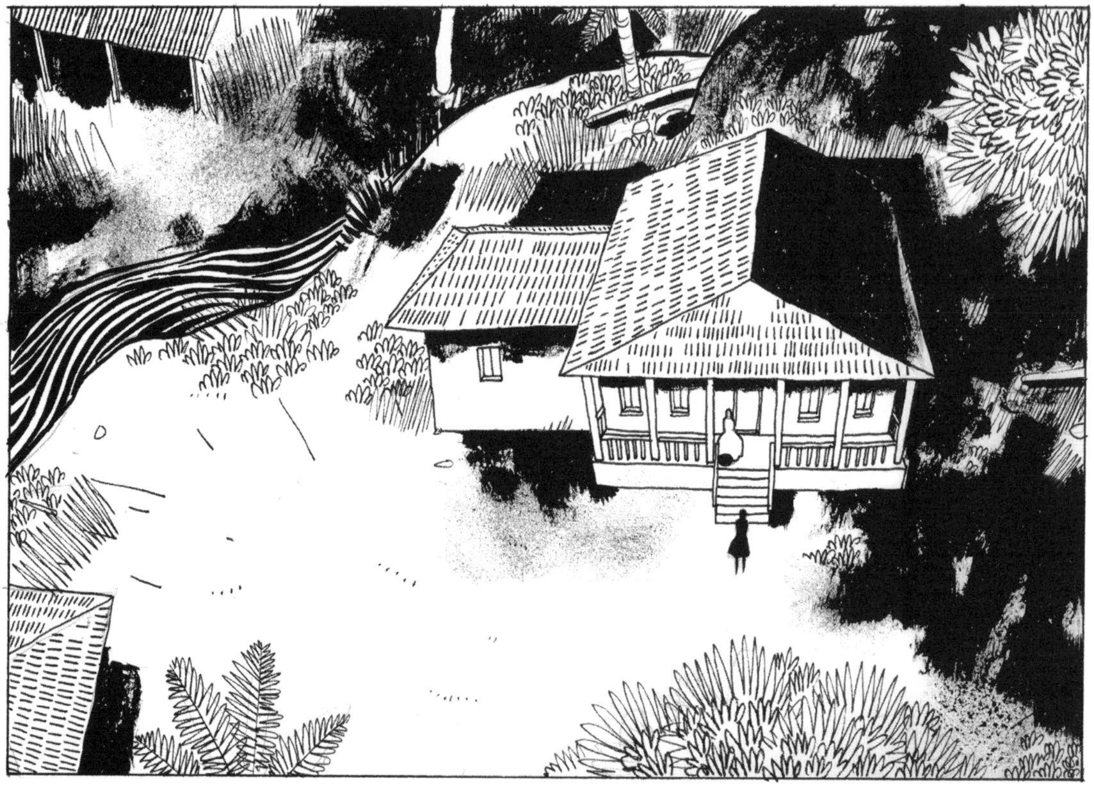

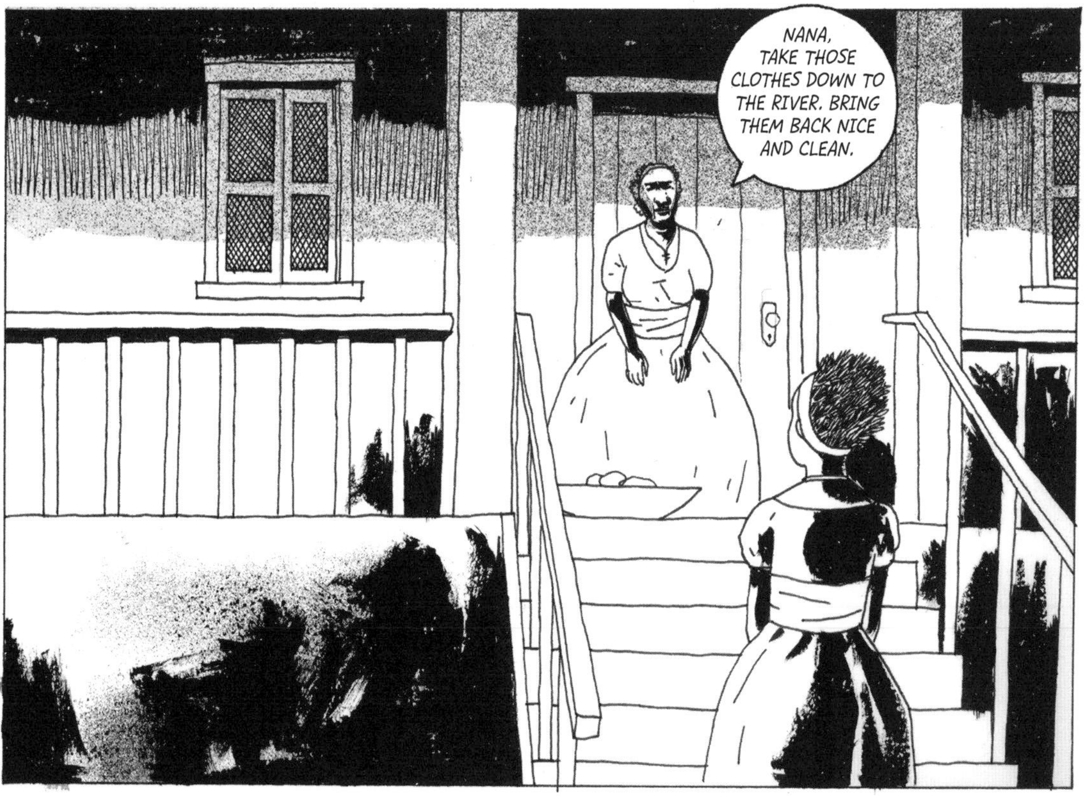
NANA, TAKE THOSE CLOTHES DOWN TO THE RIVER. BRING THEM BACK NICE AND CLEAN.

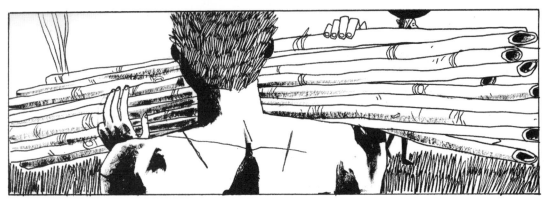

GET OVER HERE, BLACK BOY!

17

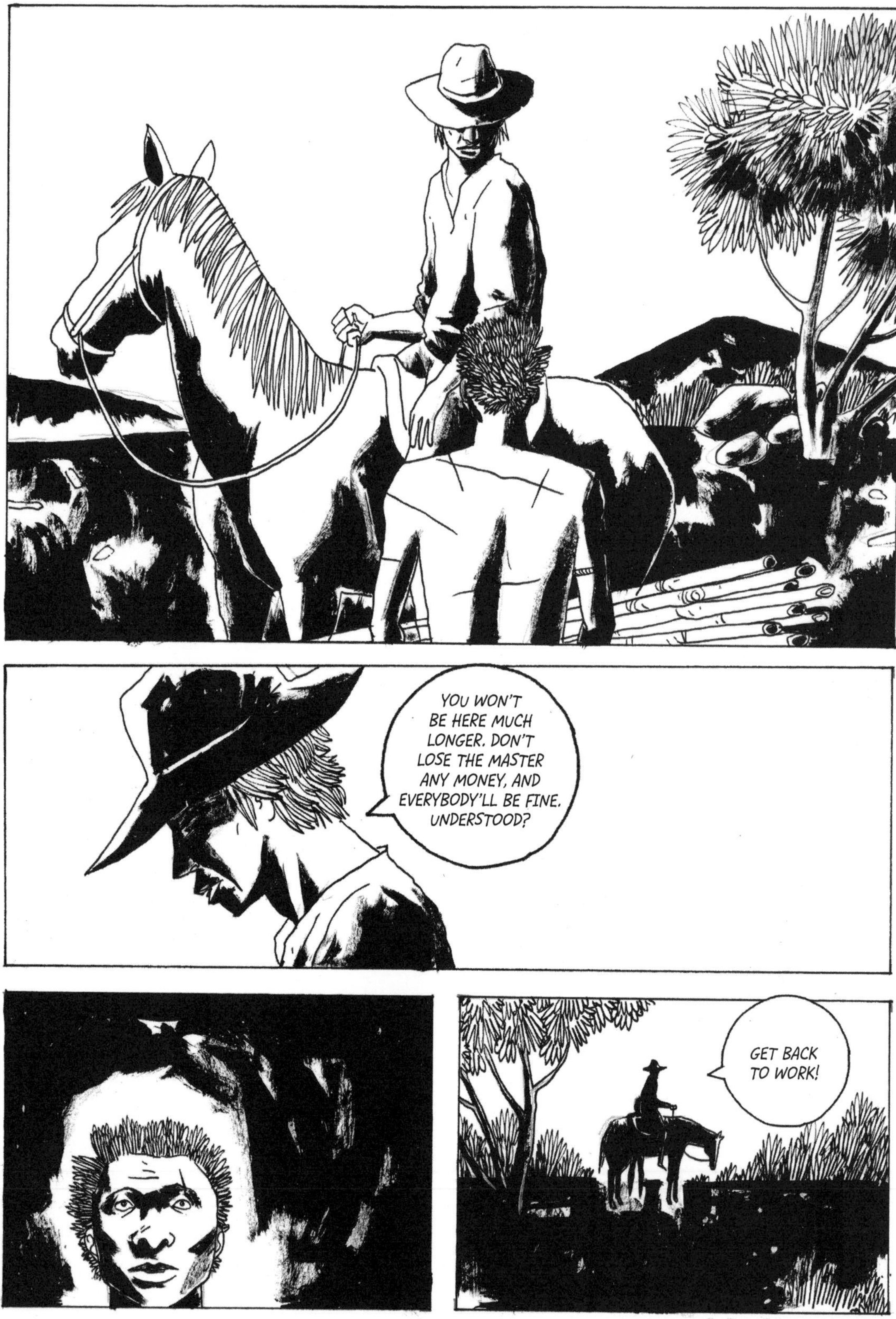
YOU WON'T BE HERE MUCH LONGER. DON'T LOSE THE MASTER ANY MONEY, AND EVERYBODY'LL BE FINE. UNDERSTOOD?
GET BACK TO WORK!

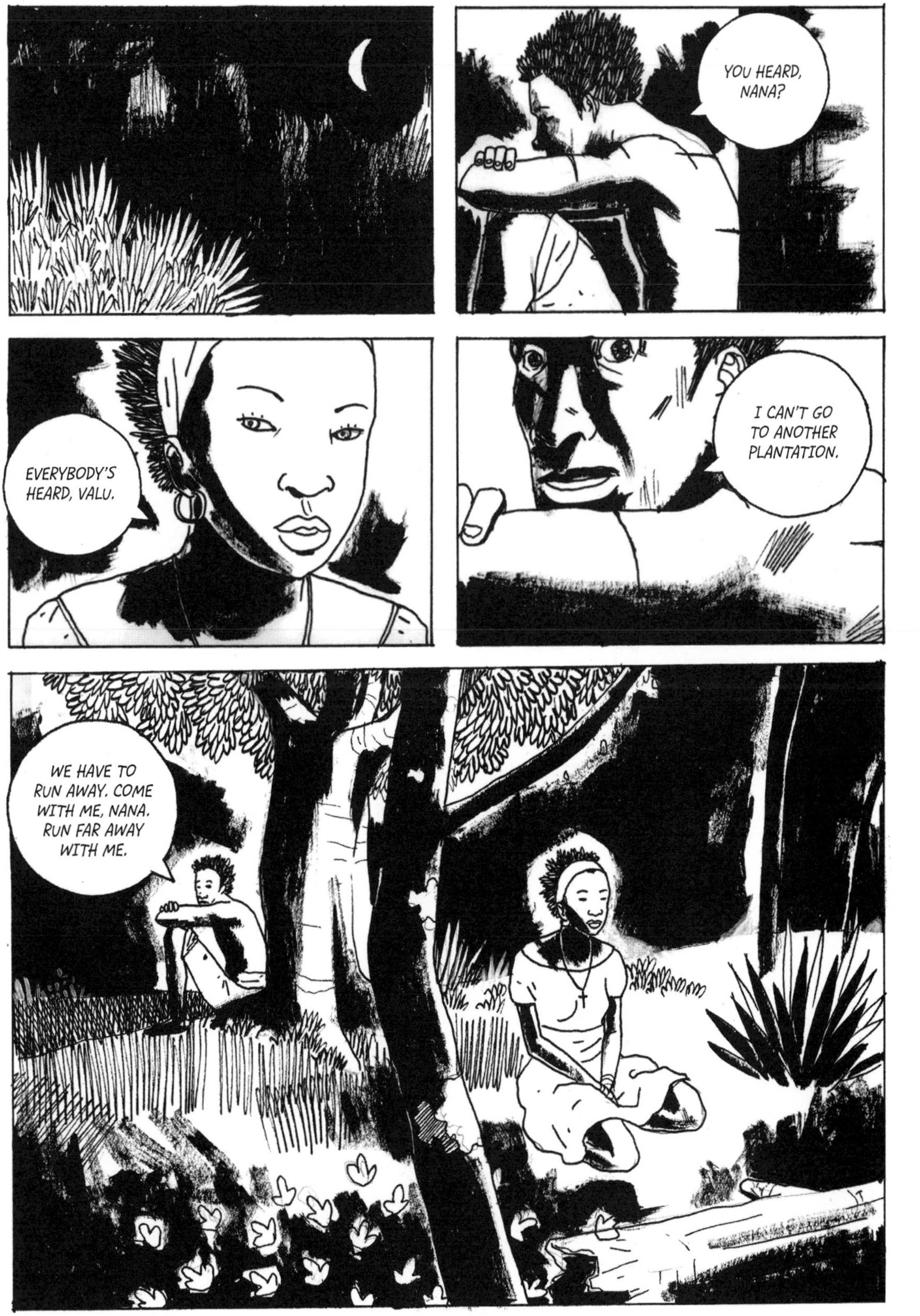
YOU HEARD, NANA?
EVERYBODY'S HEARD, VALU.
I CAN'T GO TO ANOTHER PLANTATION.
WE HAVE TO RUN AWAY. COME WITH ME, NANA. RUN FAR AWAY WITH ME.

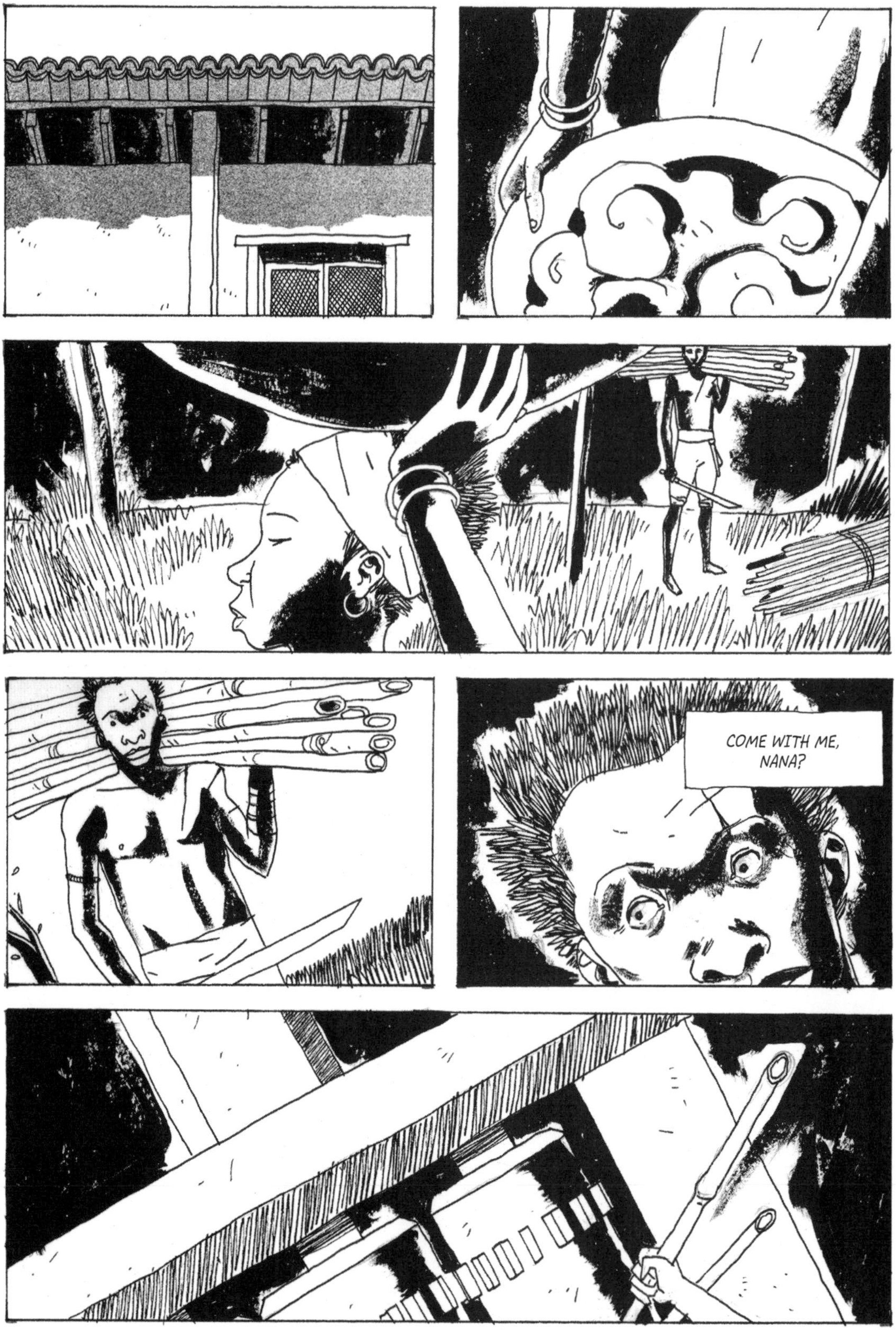
COME WITH ME,
NANA?

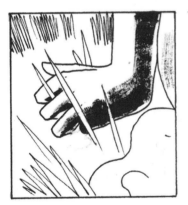

COME WITH ME?

I WAKE UP AND START WORKING. I EAT AND KEEP WORKING.

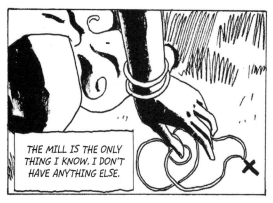

THE MILL IS THE ONLY THING I KNOW. I DON'T HAVE ANYTHING ELSE.

YOU'RE ALL I HAVE, NANA. YOU'RE MINE— YOU HAVE TO COME WITH ME.

AND FLEE THROUGH THE WILDERNESS, VALU? I WON'T MAKE IT.

YOU DON'T HAVE SCARS FROM BEING WHIPPED, NANA. YOU MAY NOT KNOW THE LAND THE WAY OTHERS DO, BUT YOU CAN STILL RUN.

THEY KNOW ME IN THE BIG HOUSE. THEY'RE GOOD TO ME.

NANA...

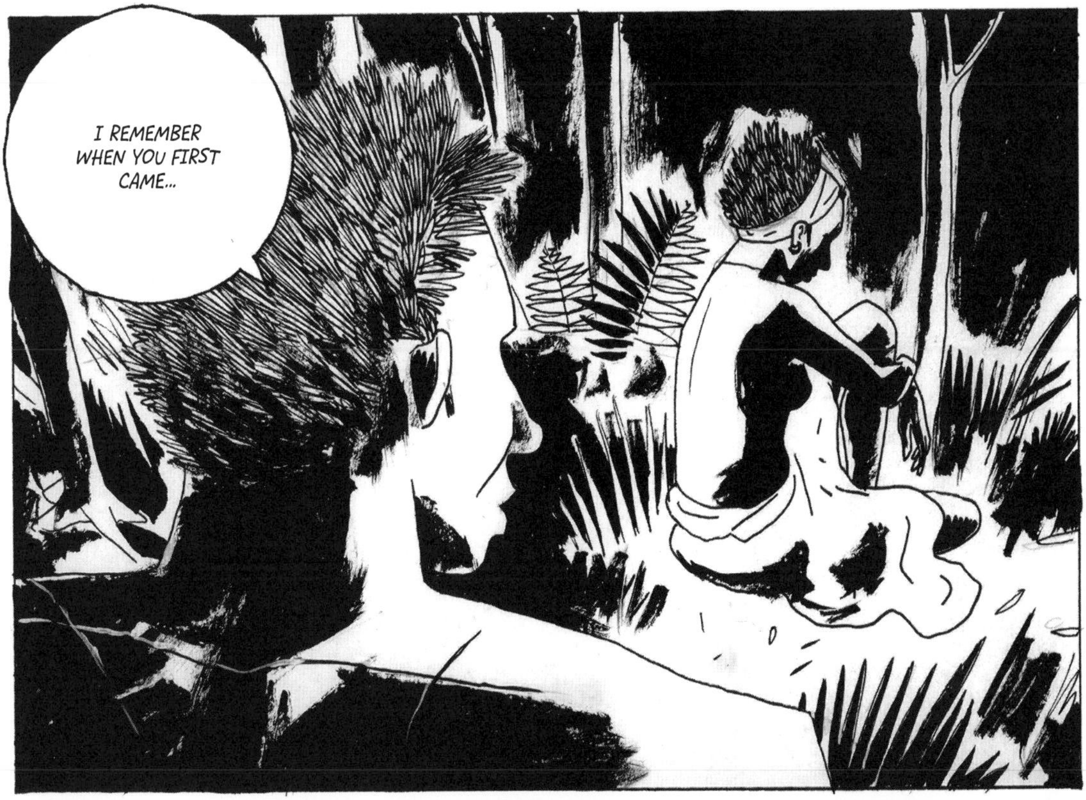
I REMEMBER WHEN YOU FIRST CAME...

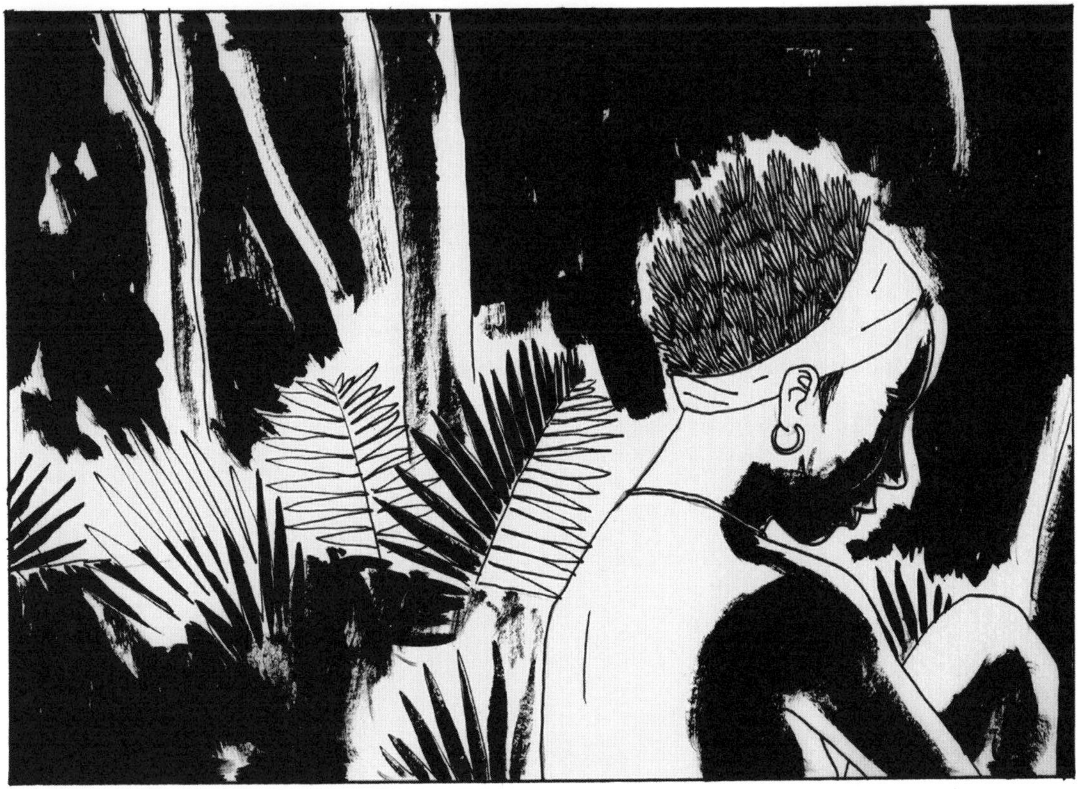

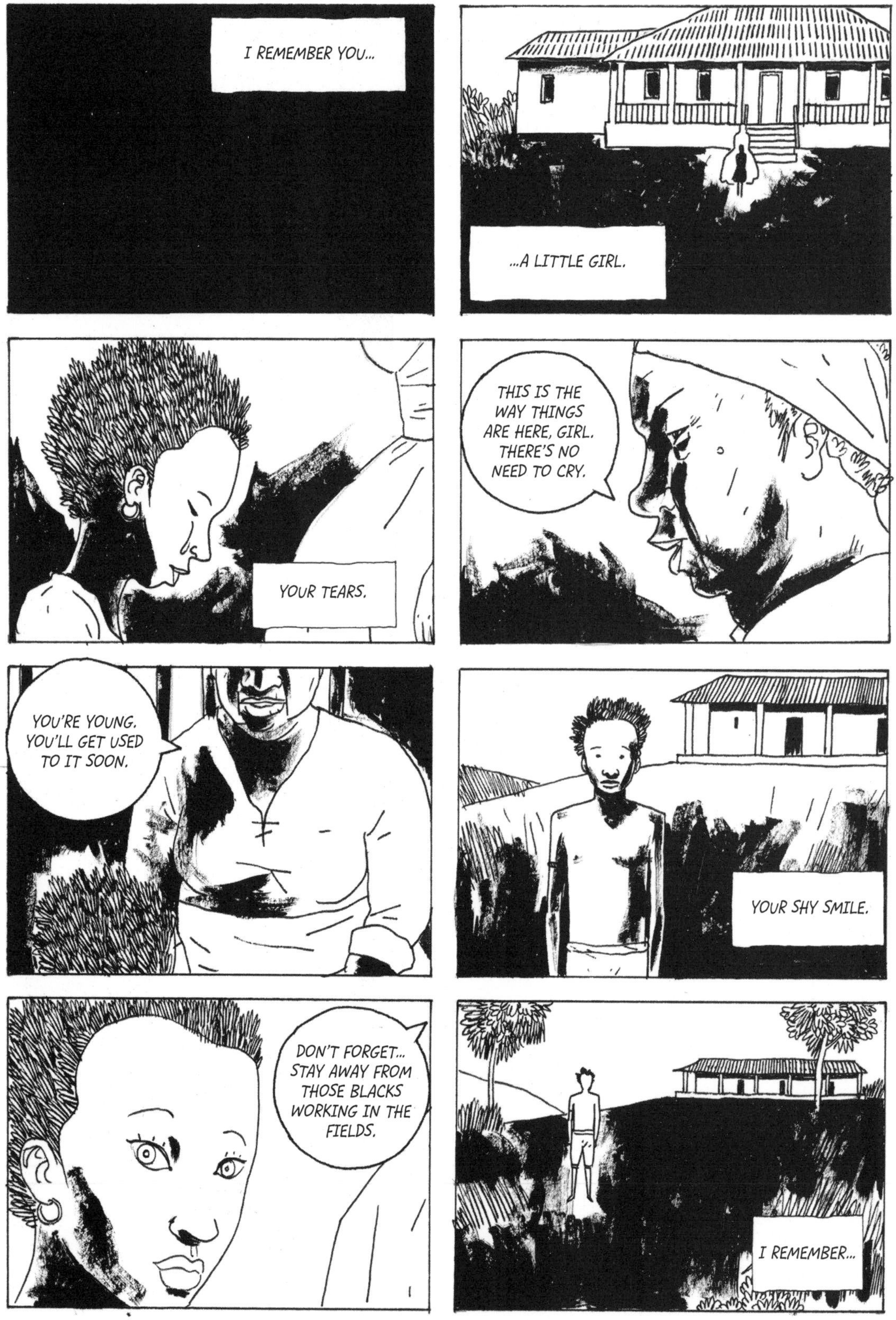
I REMEMBER YOU...
...A LITTLE GIRL.
YOUR TEARS.
THIS IS THE WAY THINGS ARE HERE, GIRL. THERE'S NO NEED TO CRY.
YOU'RE YOUNG. YOU'LL GET USED TO IT SOON.
YOUR SHY SMILE.
DON'T FORGET... STAY AWAY FROM THOSE BLACKS WORKING IN THE FIELDS.
I REMEMBER...

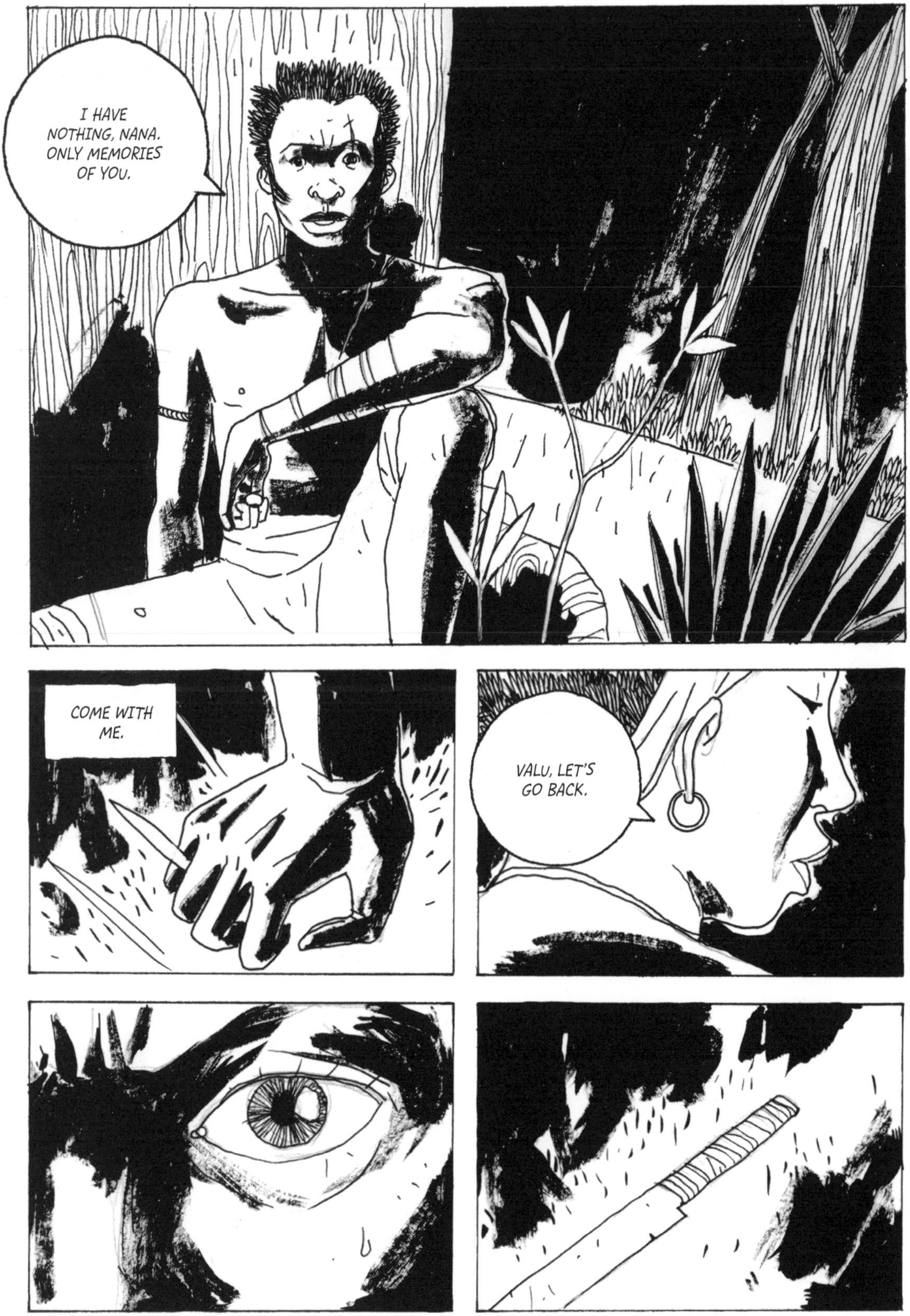
I HAVE NOTHING, NANA. ONLY MEMORIES OF YOU.
COME WITH ME.
VALU, LET'S GO BACK.

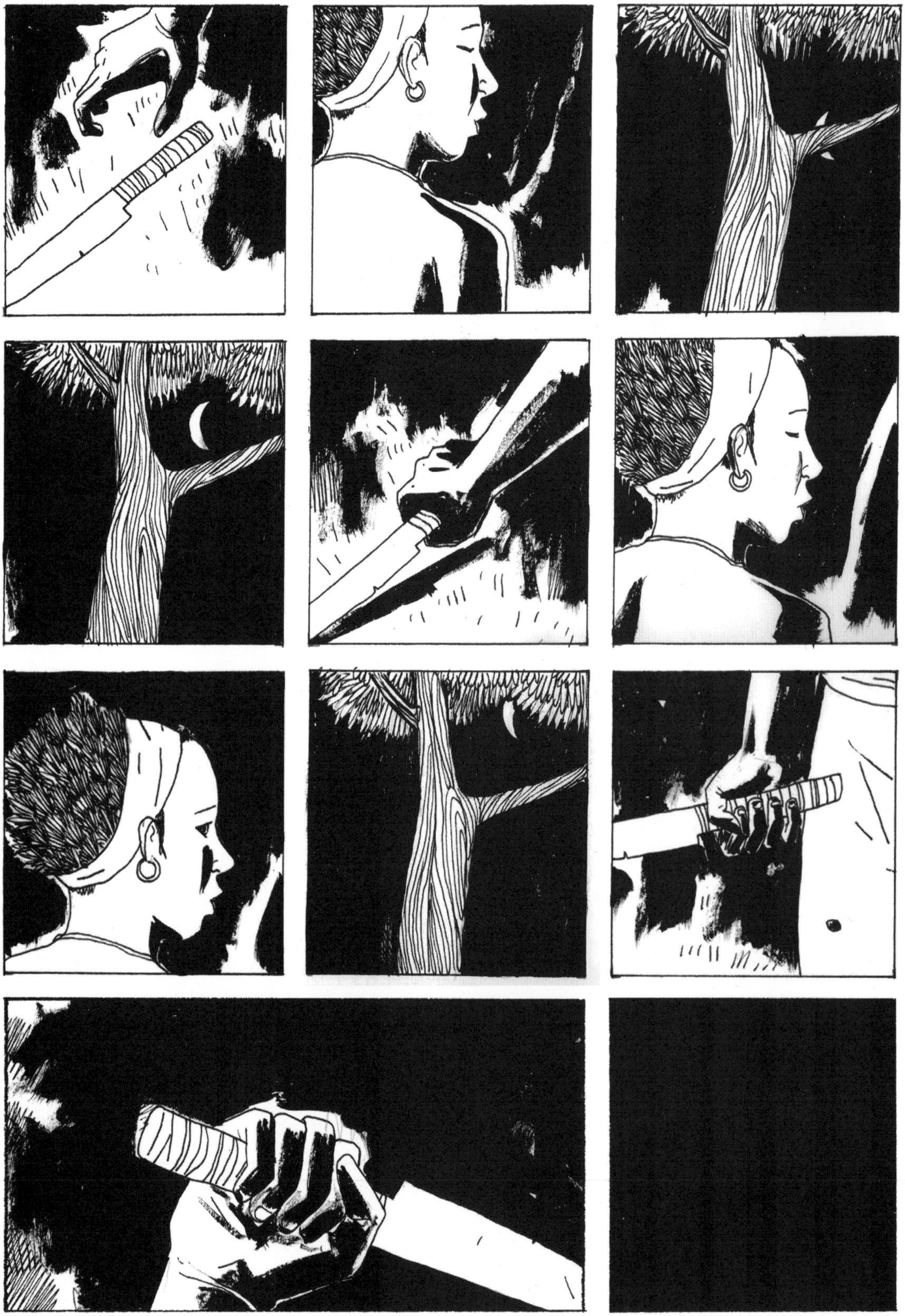

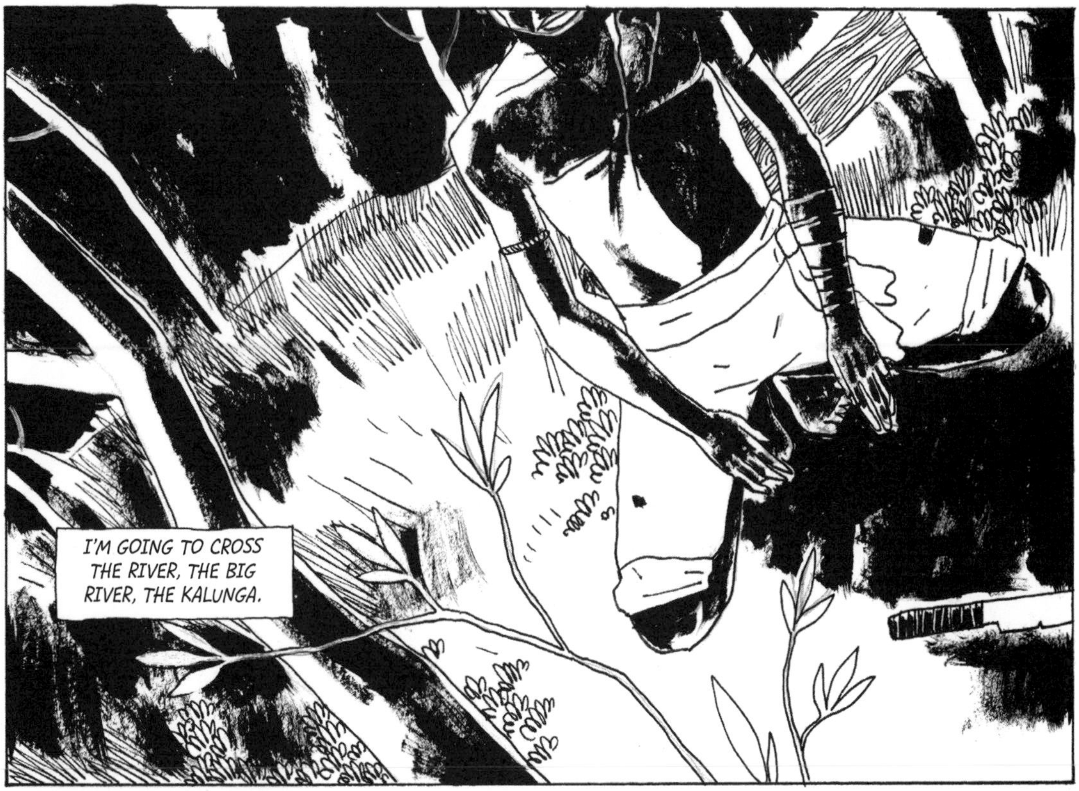
I'M GOING TO CROSS THE RIVER, THE BIG RIVER, THE KALUNGA.

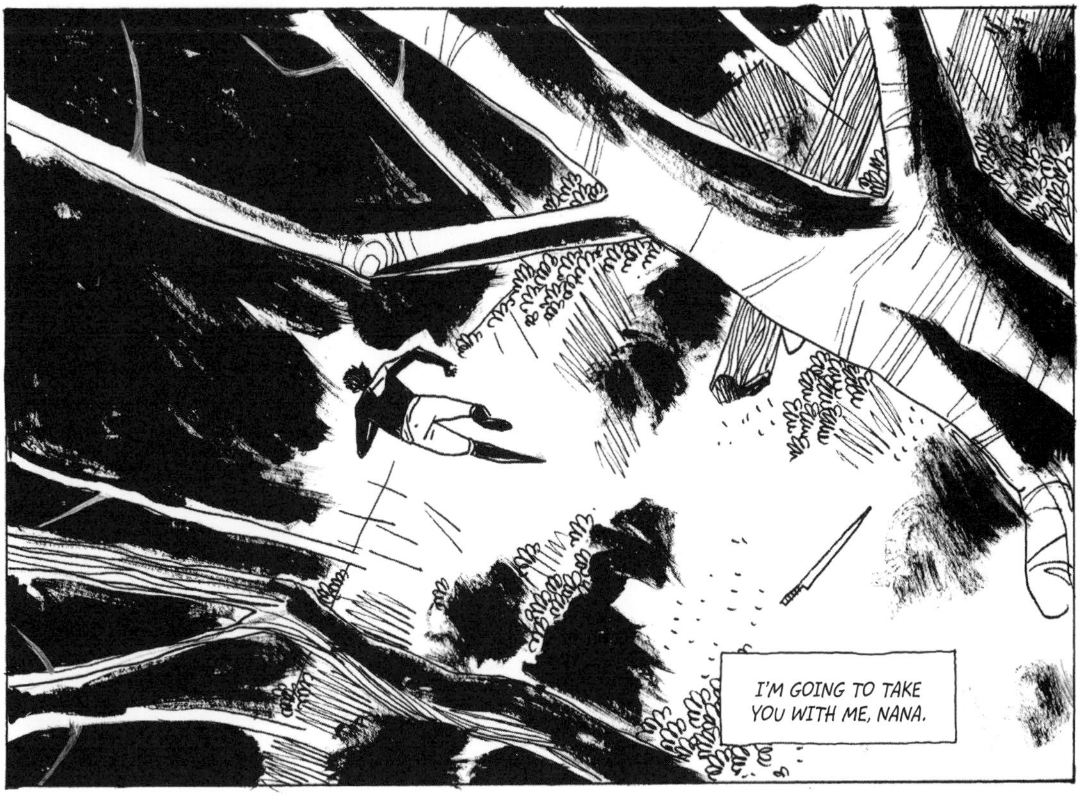
I'M GOING TO TAKE YOU WITH ME, NANA.

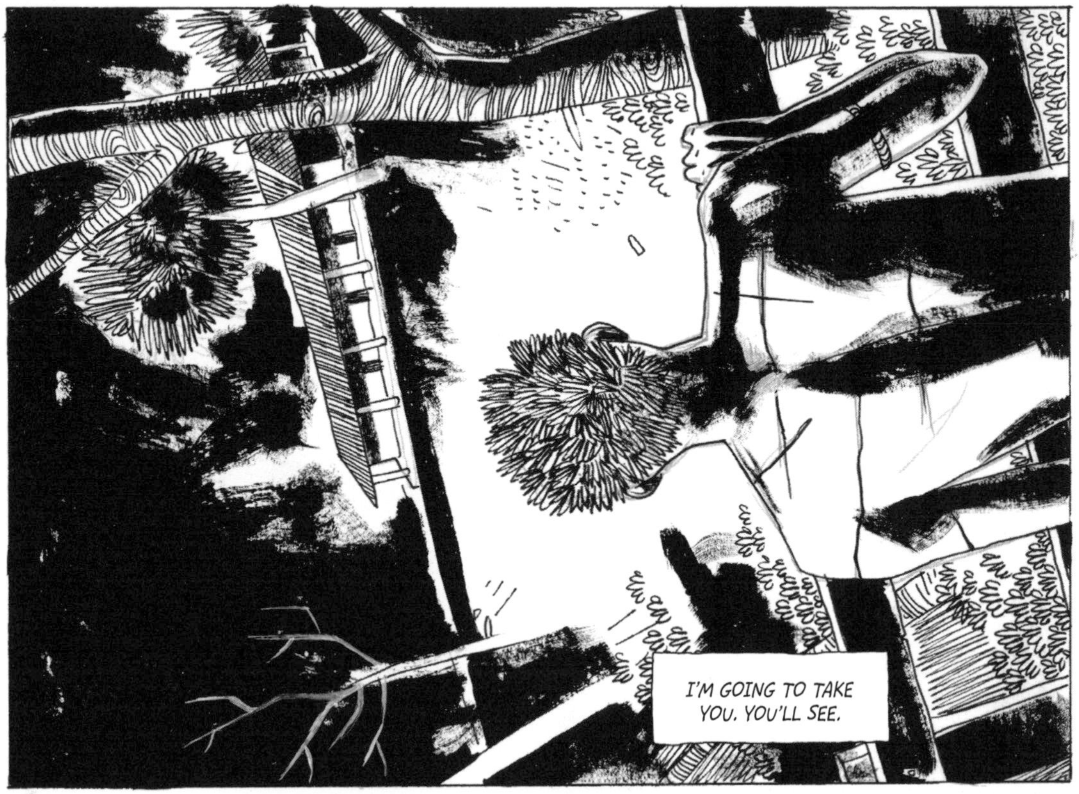
I'M GOING TO TAKE YOU. YOU'LL SEE.

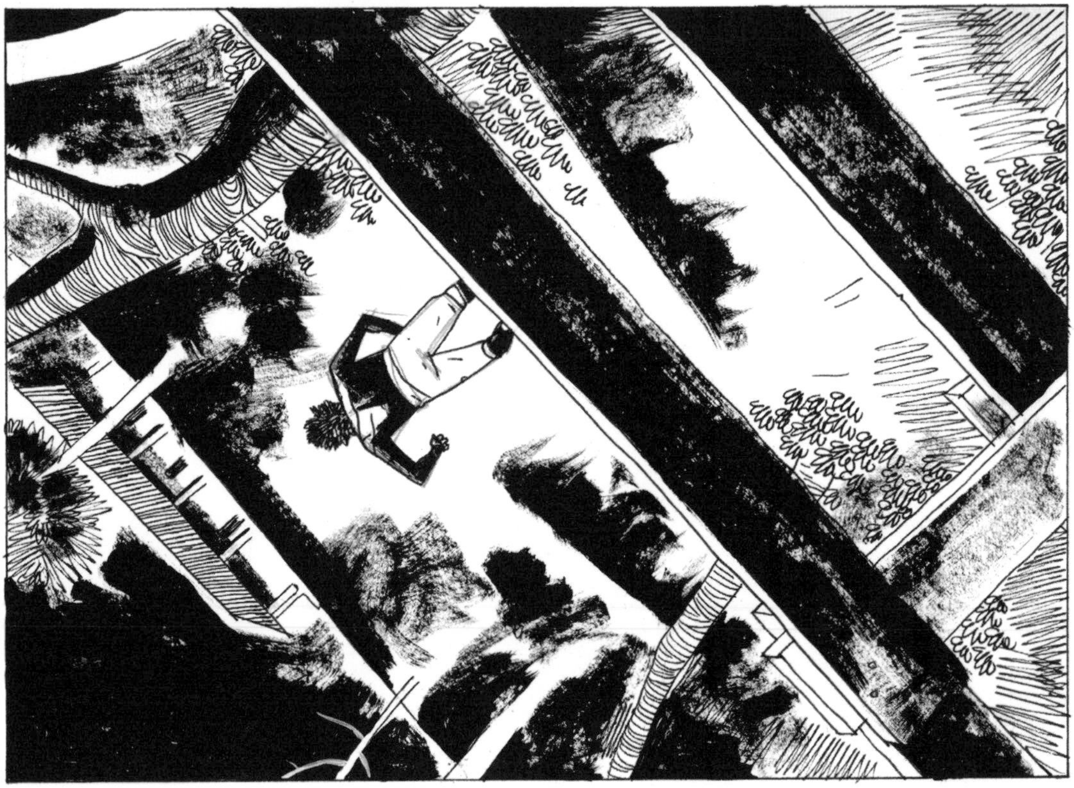

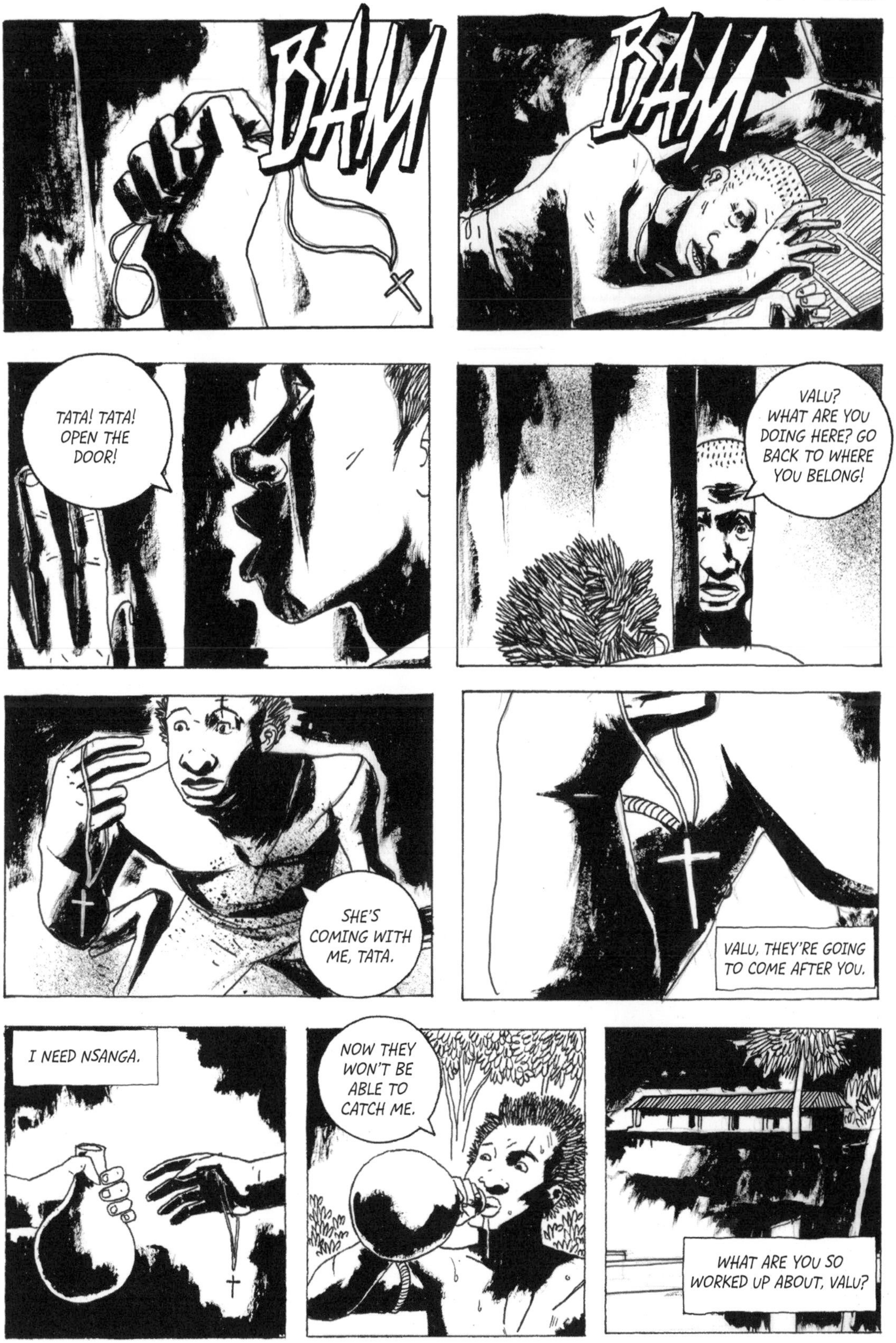
BAM
BAM
TATA! TATA! OPEN THE DOOR!
VALU? WHAT ARE YOU DOING HERE? GO BACK TO WHERE YOU BELONG!
SHE'S COMING WITH ME, TATA.
VALU, THEY'RE GOING TO COME AFTER YOU.
I NEED NSANGA.
NOW THEY WON'T BE ABLE TO CATCH ME.
WHAT ARE YOU SO WORKED UP ABOUT, VALU?

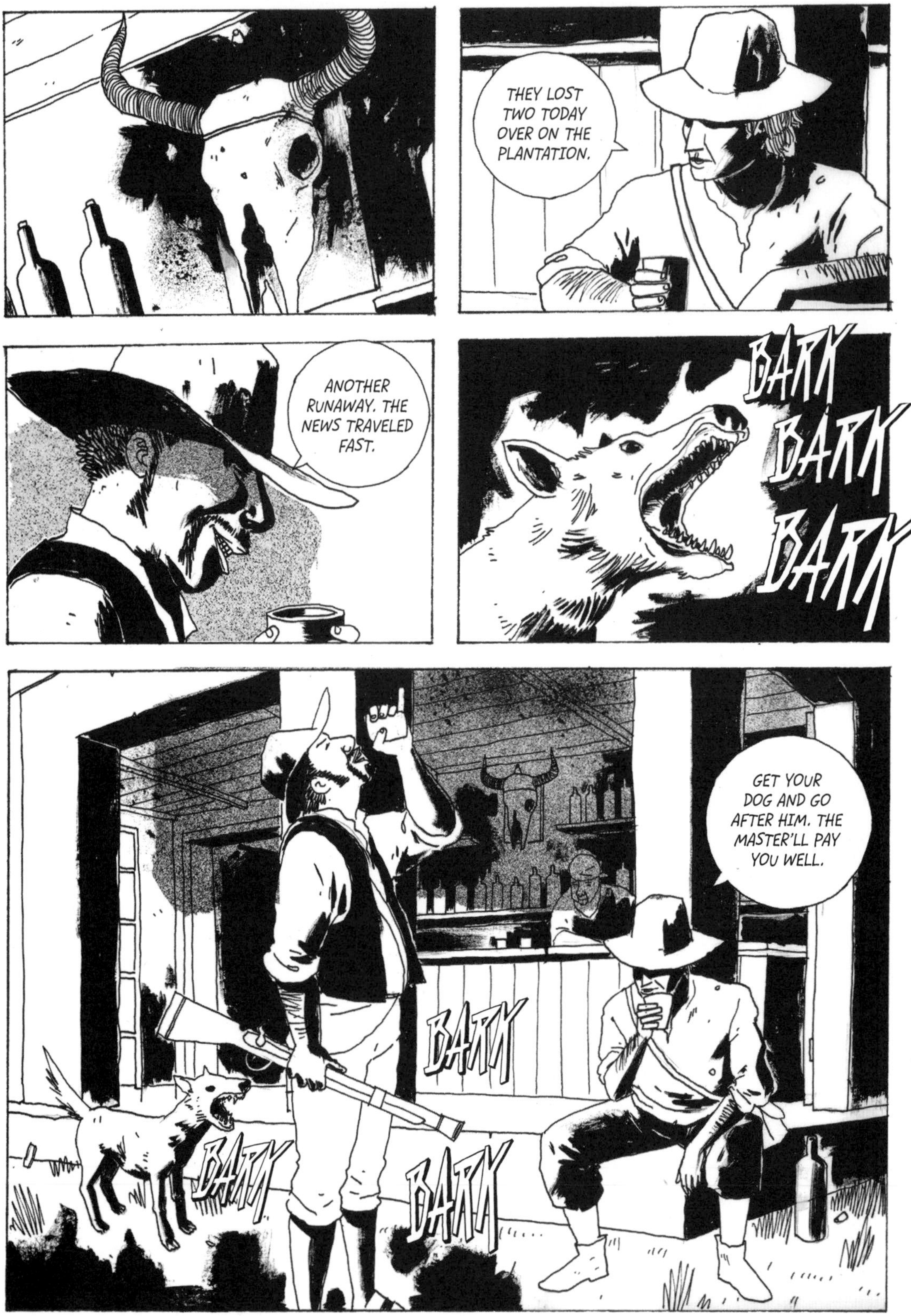
THEY LOST TWO TODAY OVER ON THE PLANTATION.
ANOTHER RUNAWAY. THE NEWS TRAVELED FAST.
BARK
BARK
BARK
GET YOUR DOG AND GO AFTER HIM. THE MASTER'LL PAY YOU WELL.
BARK
BARK
BARK

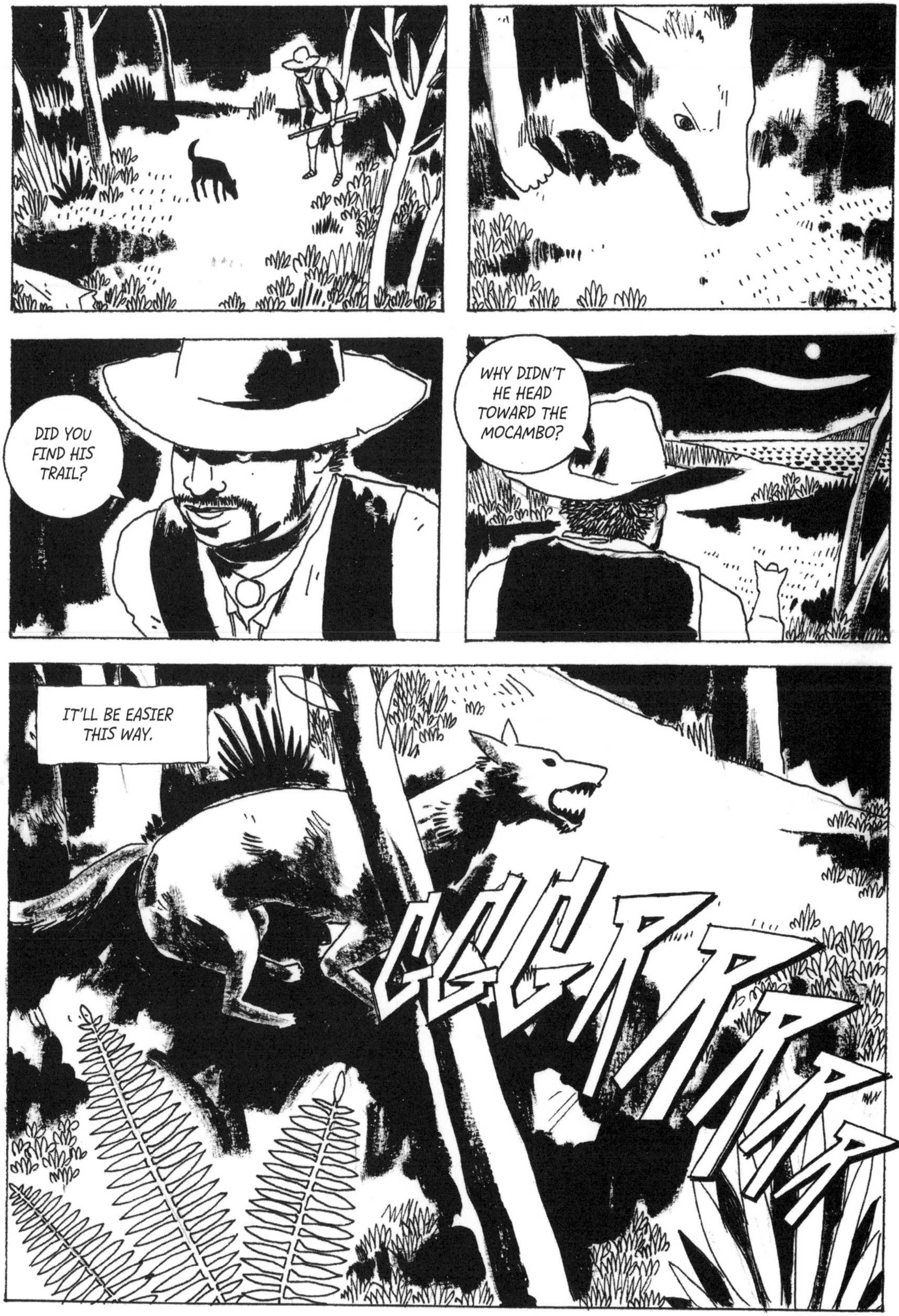

DID YOU FIND HIS TRAIL?
WHY DIDN'T HE HEAD TOWARD THE MOCAMBO?
IT'LL BE EASIER THIS WAY.
GGGRRRRR

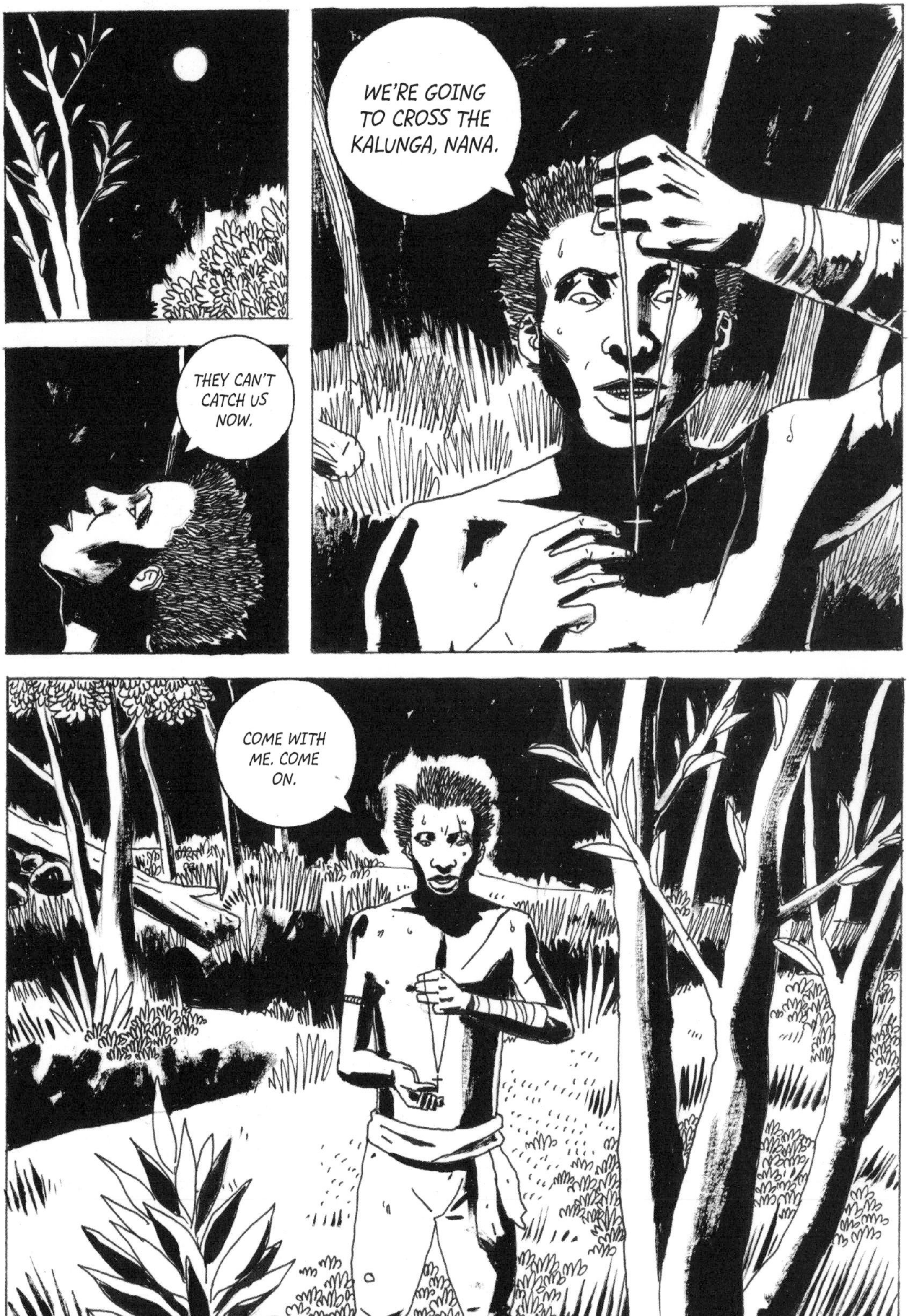
THEY CAN'T CATCH US NOW.
WE'RE GOING TO CROSS THE KALUNGA, NANA.
COME WITH ME. COME ON.

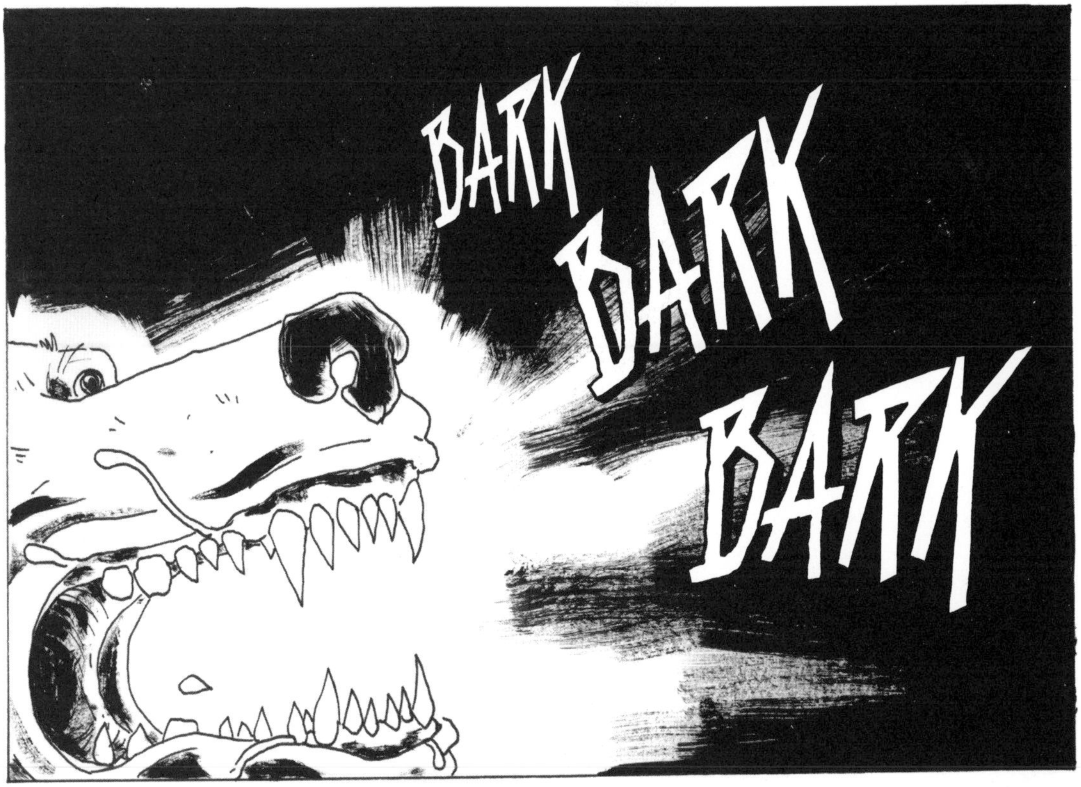
BARK
BARK
BARK

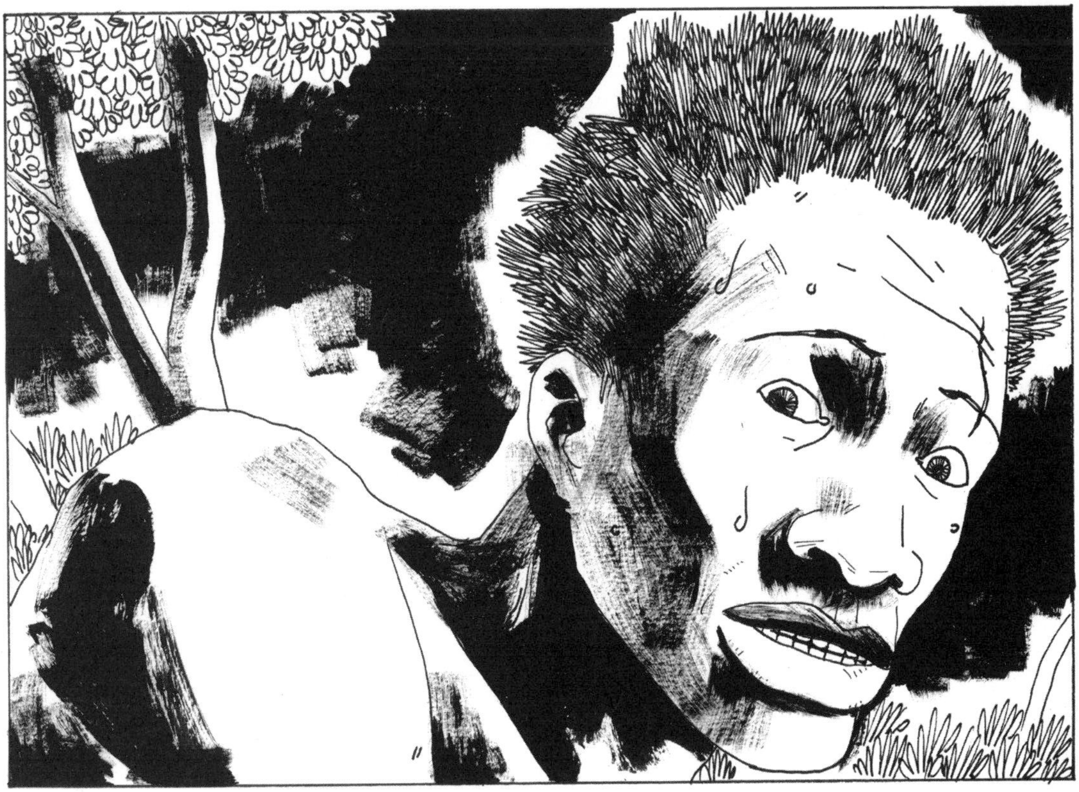

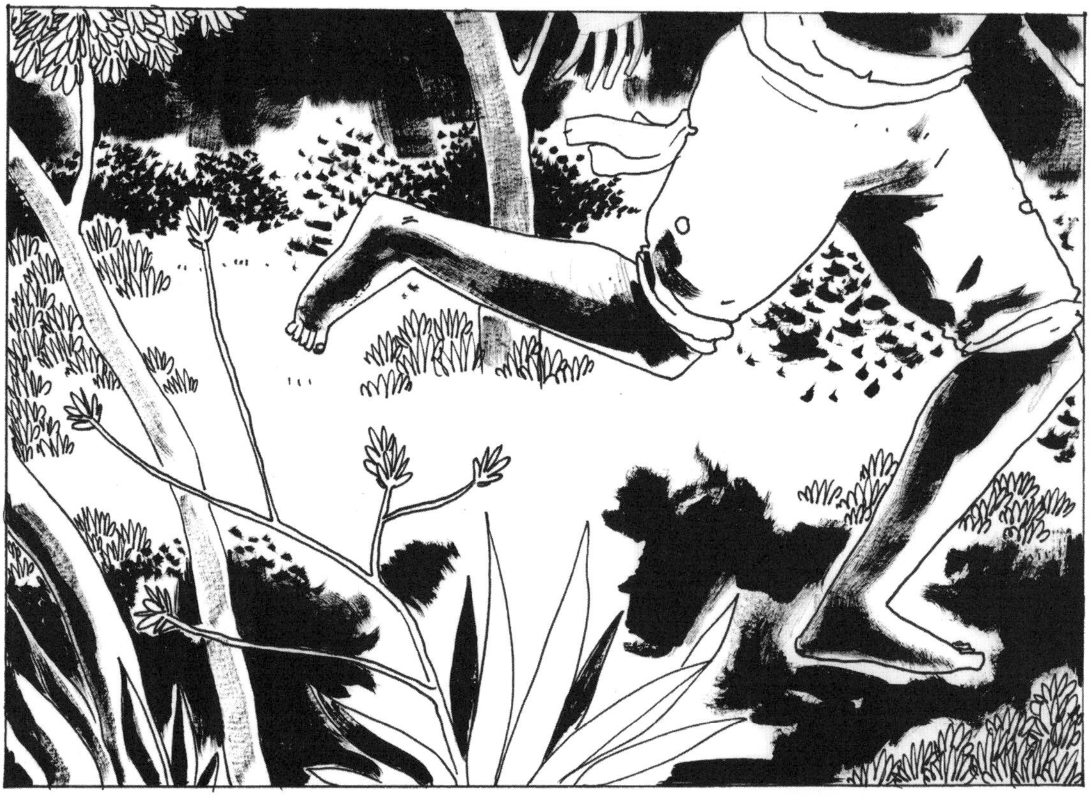

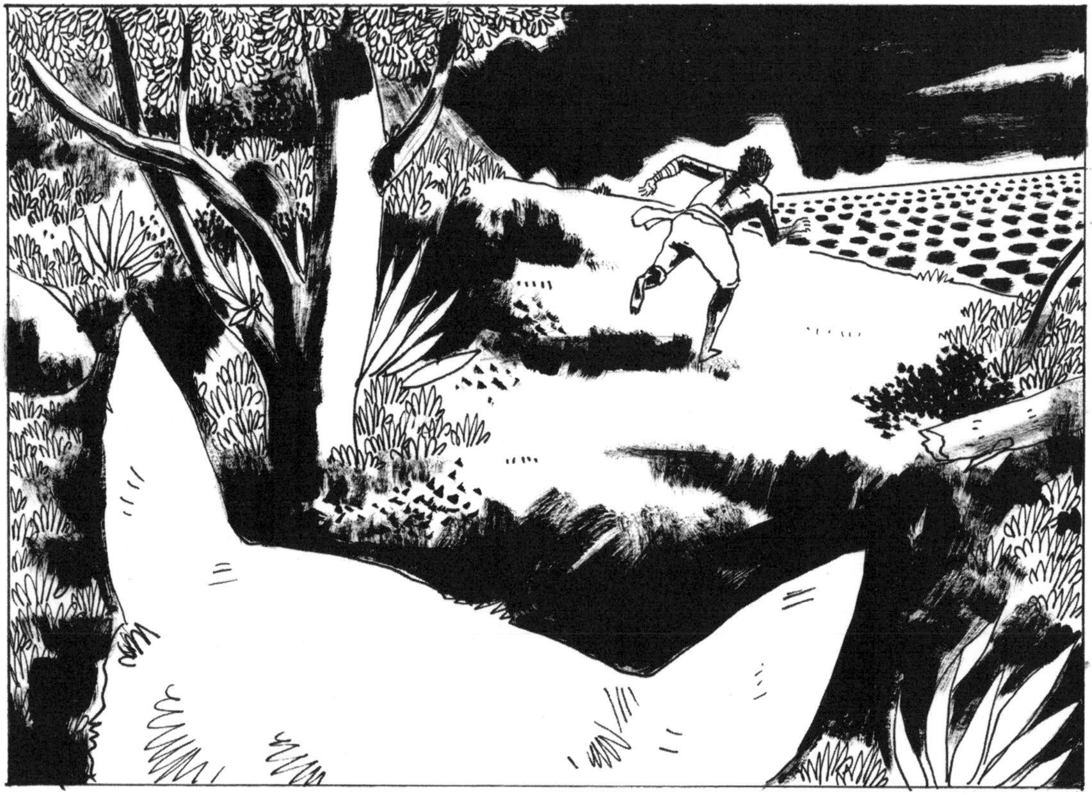

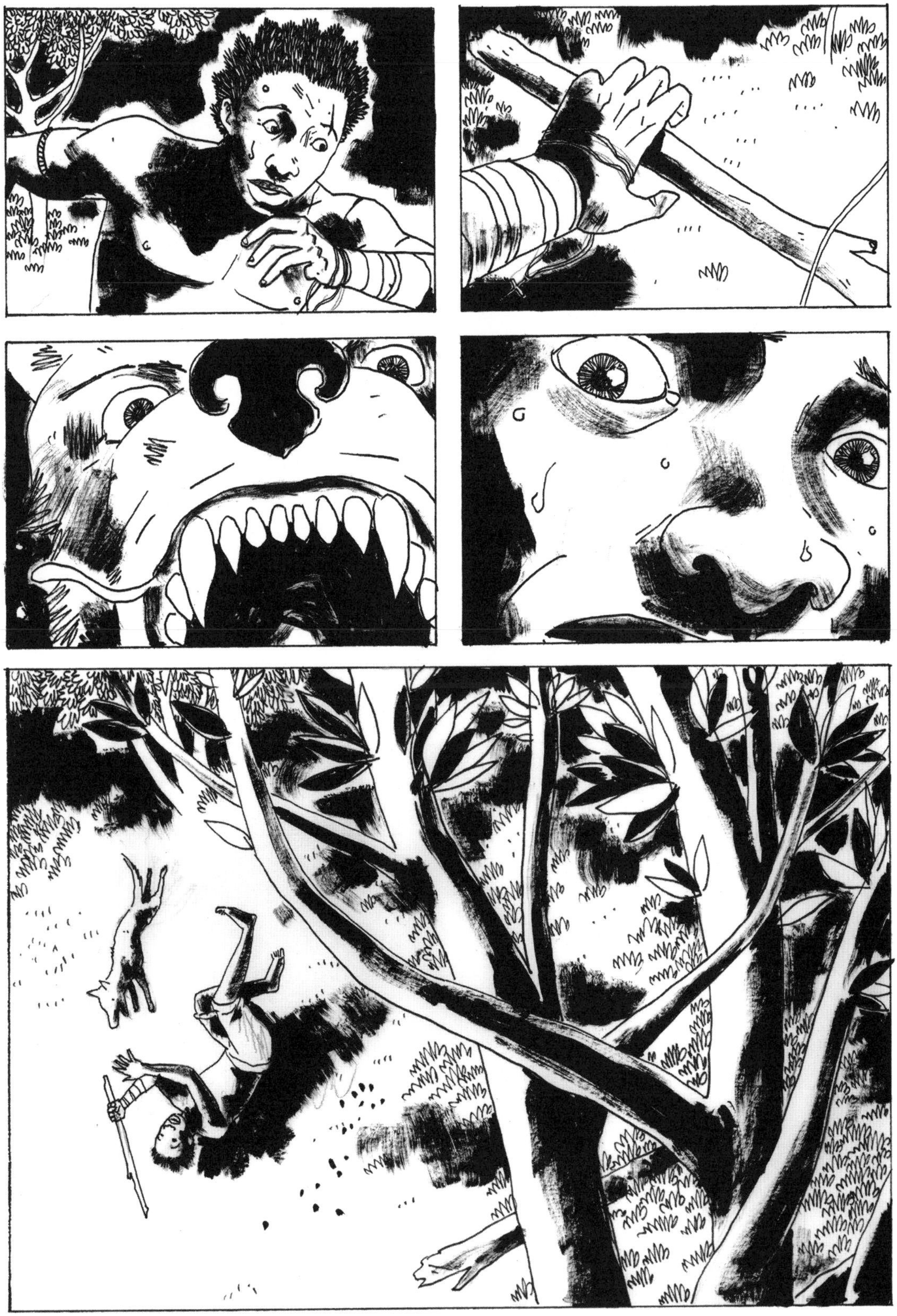

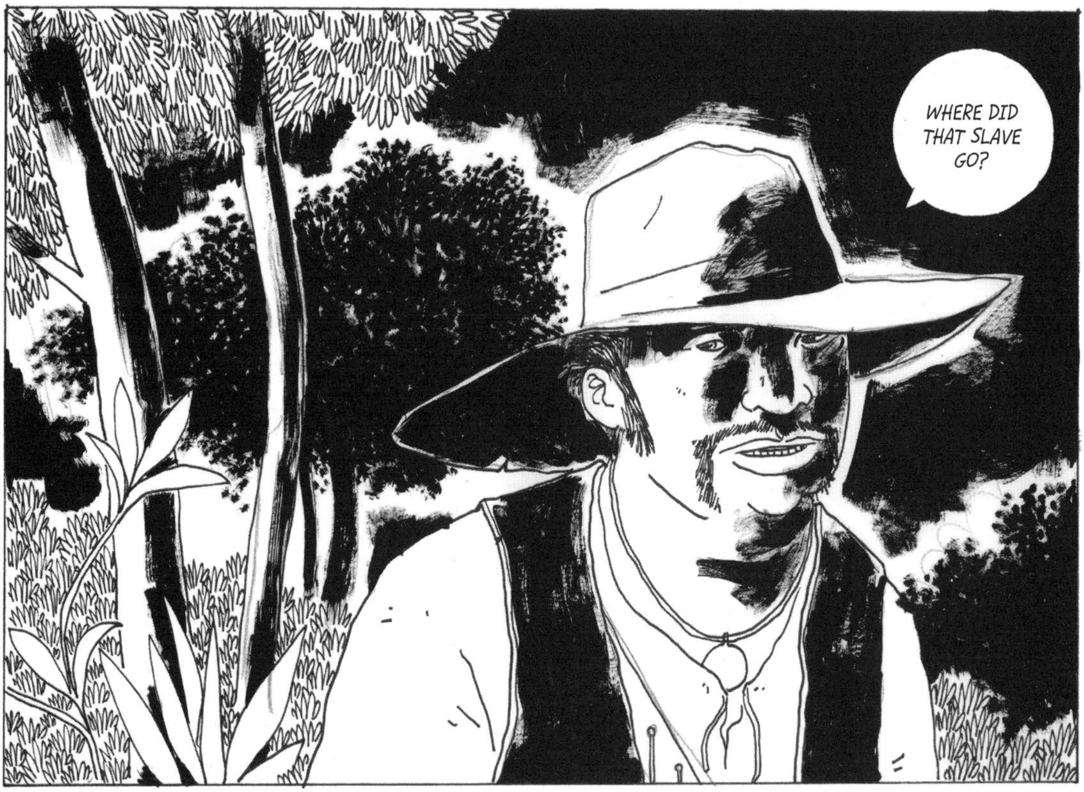
WHERE DID THAT SLAVE GO?

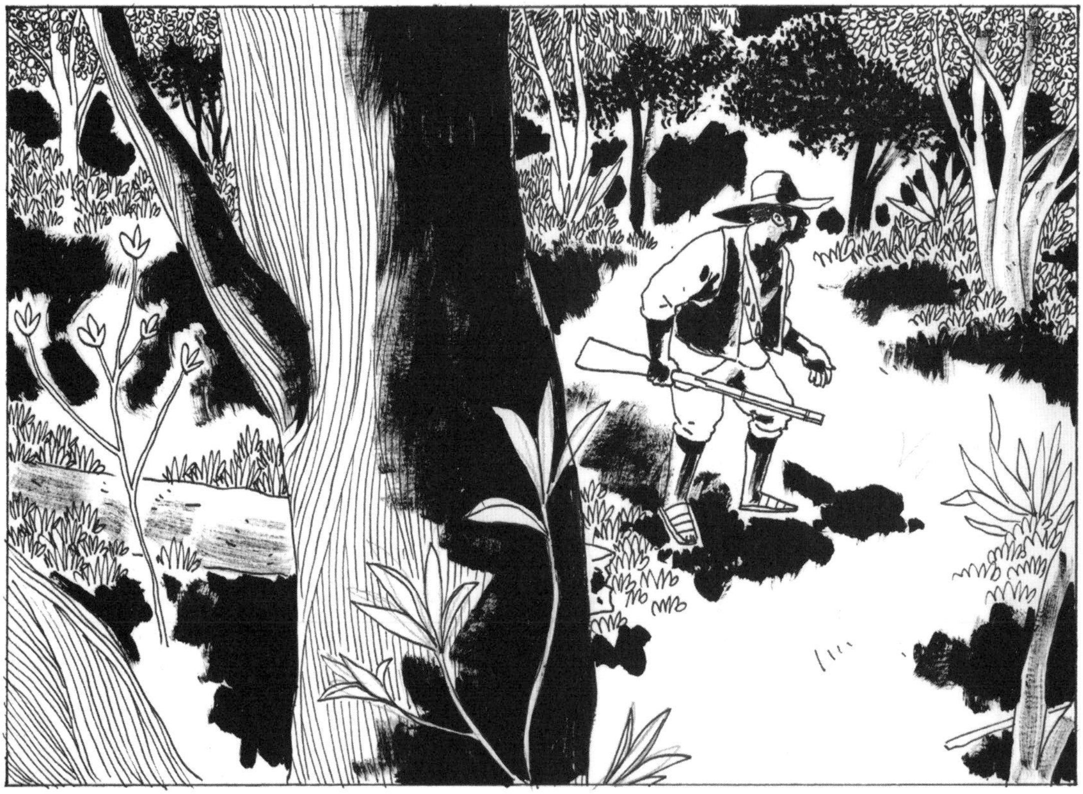

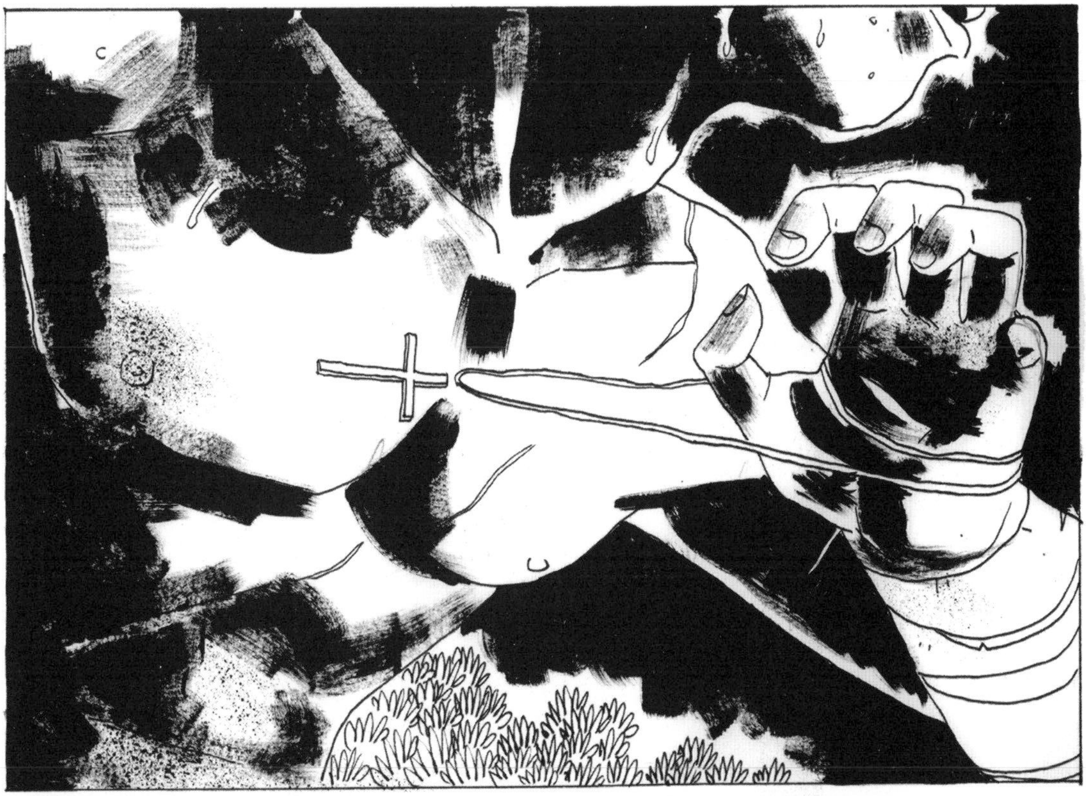

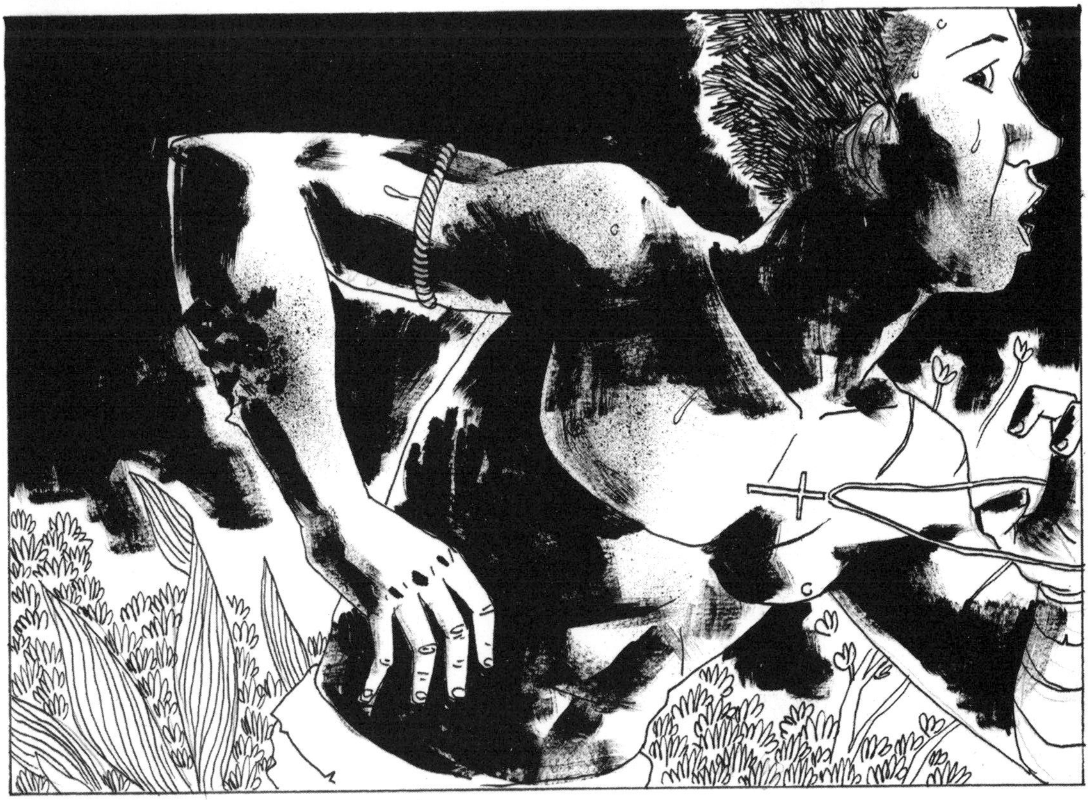

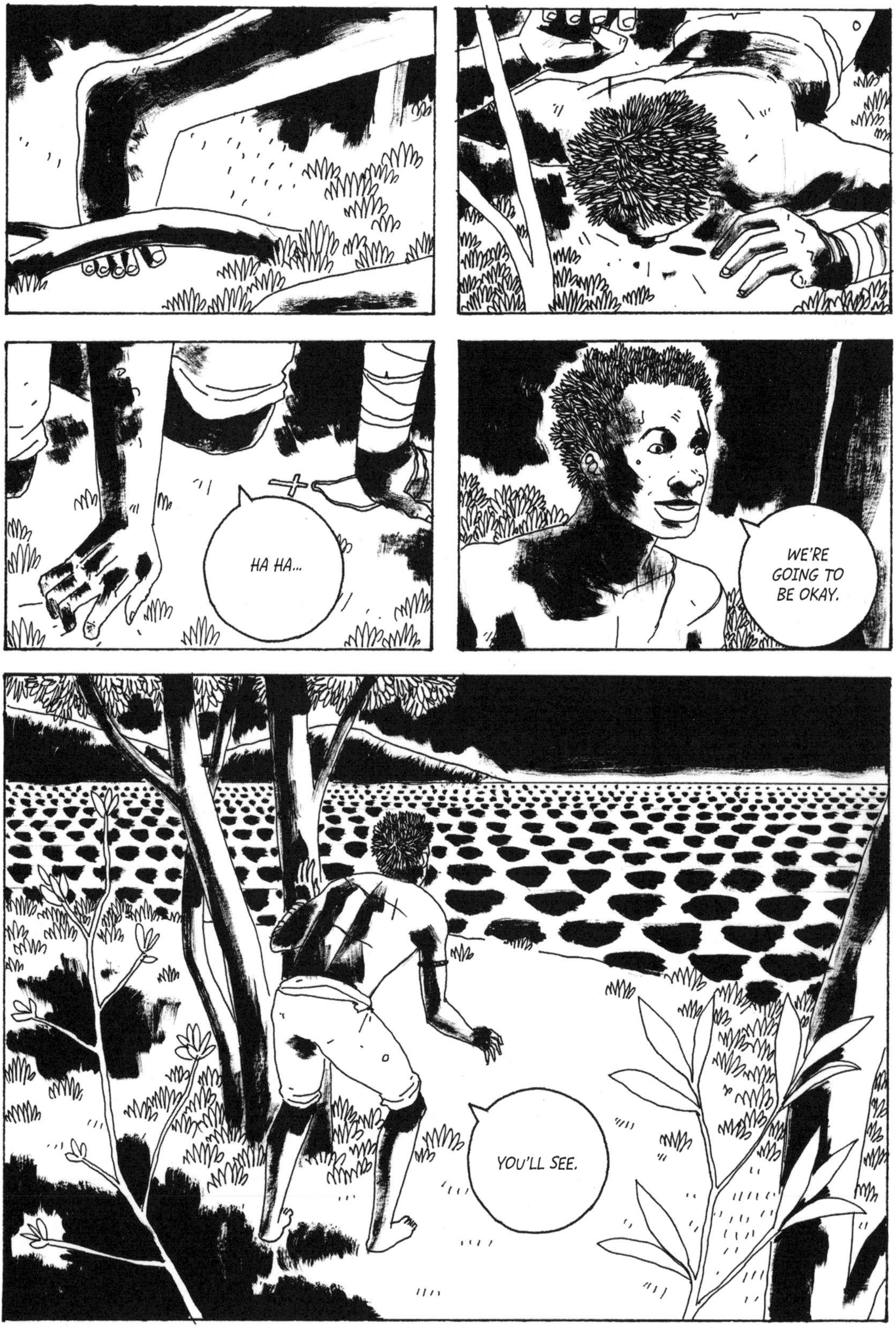
HA HA...
WE'RE GOING TO BE OKAY.
YOU'LL SEE.

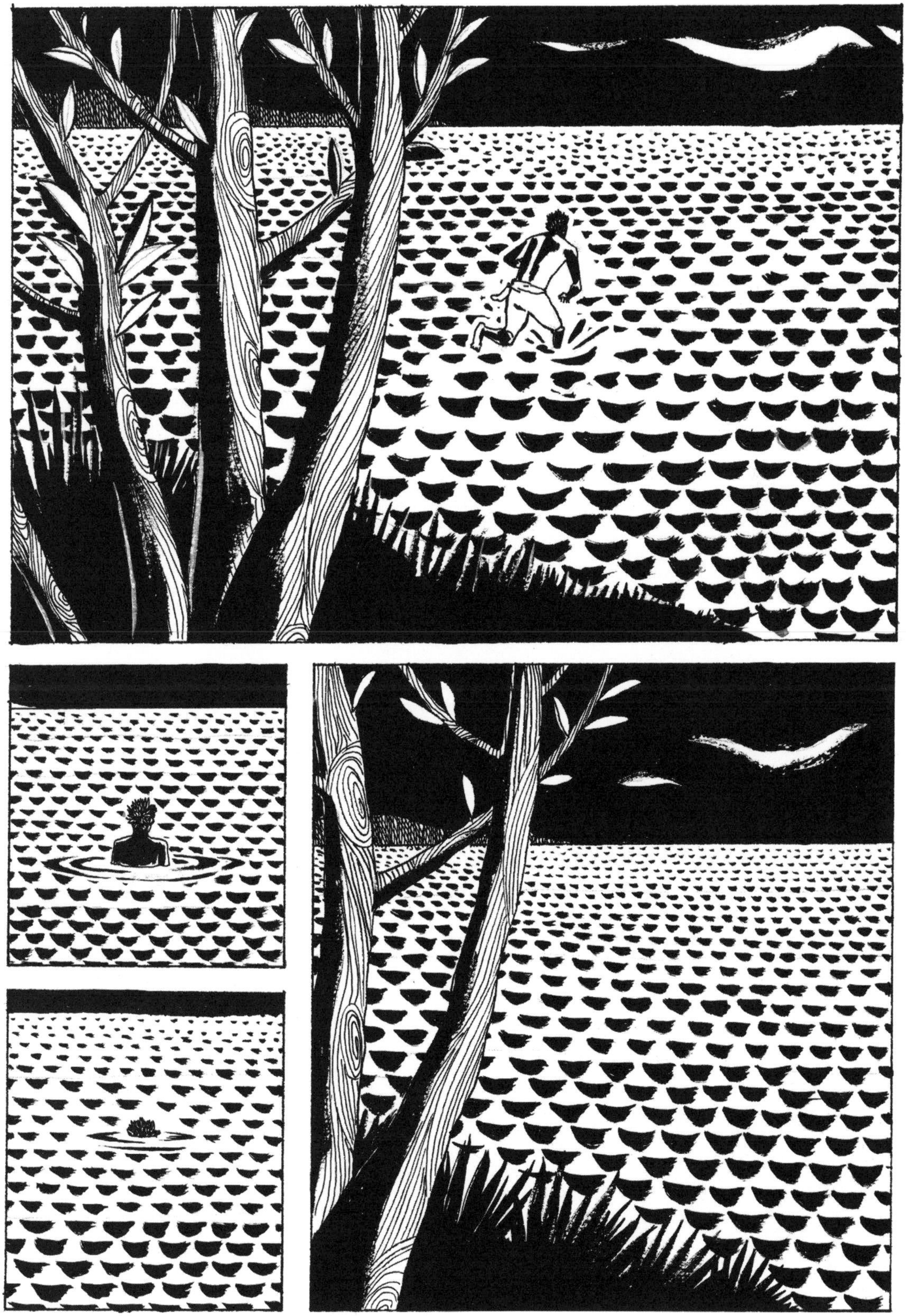

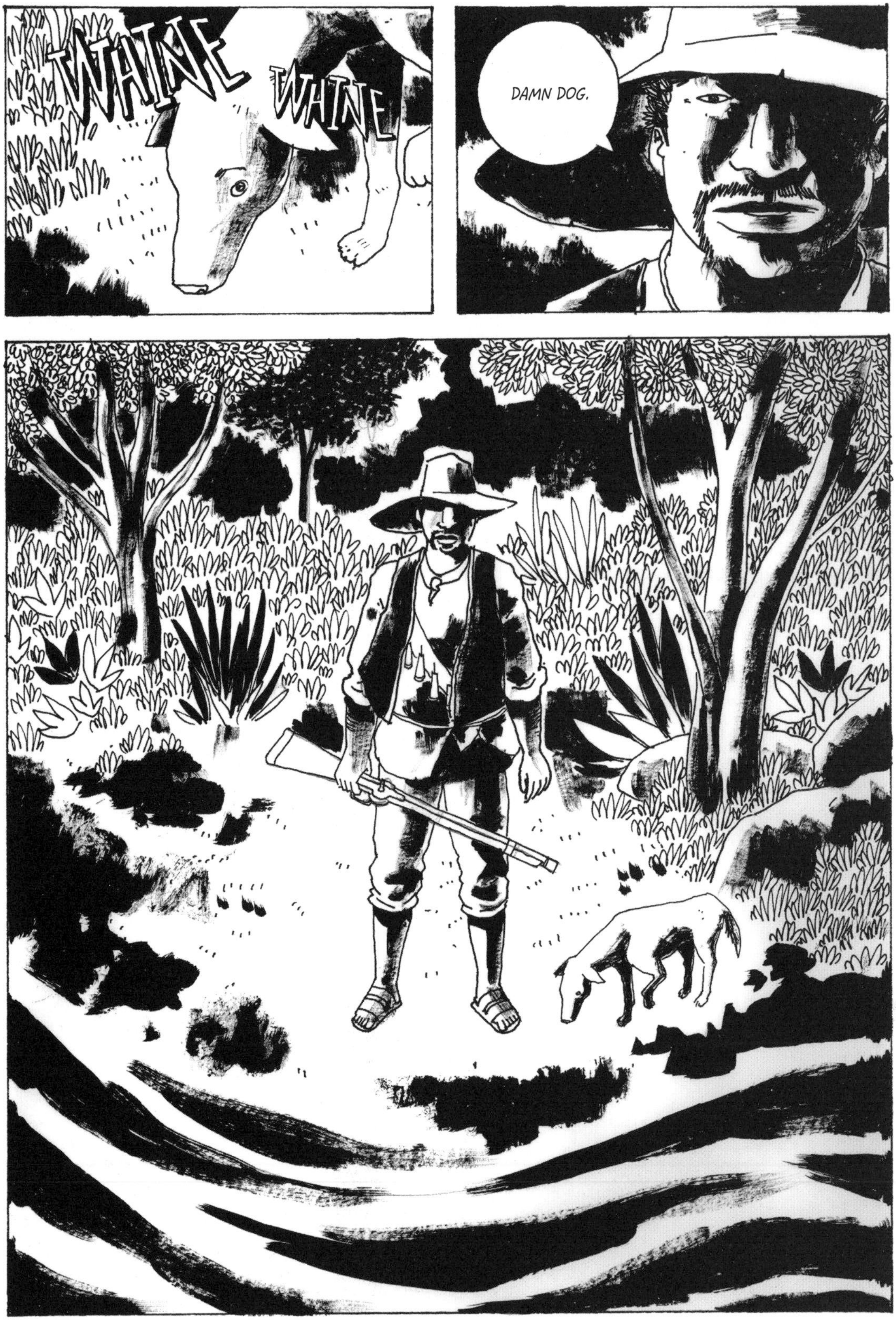
WHINE
WHINE
DAMN DOG.

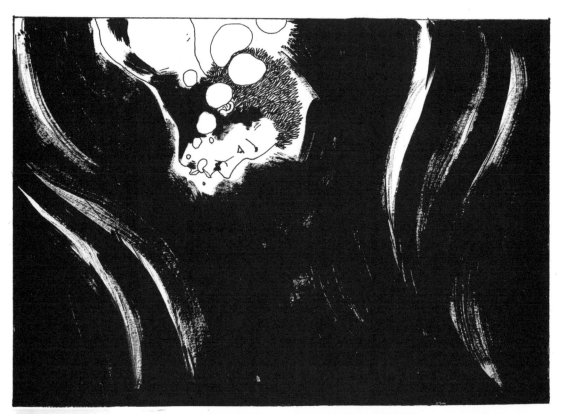

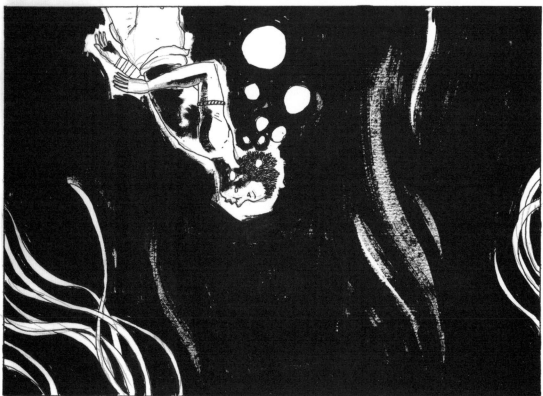

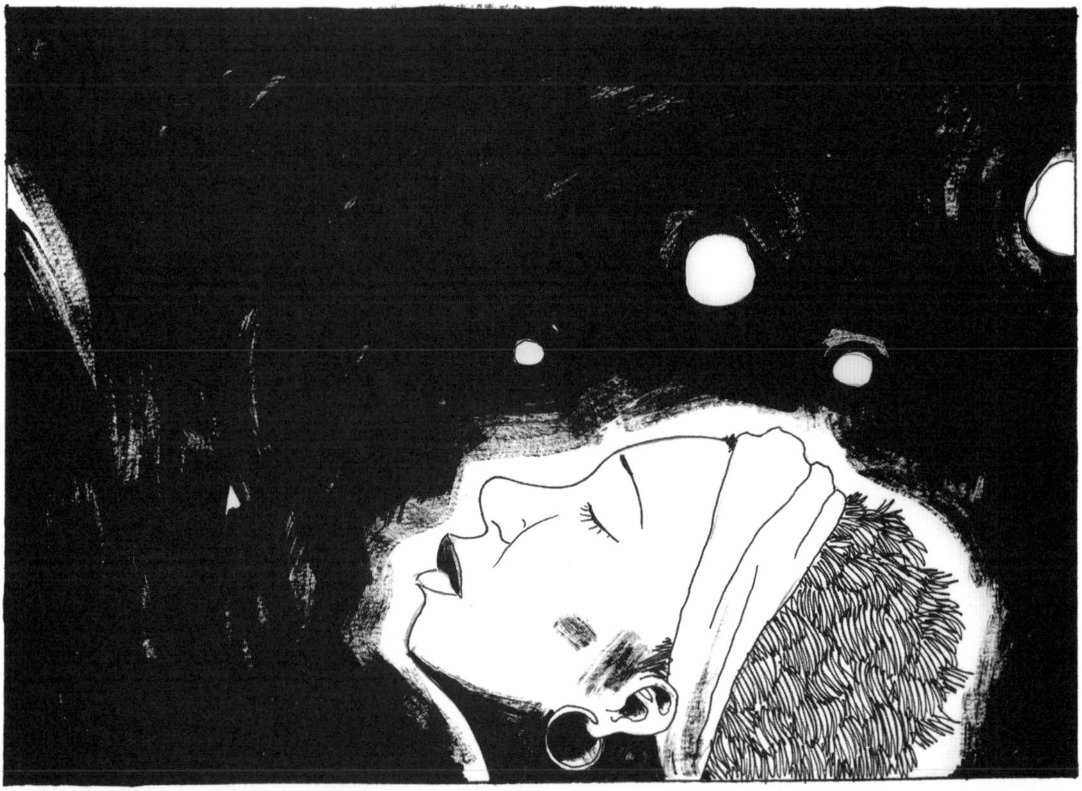

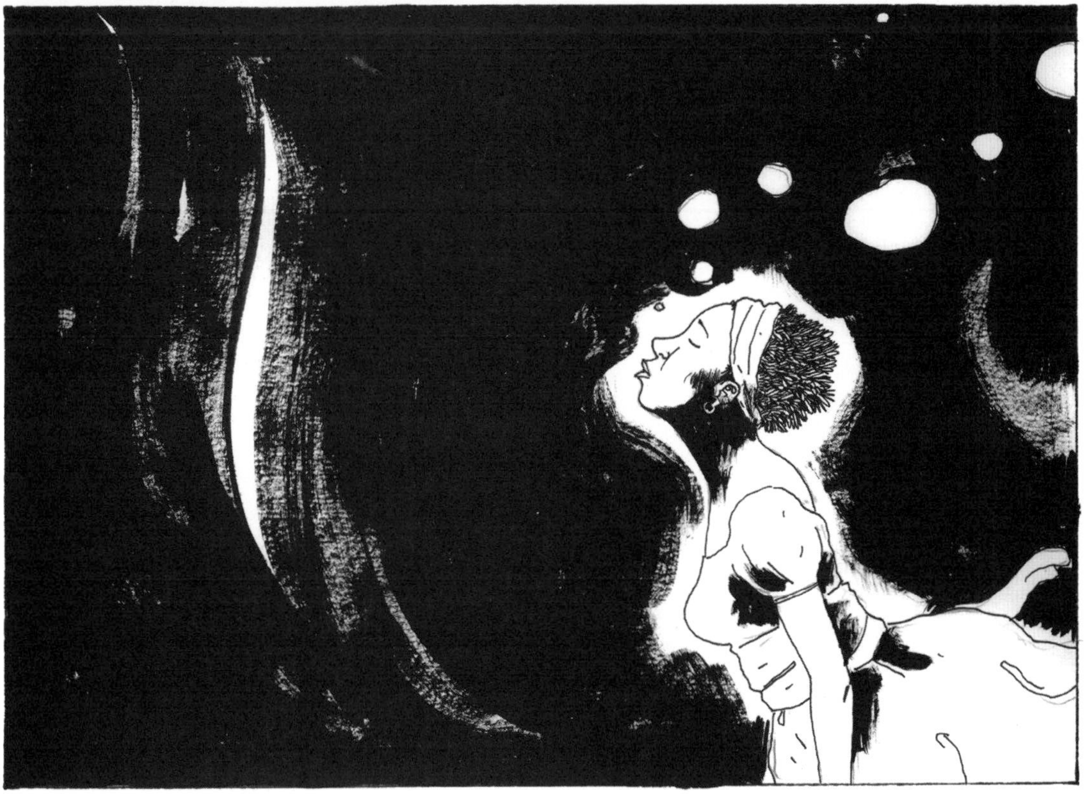

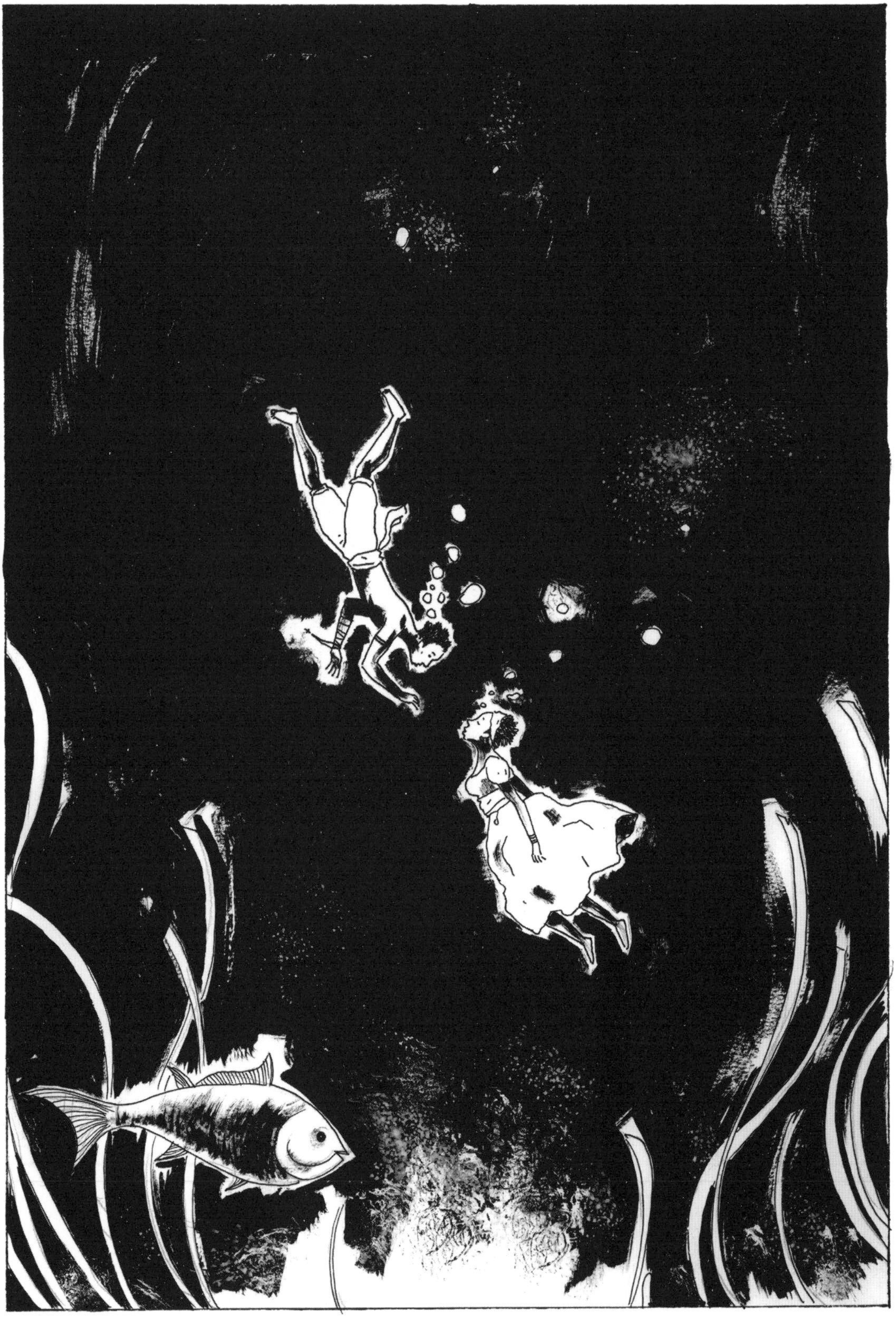

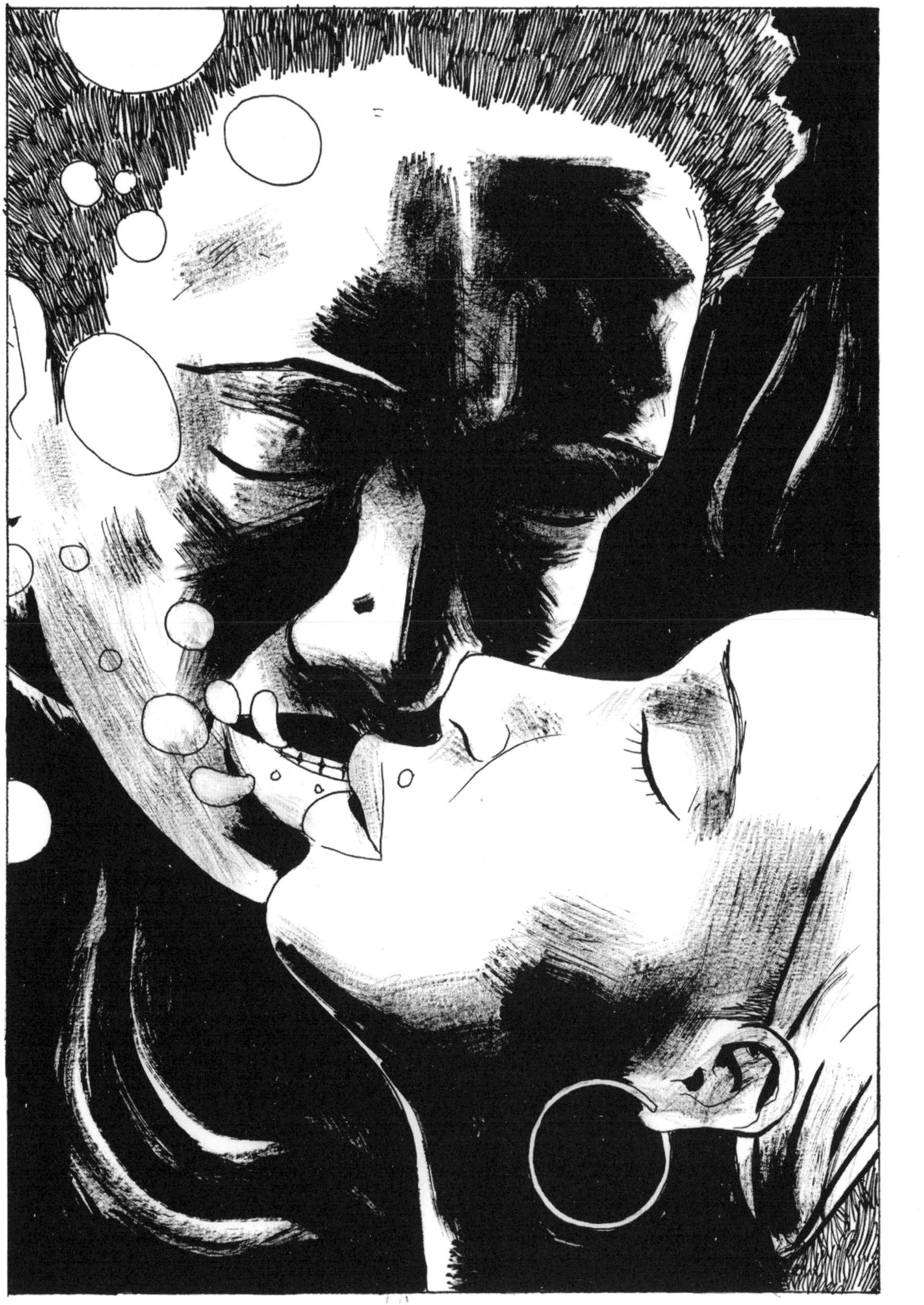

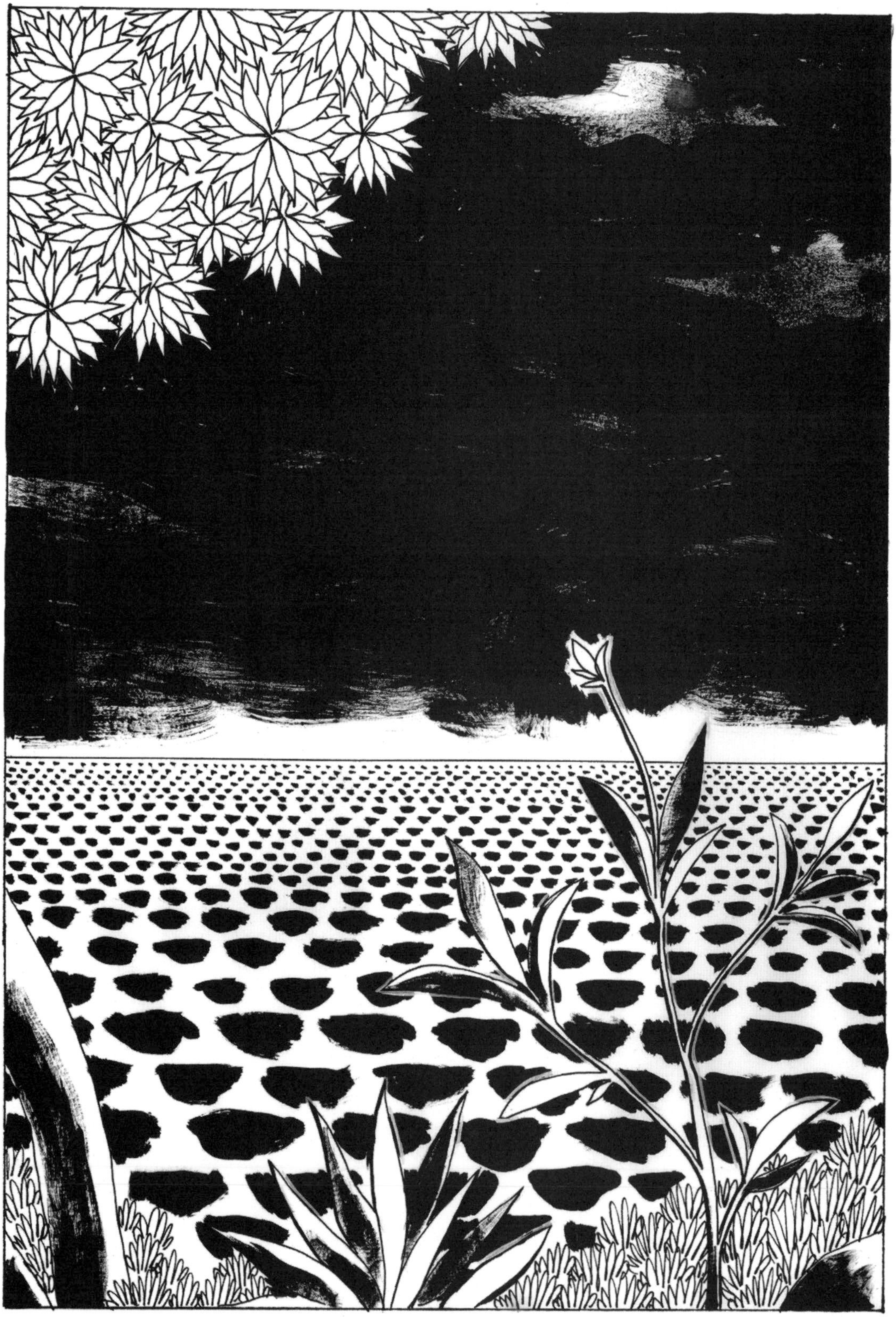

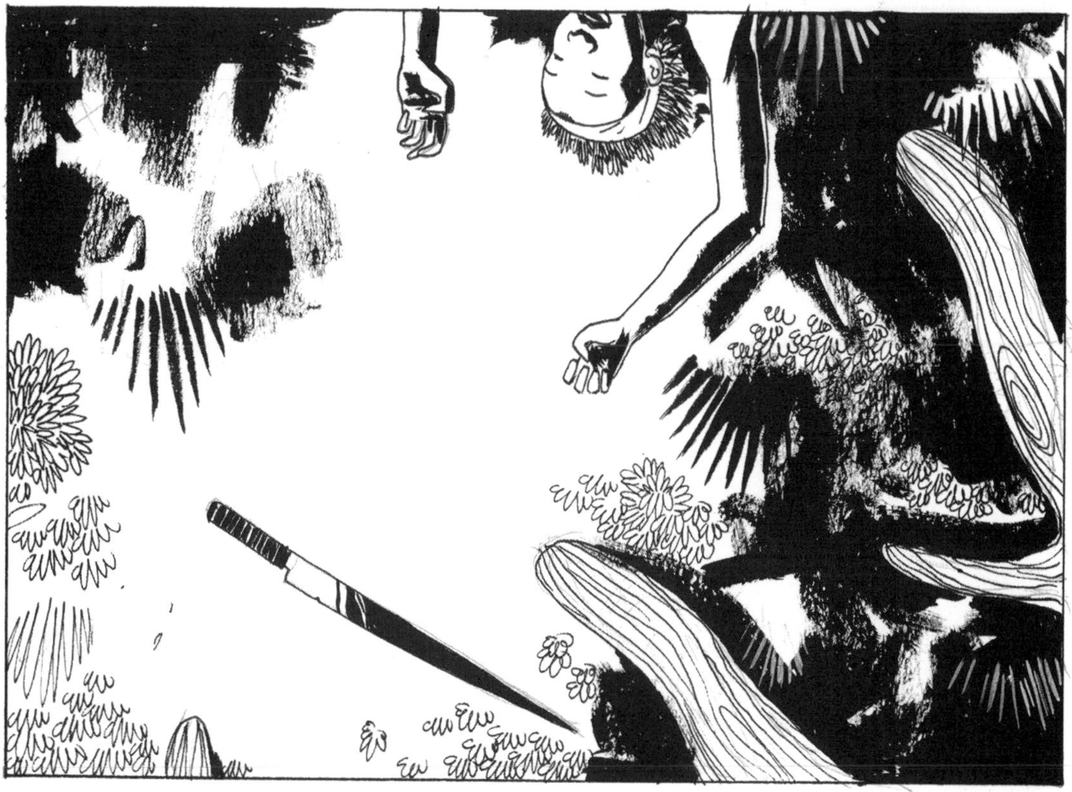

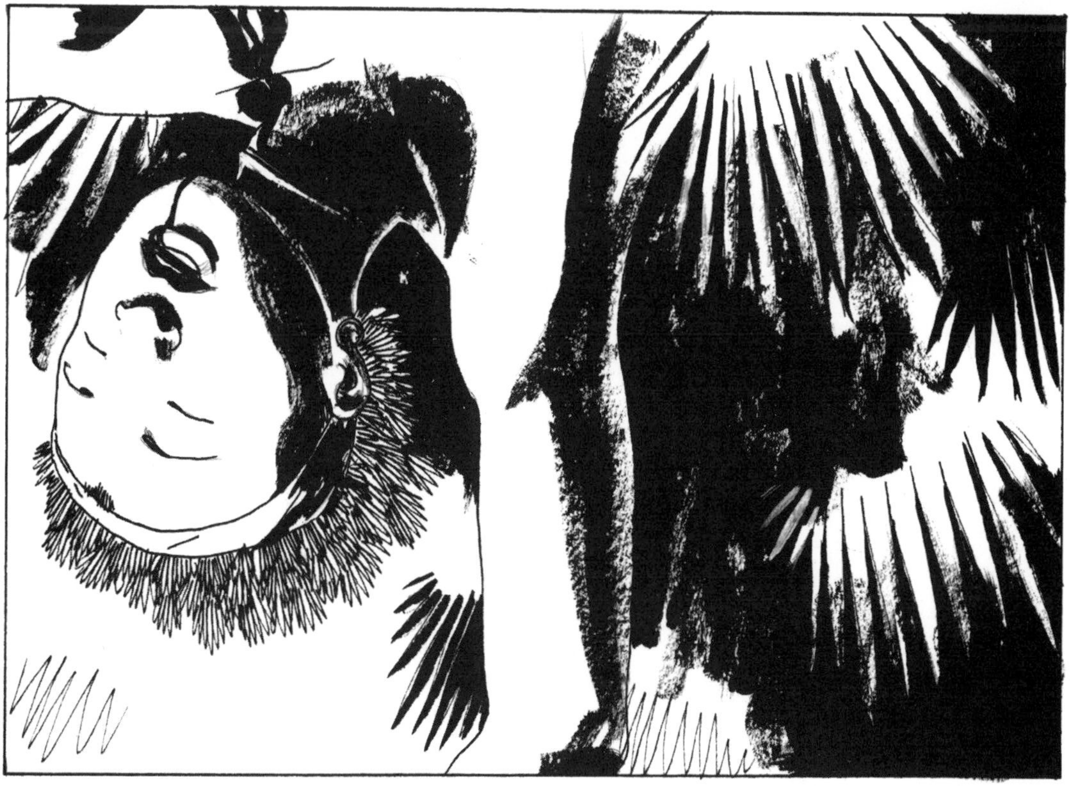

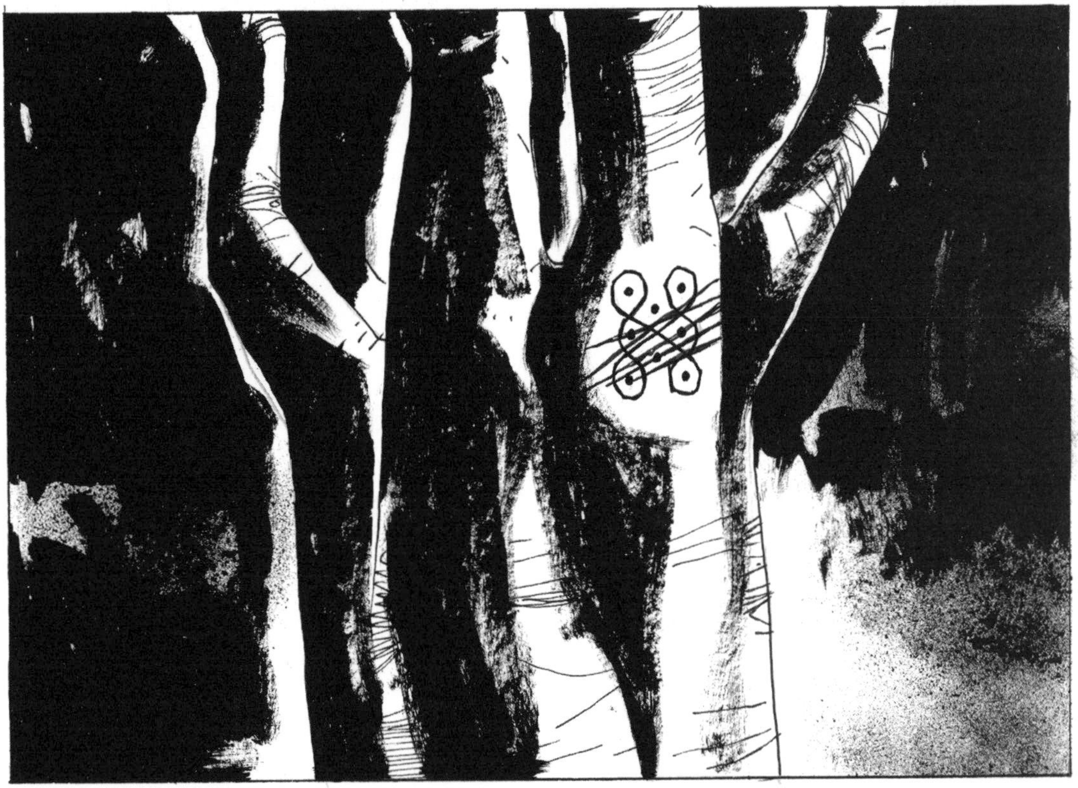

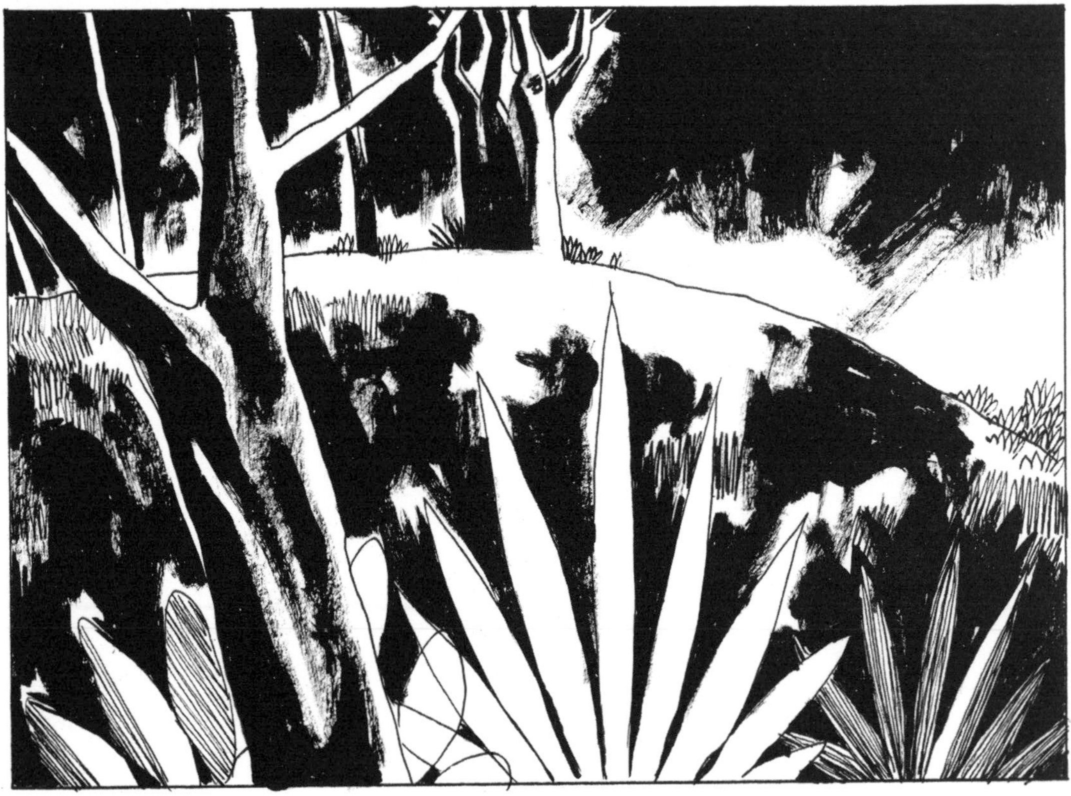

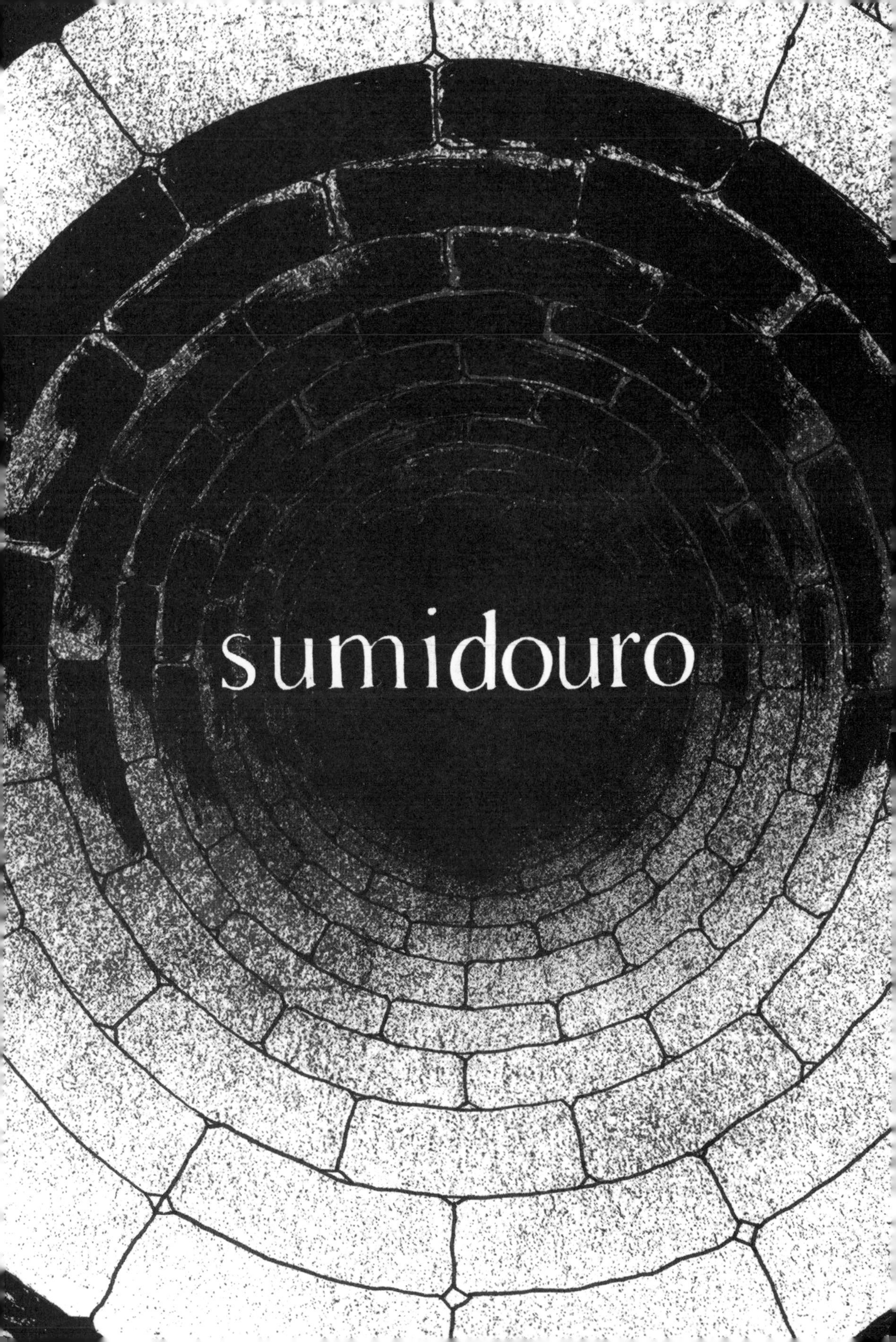
sumidouro

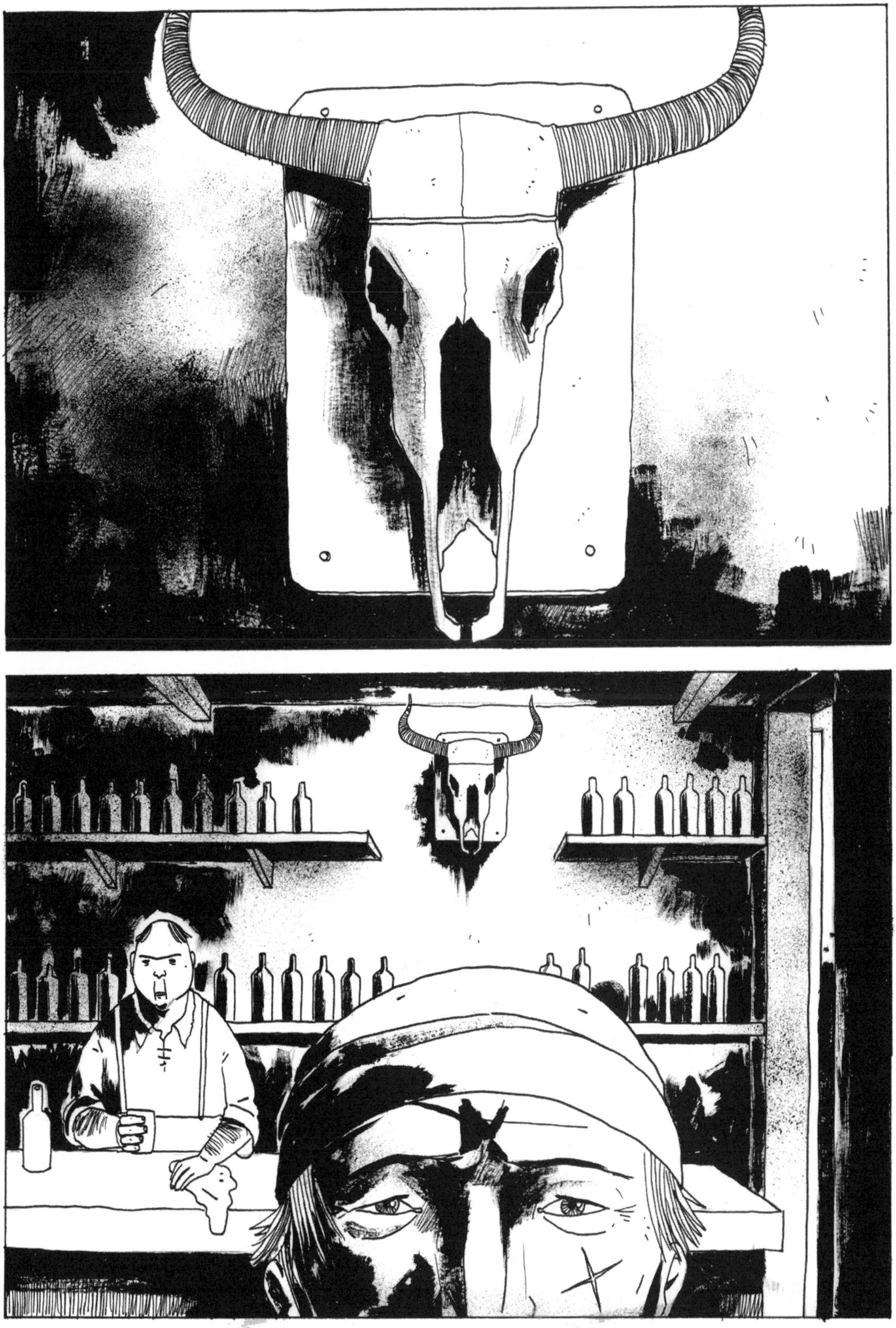

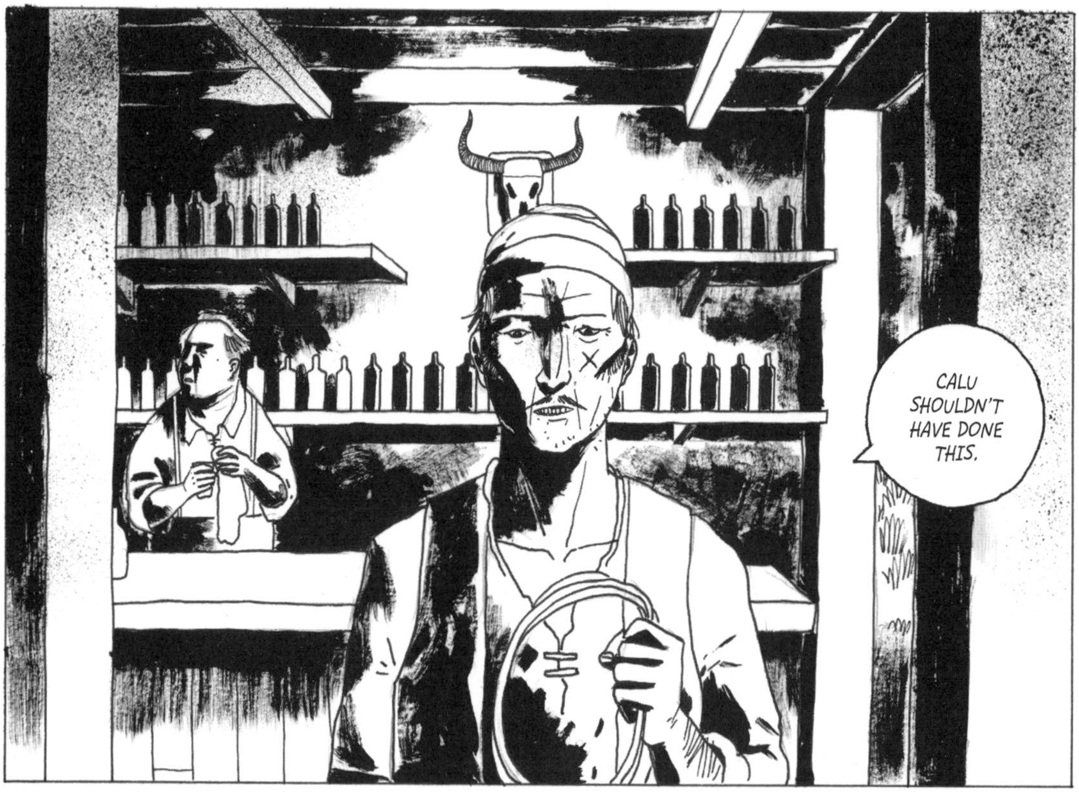
CALU SHOULDN'T HAVE DONE THIS.

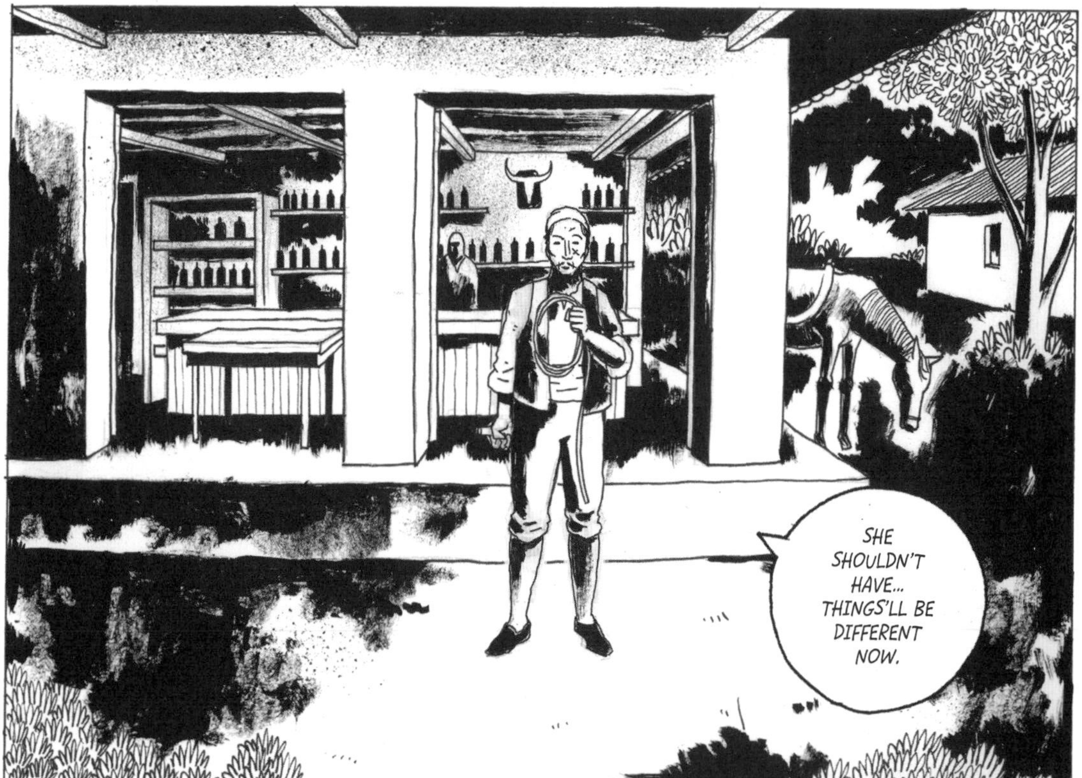
SHE SHOULDN'T HAVE... THINGS'LL BE DIFFERENT NOW.

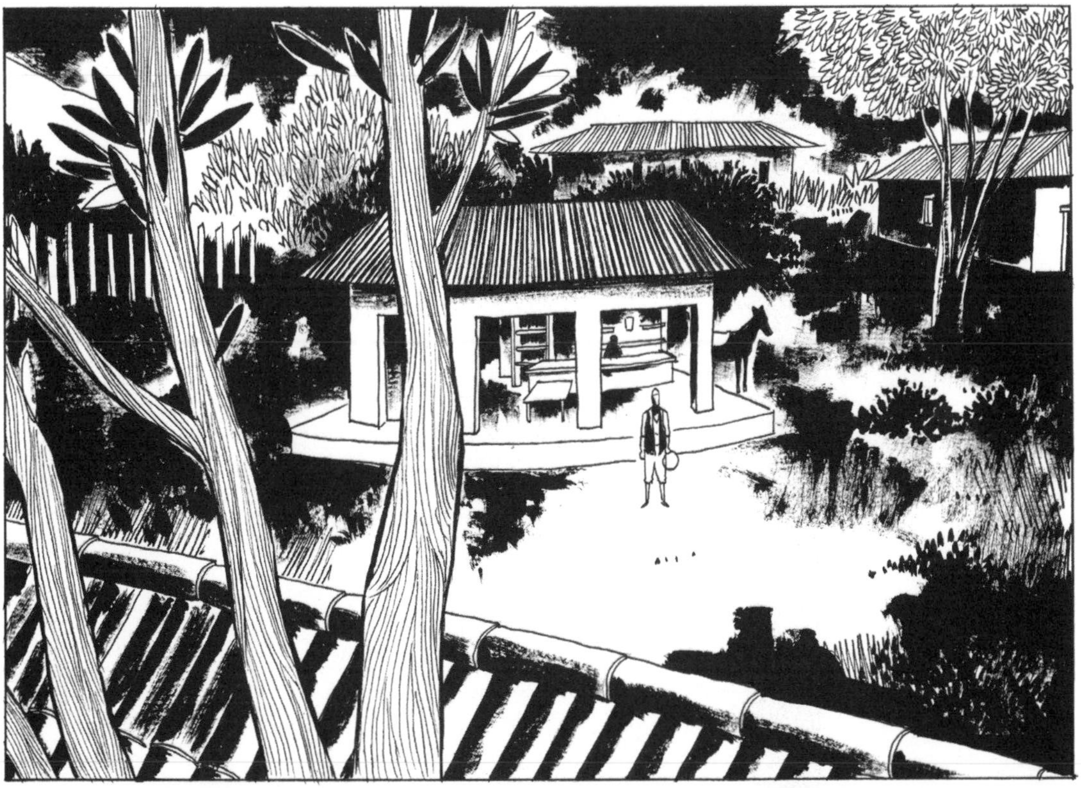

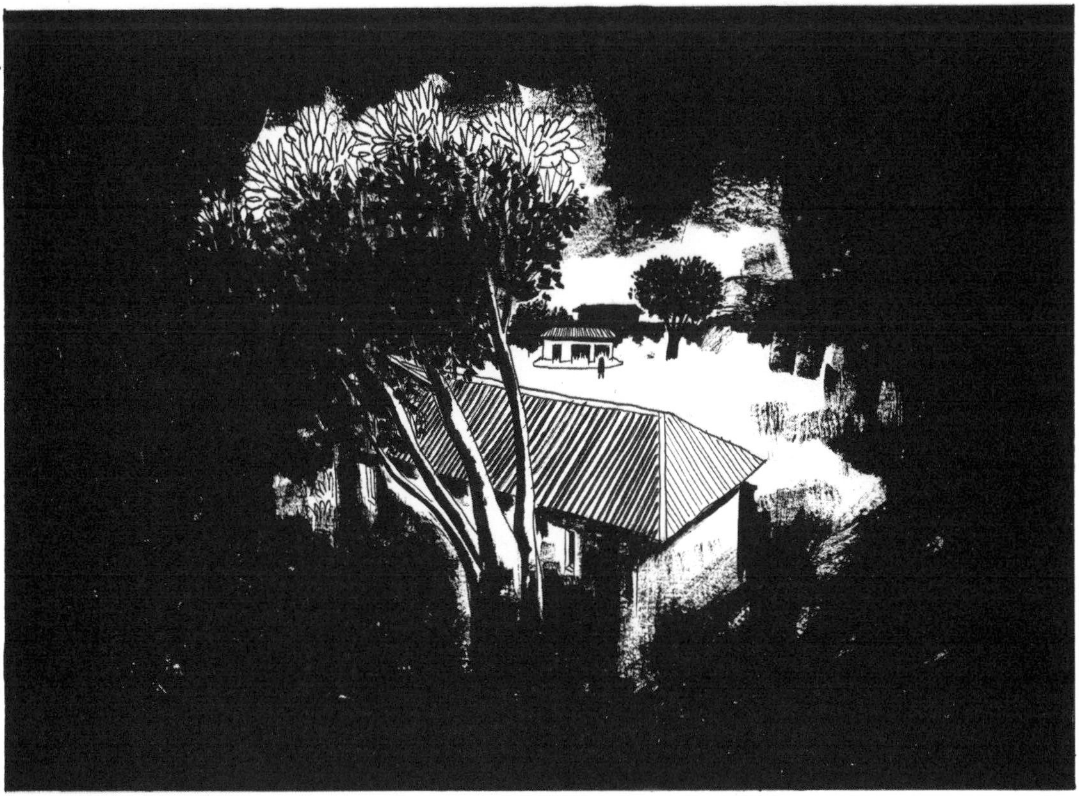

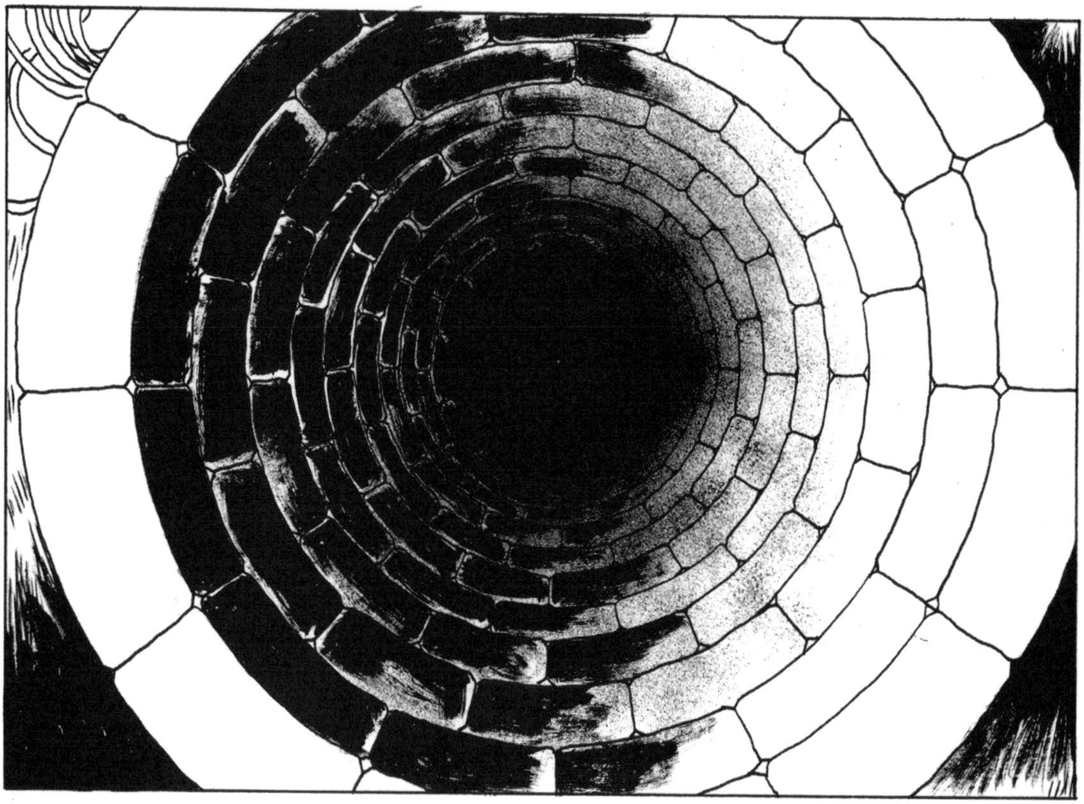

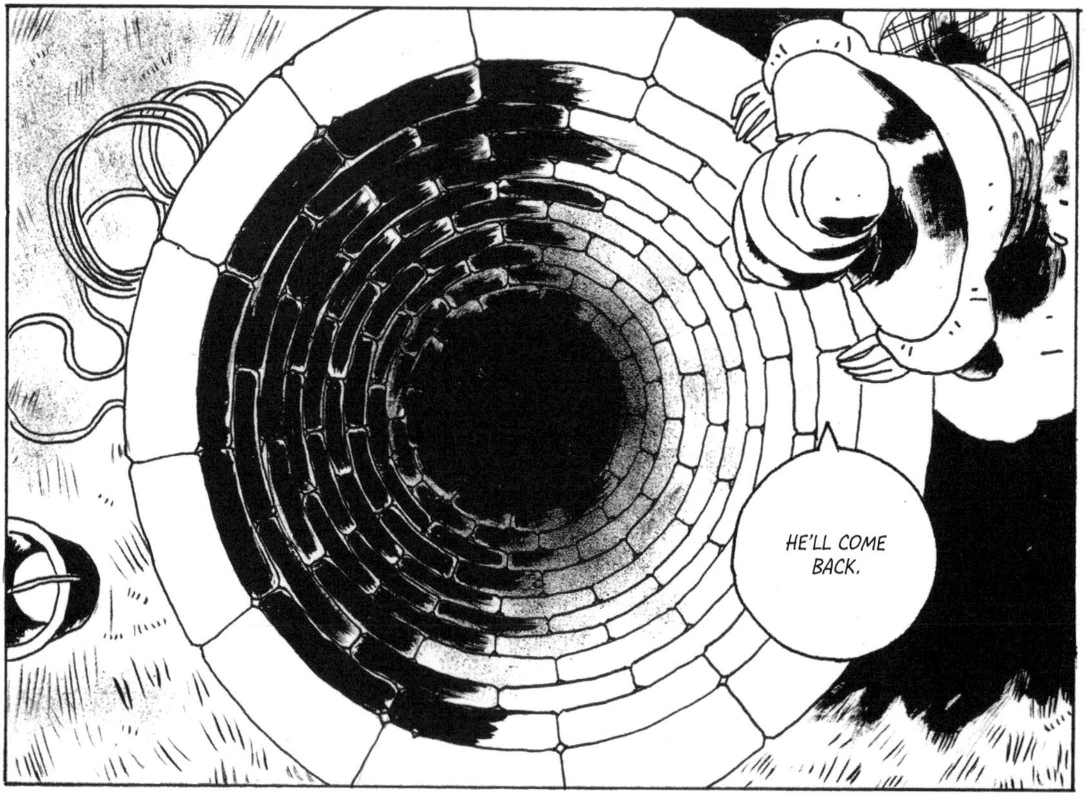
HE'LL COME BACK.

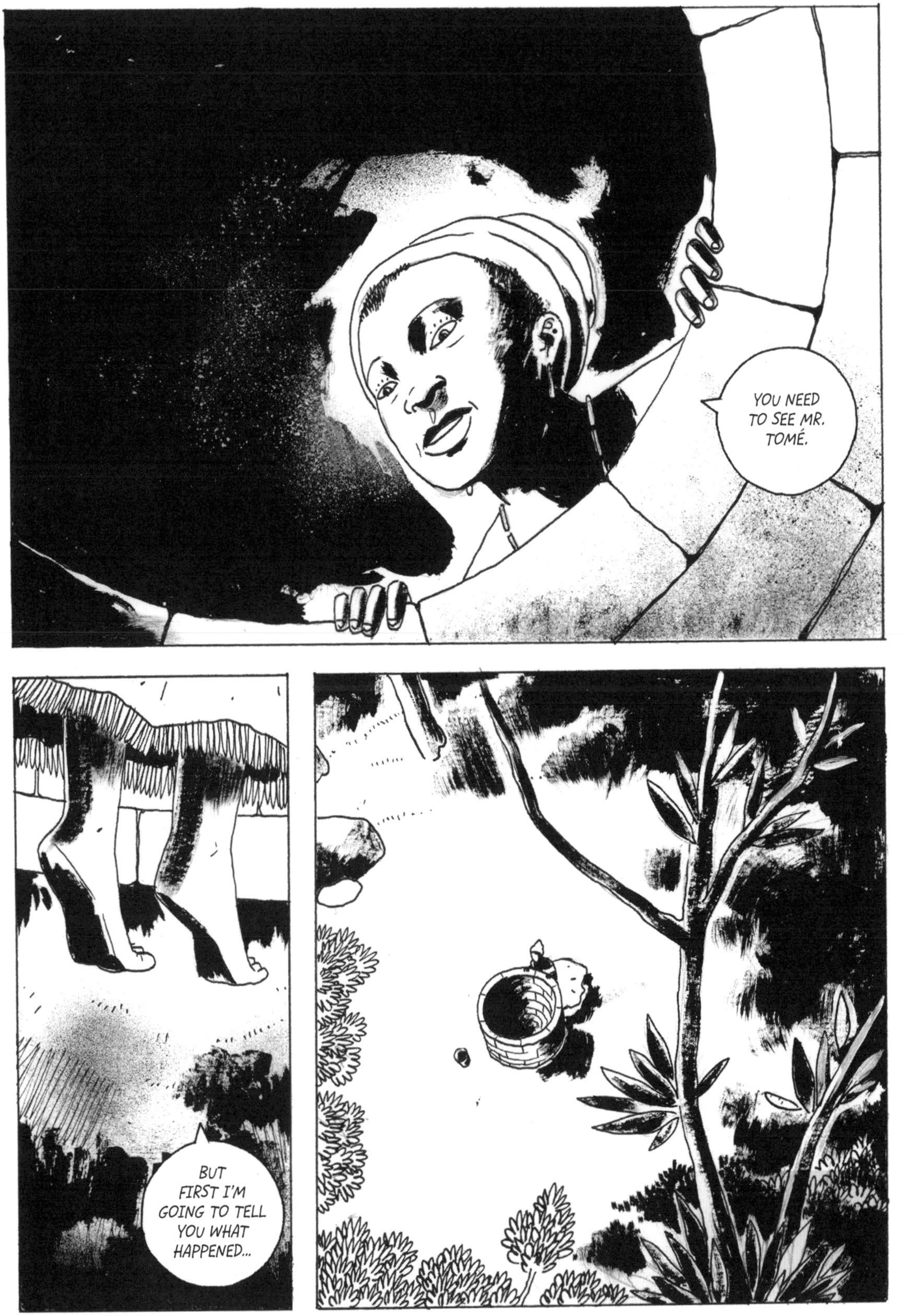
YOU NEED TO SEE MR. TOMÉ.
BUT FIRST I'M GOING TO TELL YOU WHAT HAPPENED...

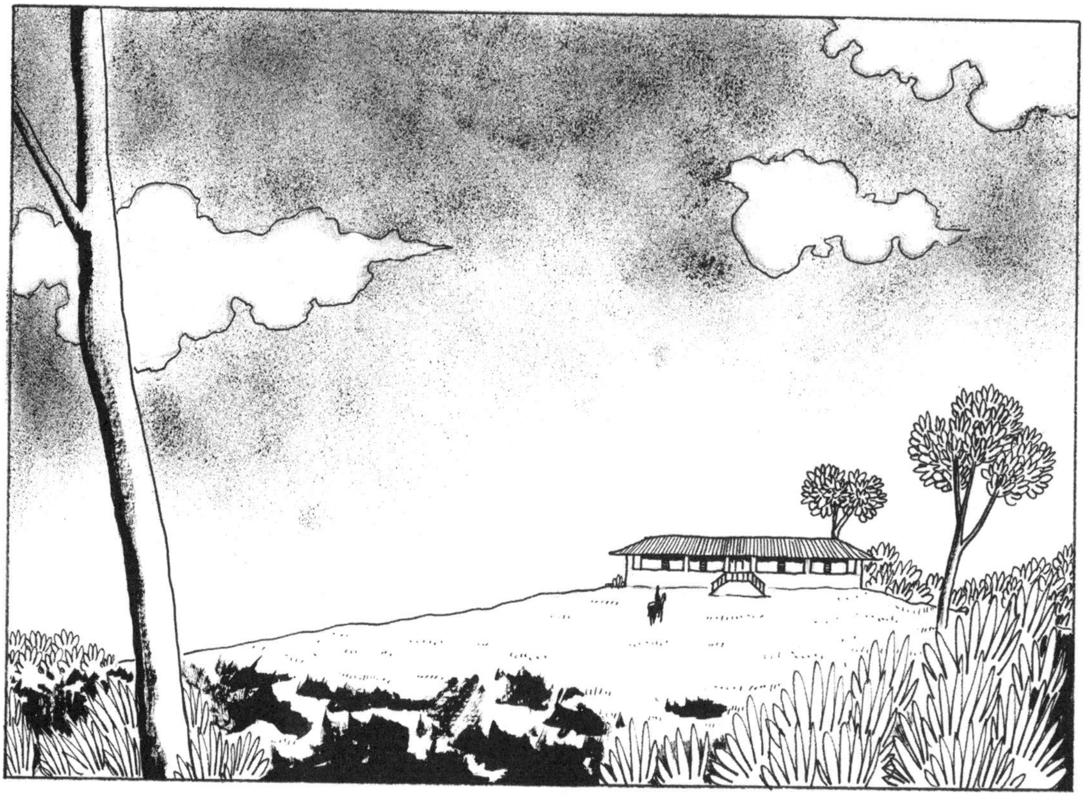

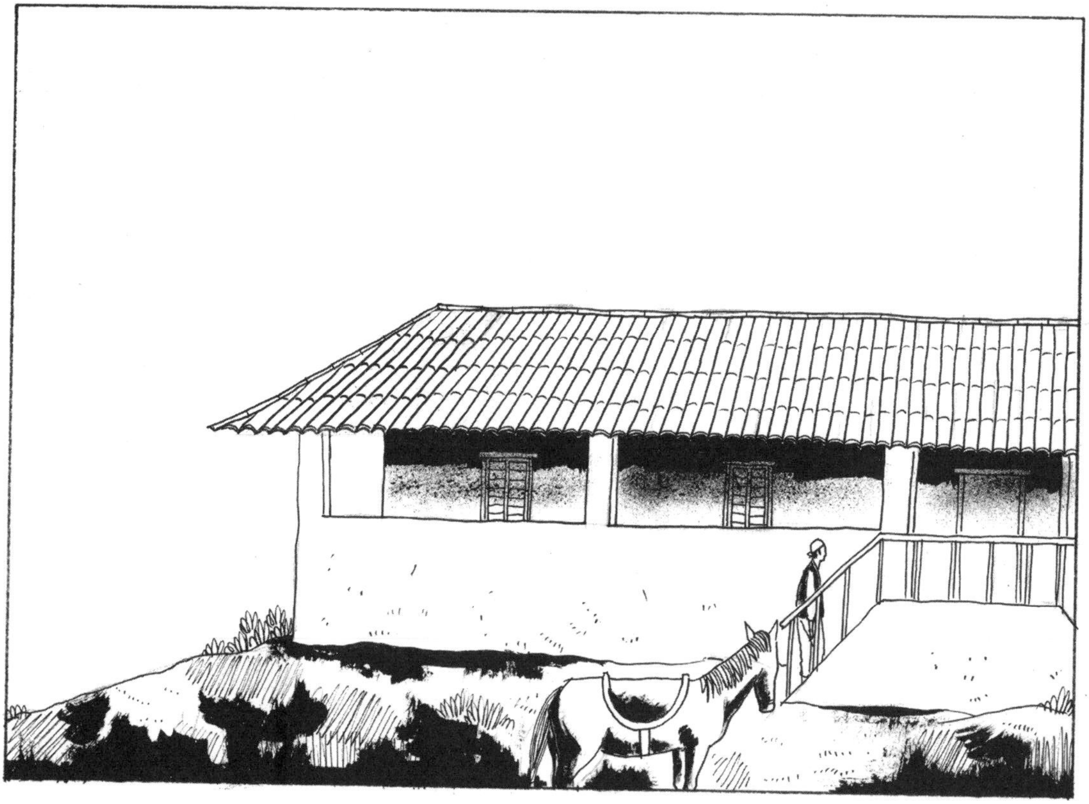

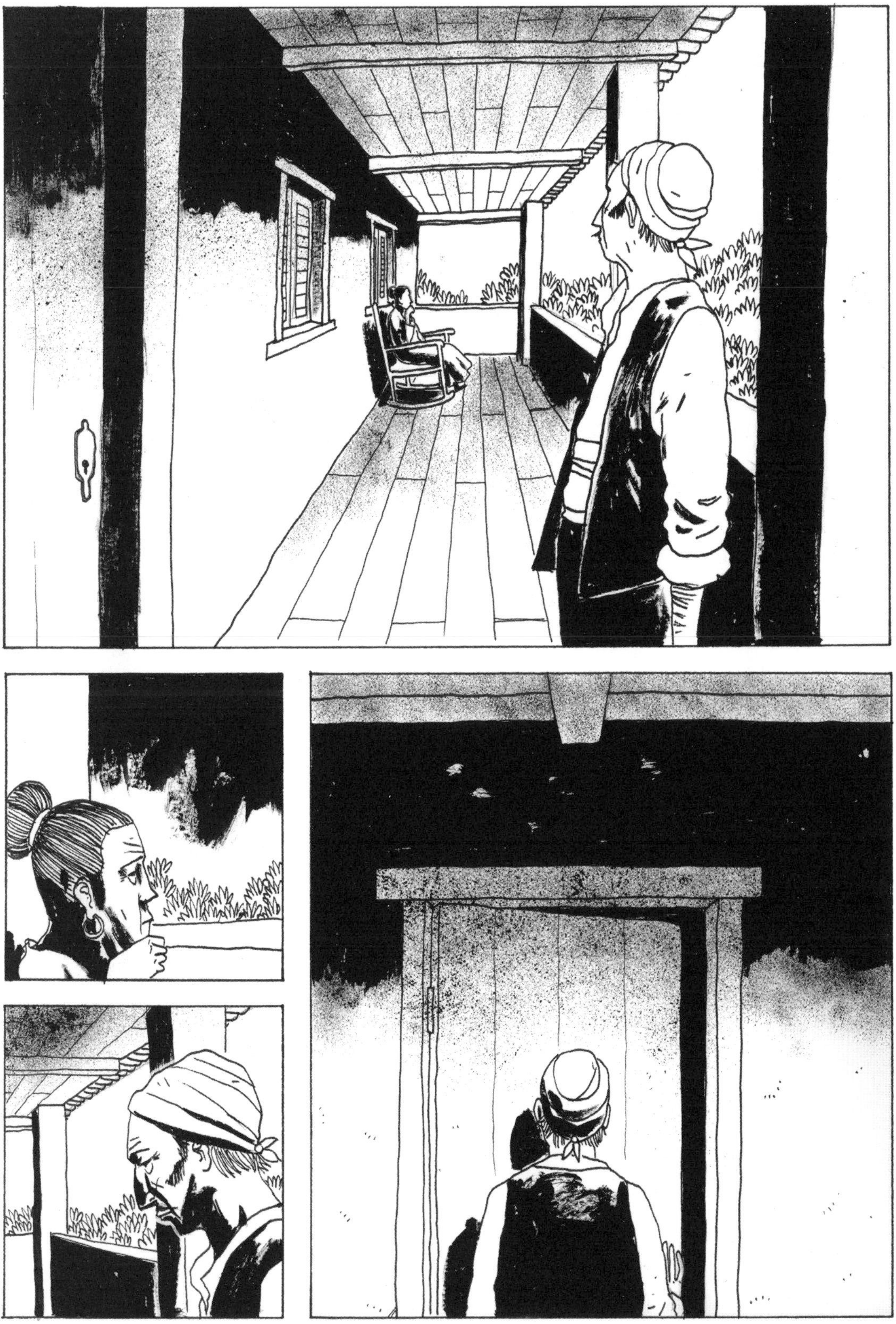

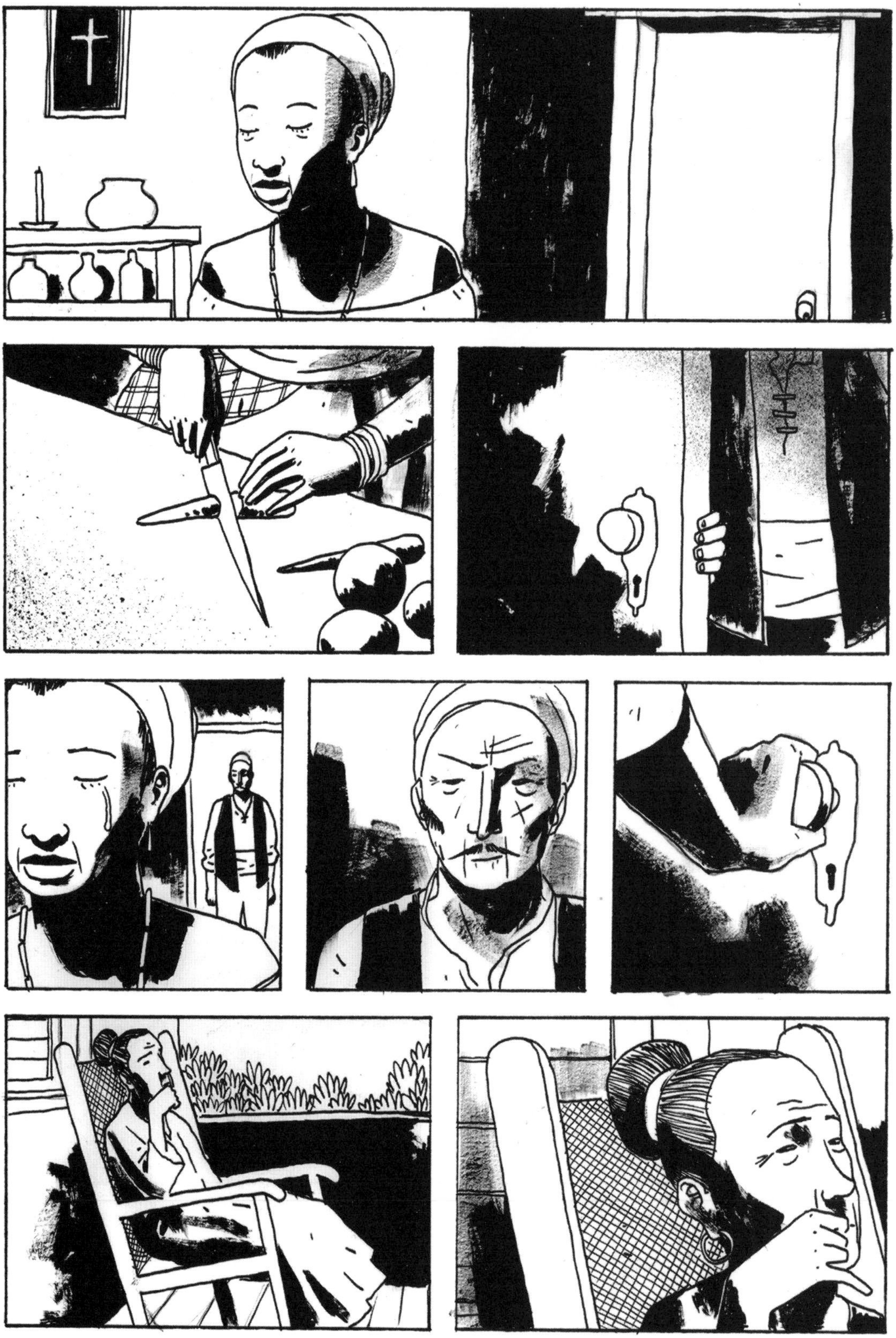

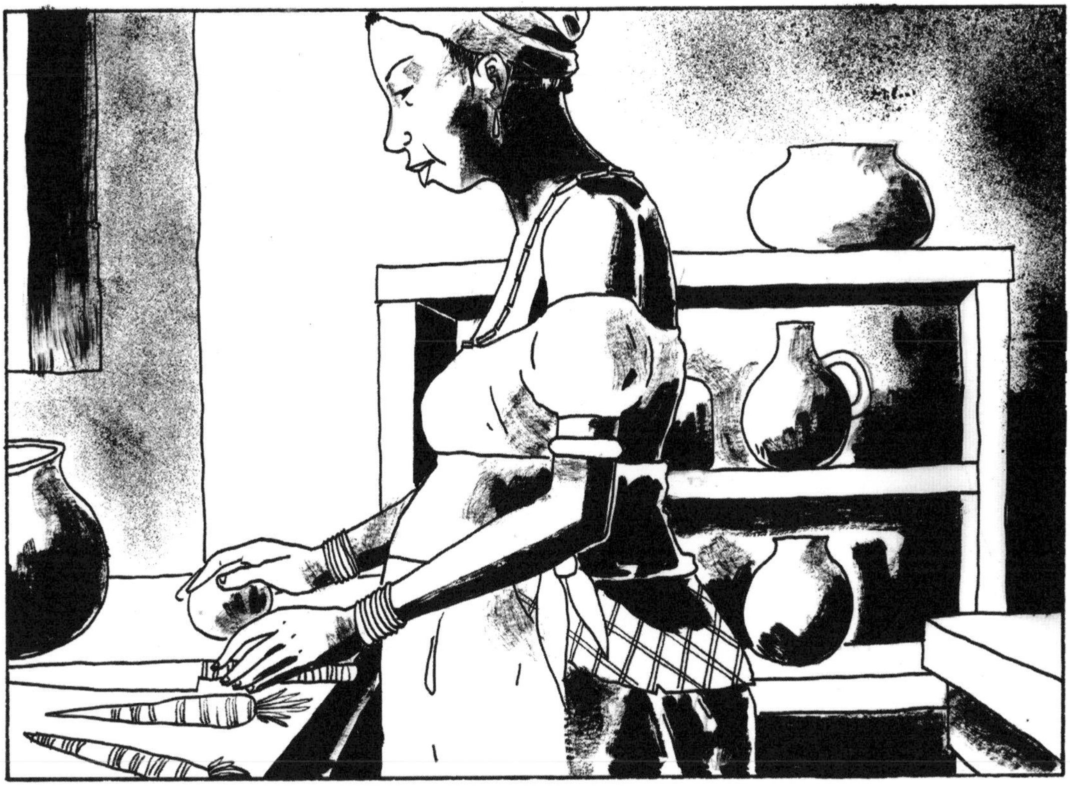
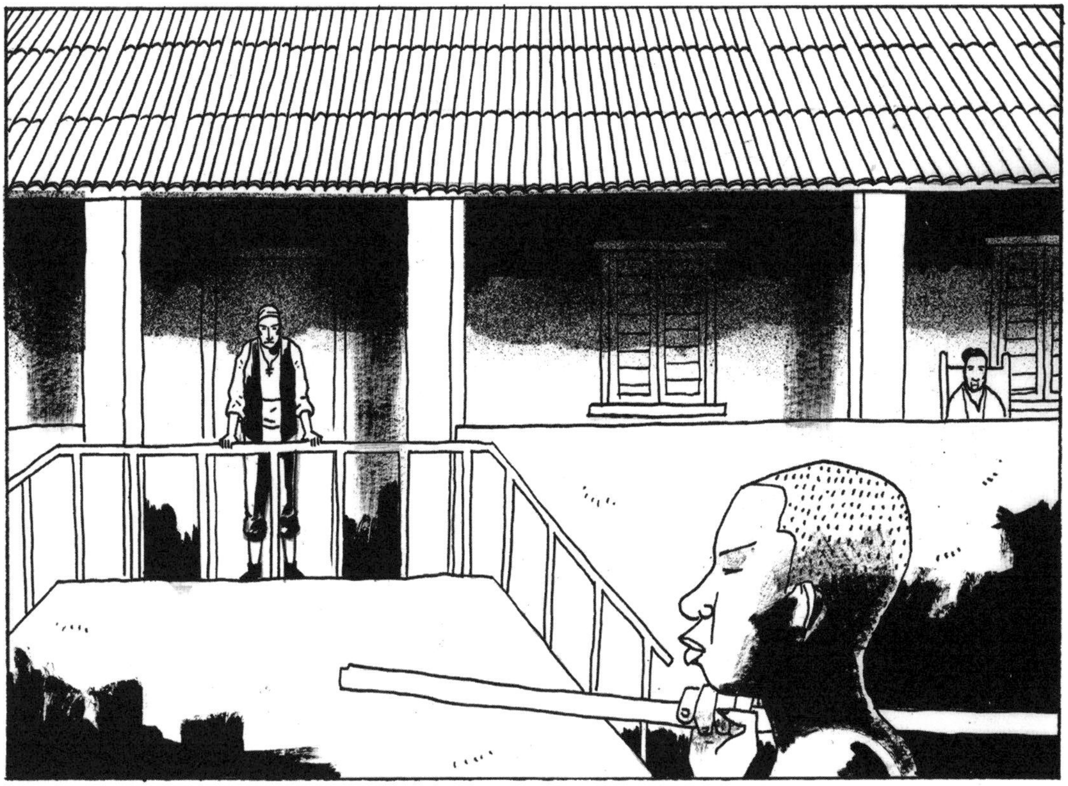

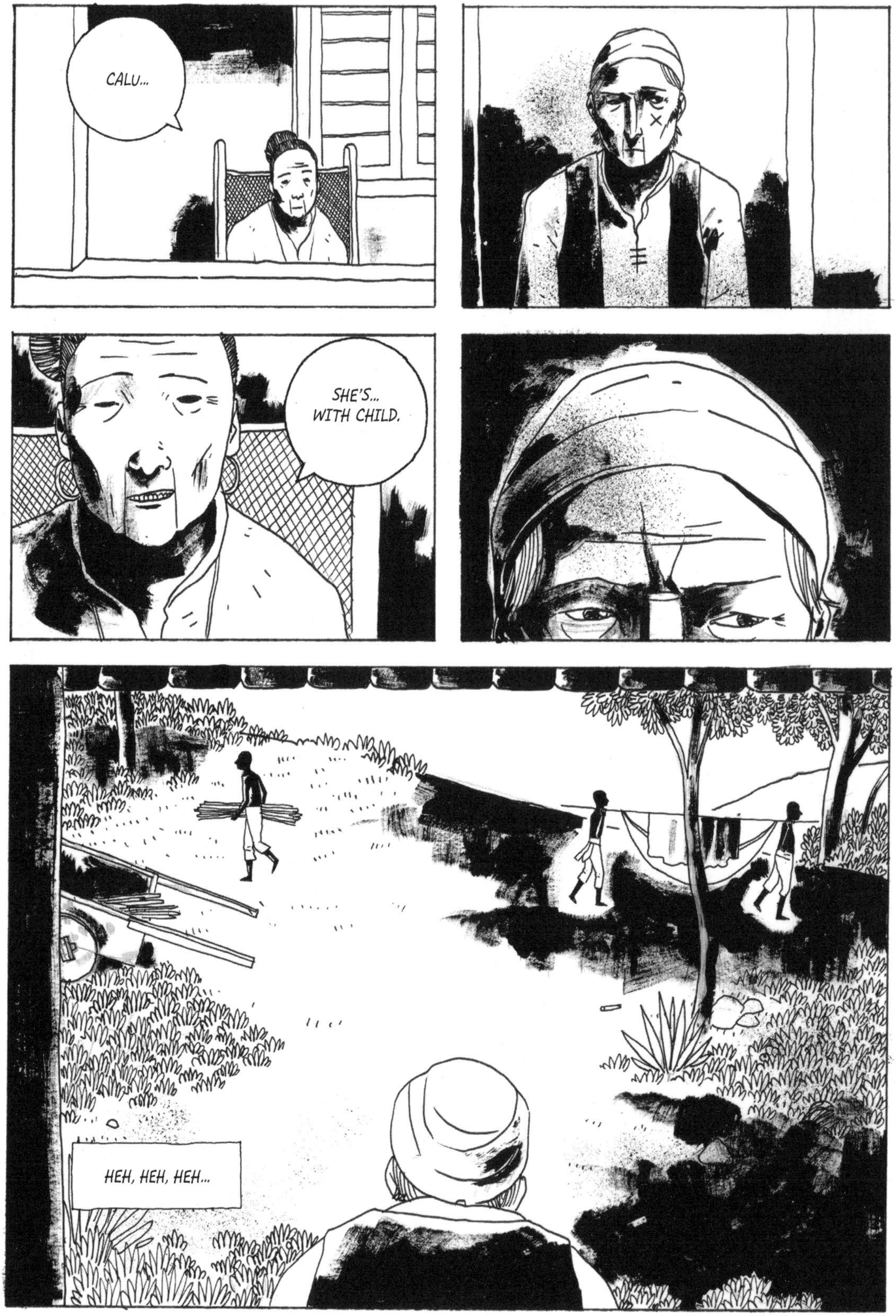
CALU...
SHE'S... WITH CHILD.
HEH, HEH, HEH...

GO ON,
PUSH!
HARDER!

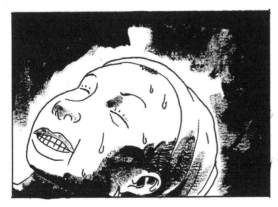

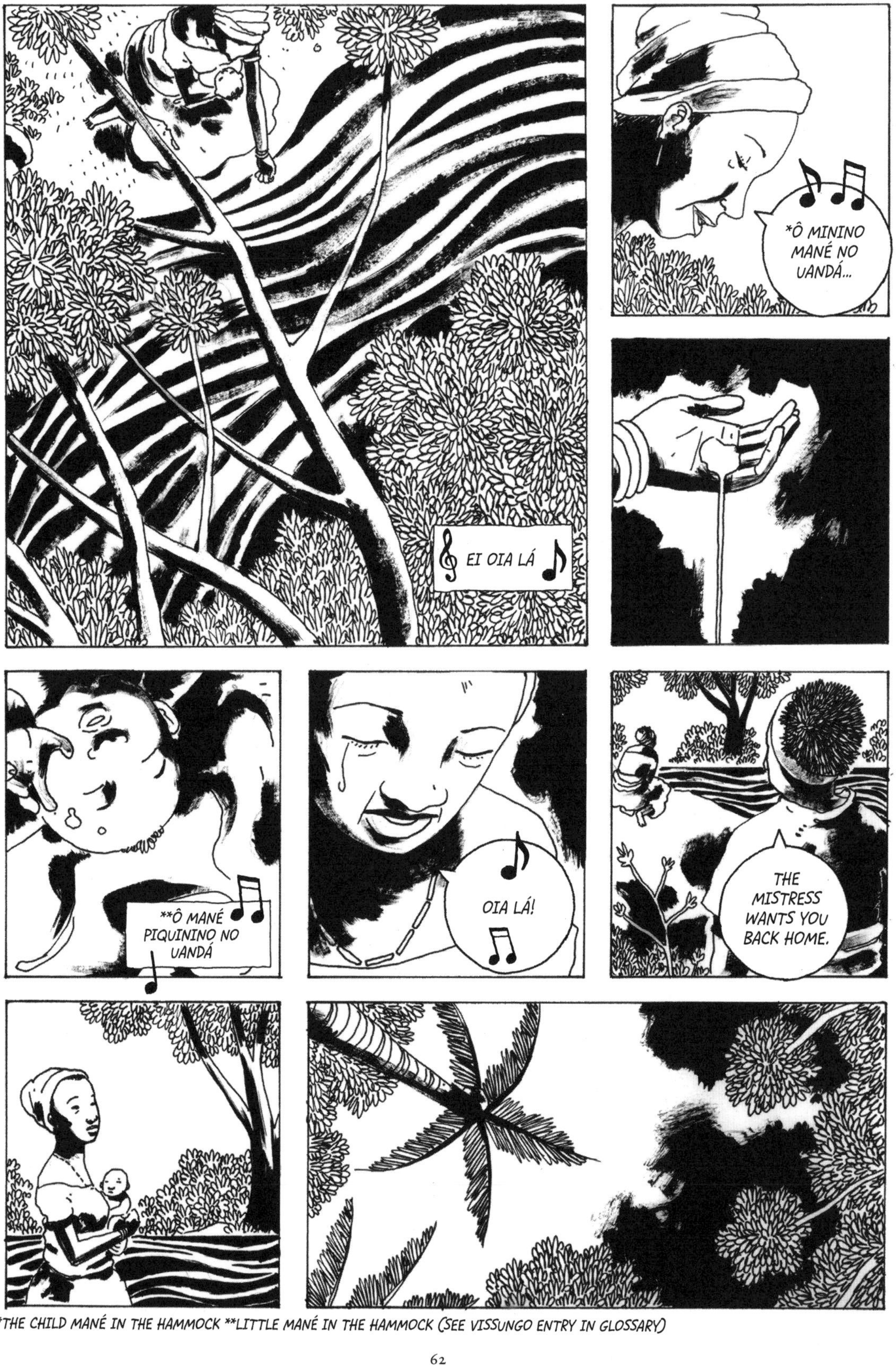
EI OIA LÁ
*Ô MININO MANÉ NO UANDÁ...
**Ô MANÉ PIQUININO NO UANDÁ
OIA LÁ!
THE MISTRESS WANTS YOU BACK HOME.

*THE CHILD MANÉ IN THE HAMMOCK **LITTLE MANÉ IN THE HAMMOCK (SEE VISSUNGO ENTRY IN GLOSSARY)

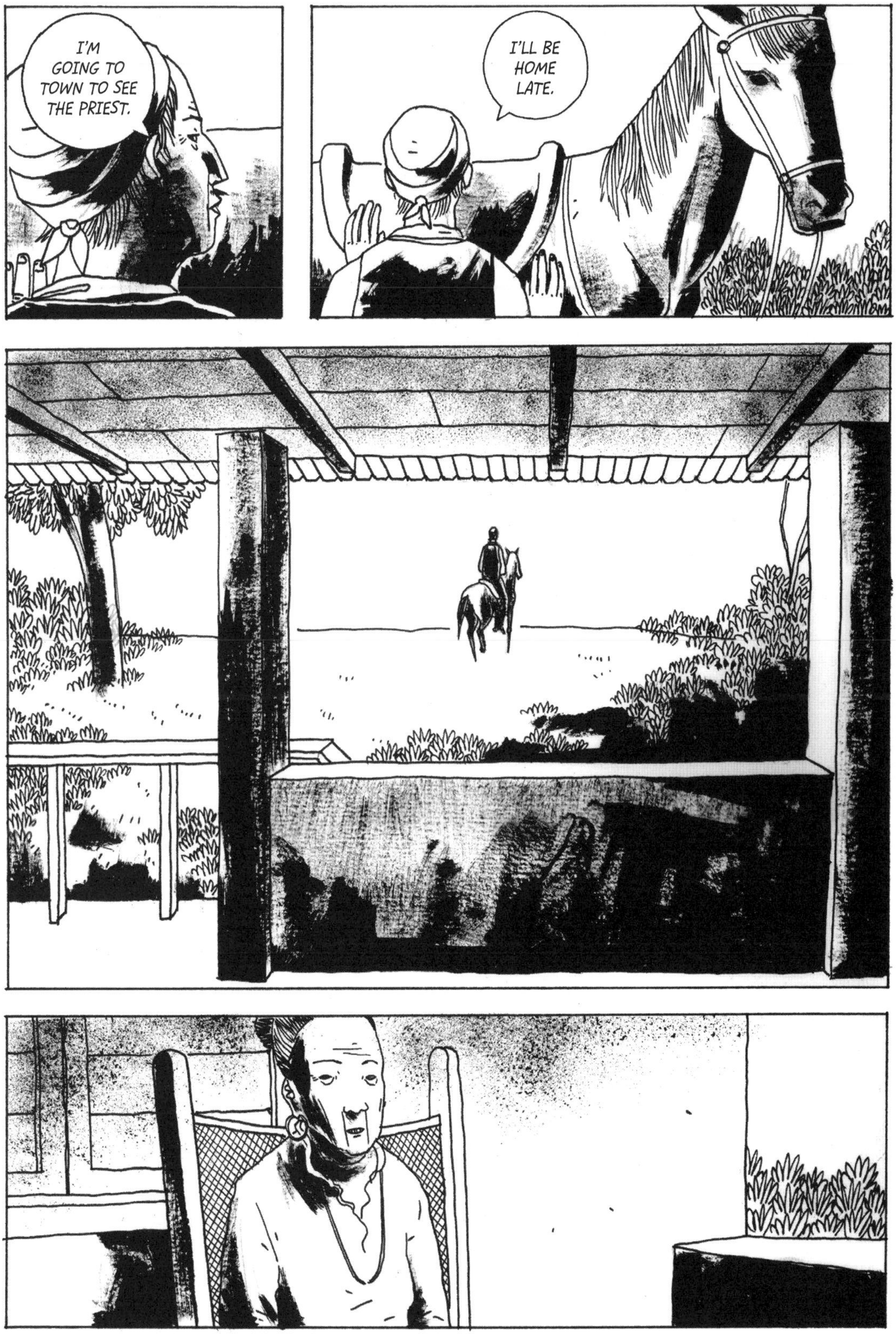
I'M GOING TO TOWN TO SEE THE PRIEST.
I'LL BE HOME LATE.

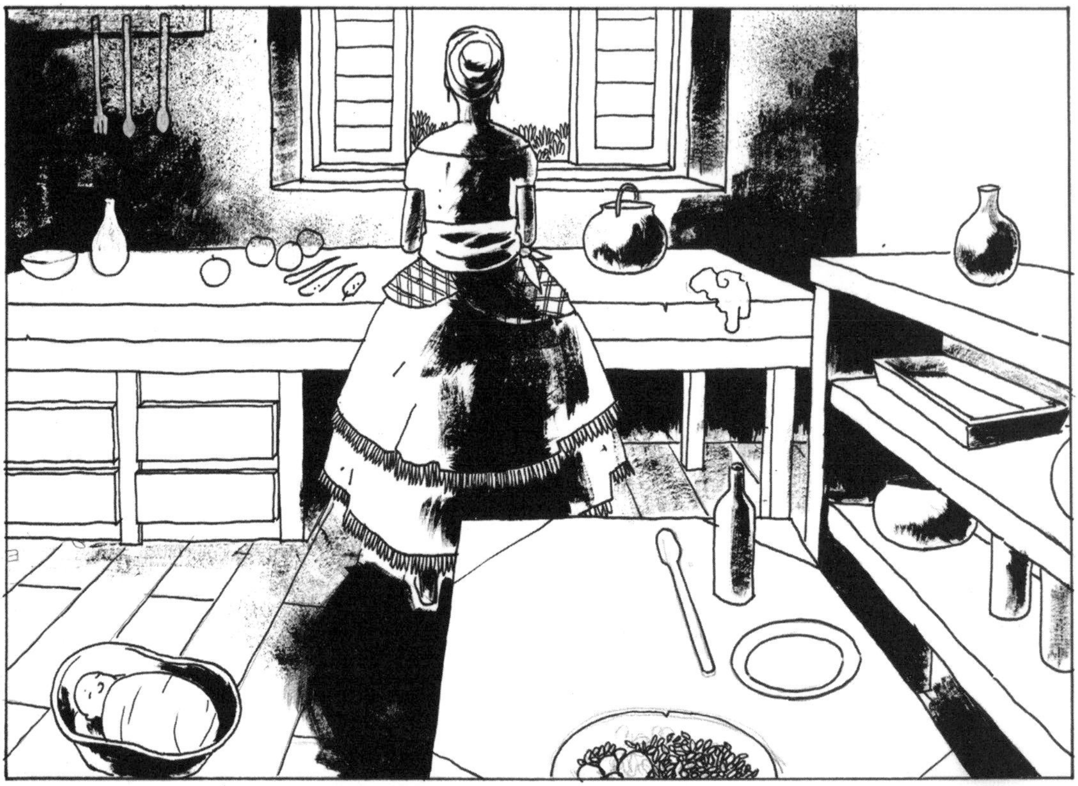

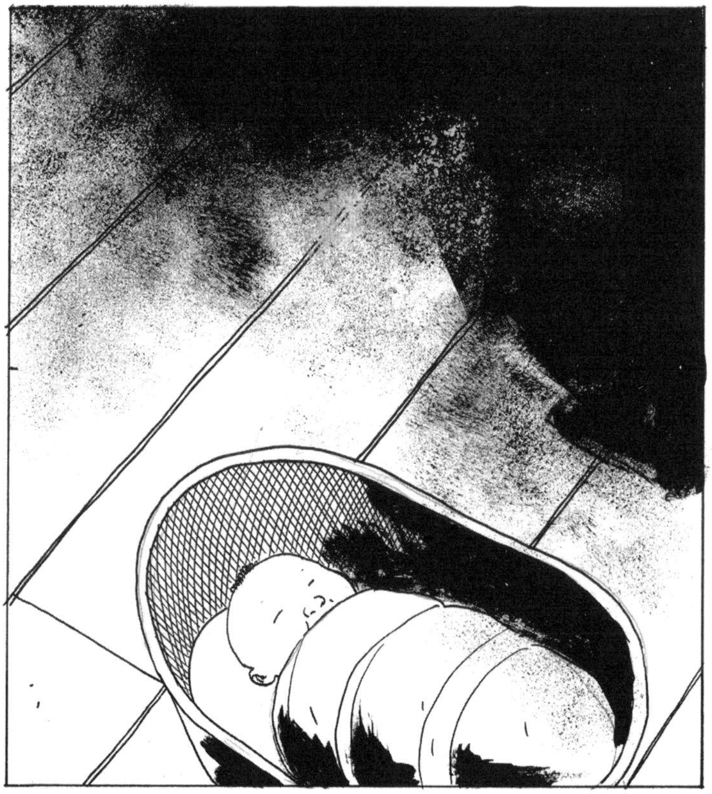

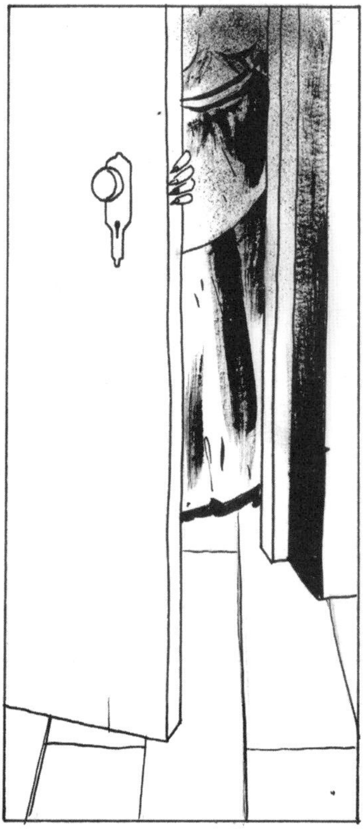

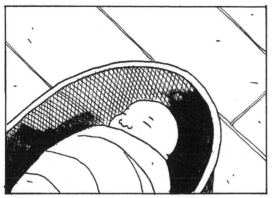

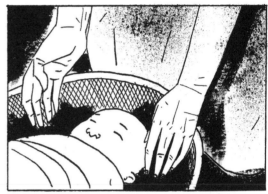

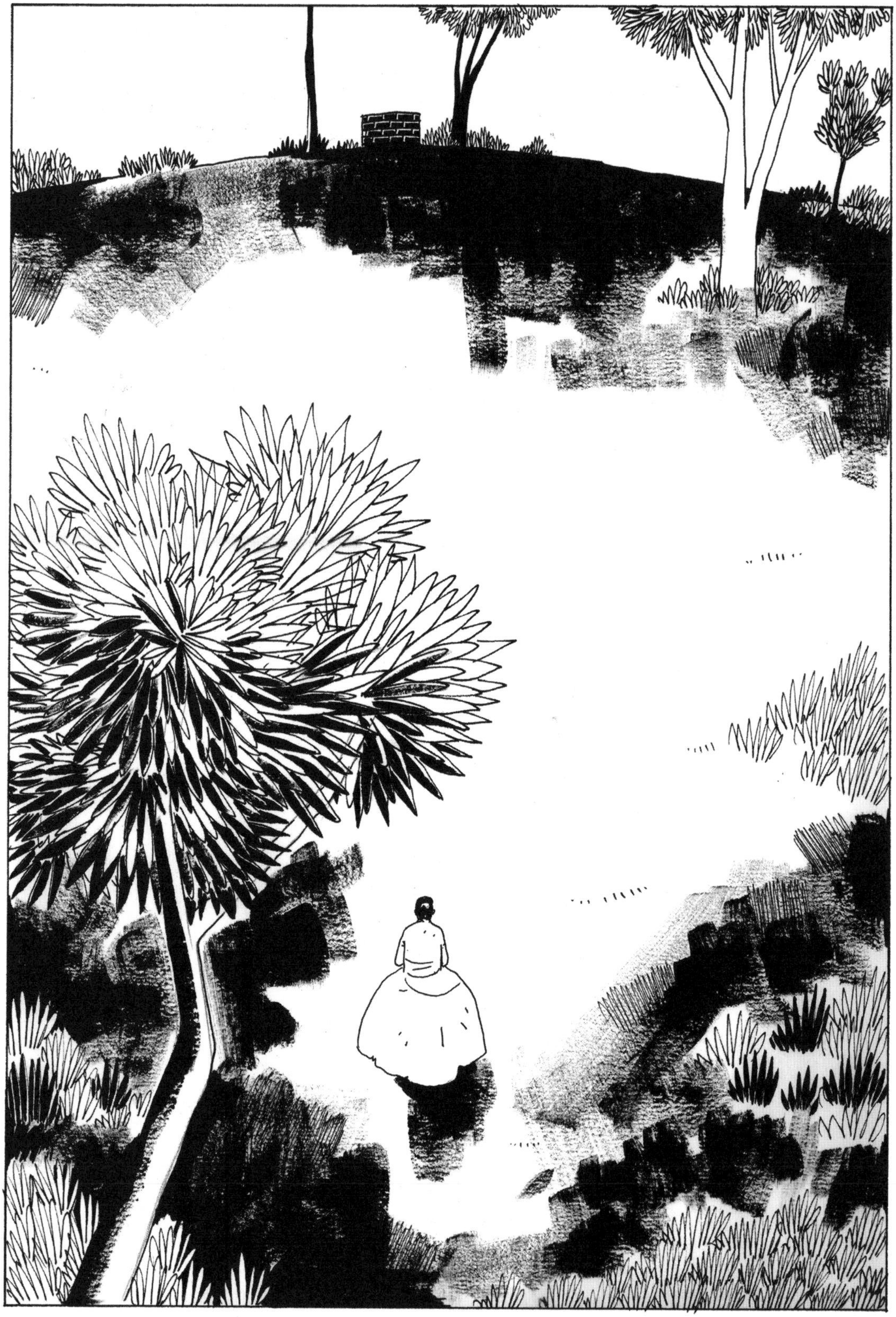

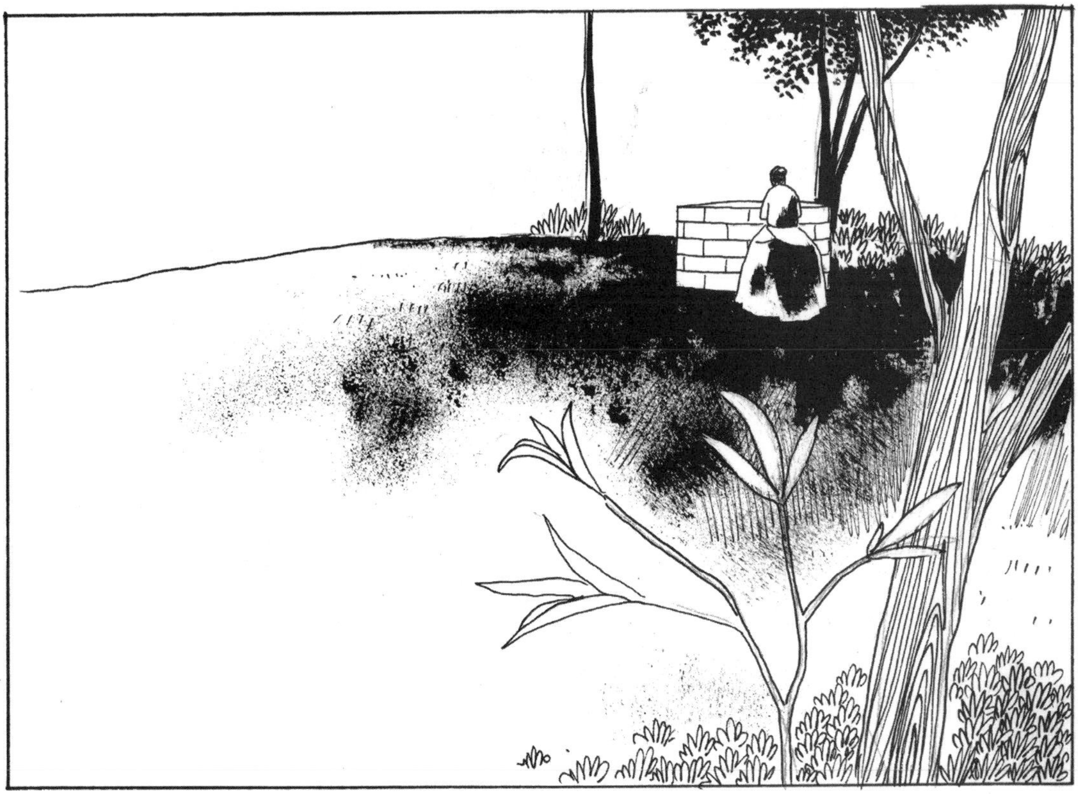

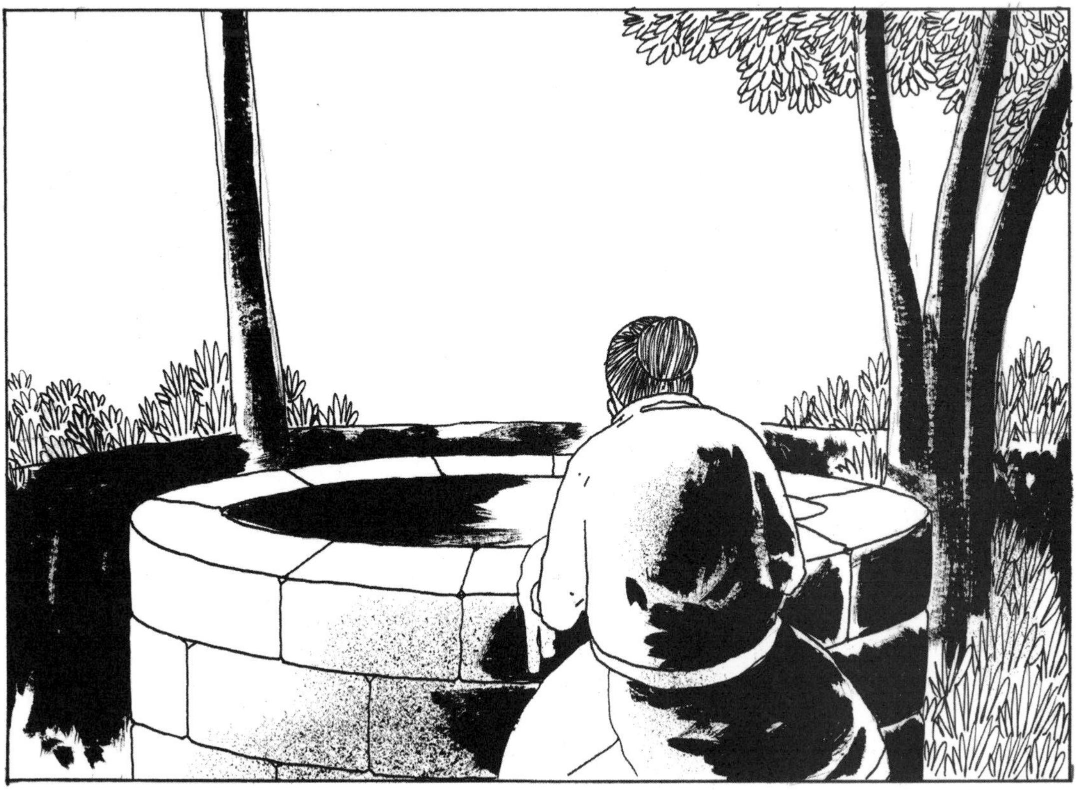

?!?!

WHAT'S GOING ON, CALU?

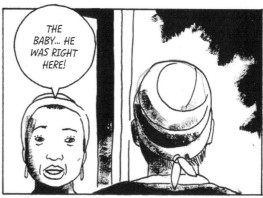

THE BABY... HE WAS RIGHT HERE!

THE
SUMID...

THE
SUMIDOURO
IS DEEP.

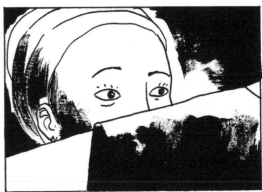

REALLY DEEP...

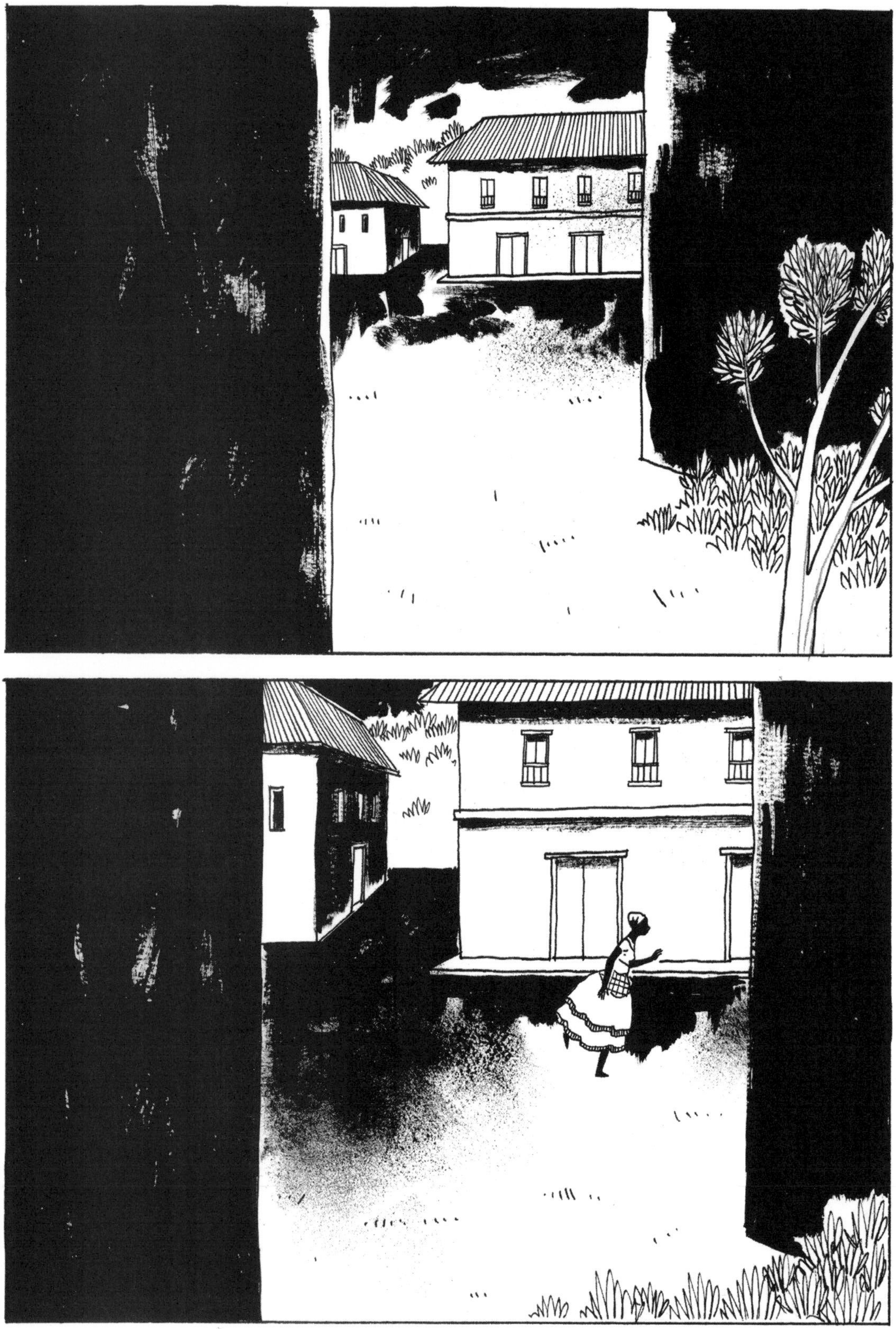

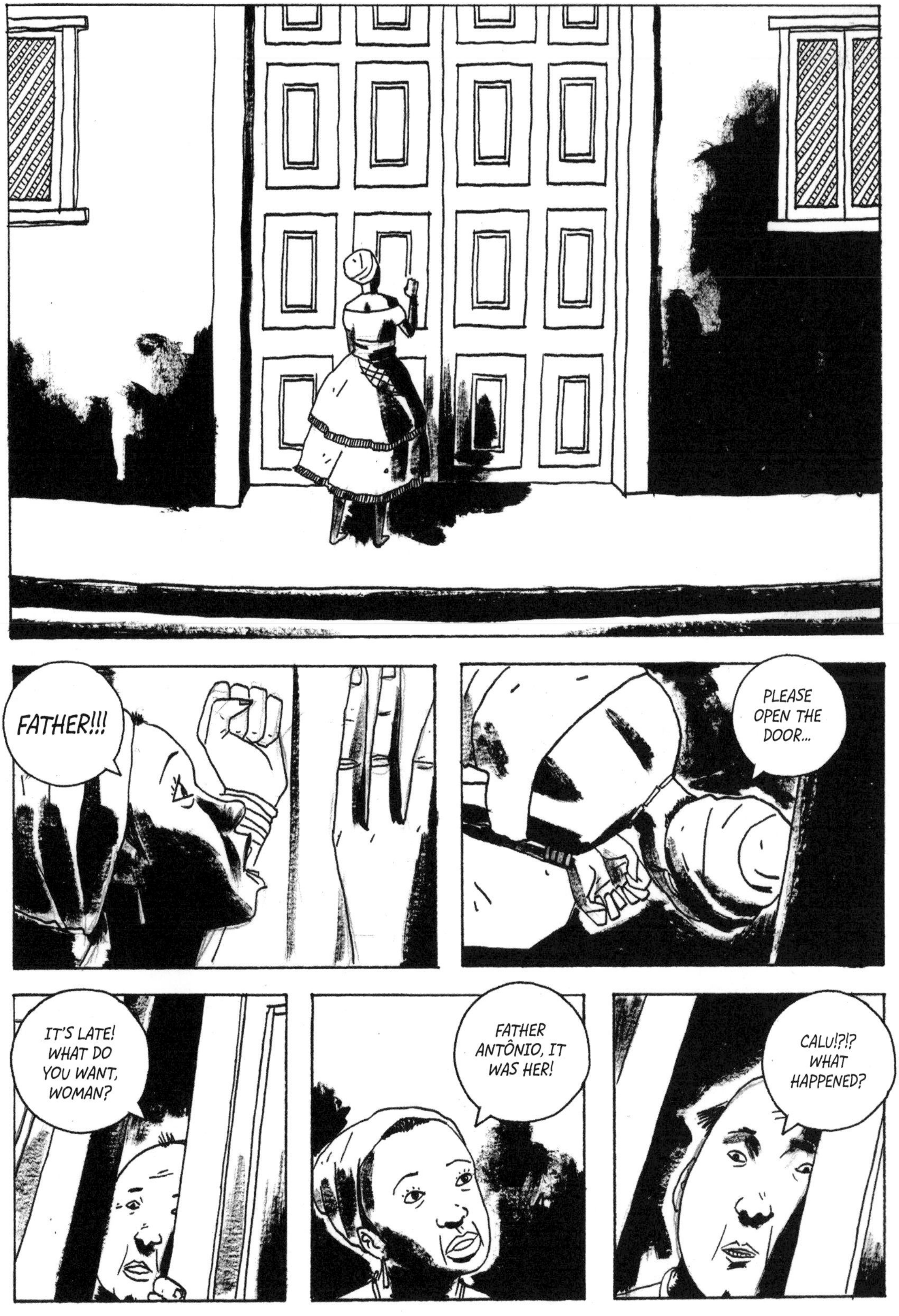
FATHER!!!
PLEASE OPEN THE DOOR...
IT'S LATE! WHAT DO YOU WANT, WOMAN?
FATHER ANTÔNIO, IT WAS HER!
CALU!?!? WHAT HAPPENED?

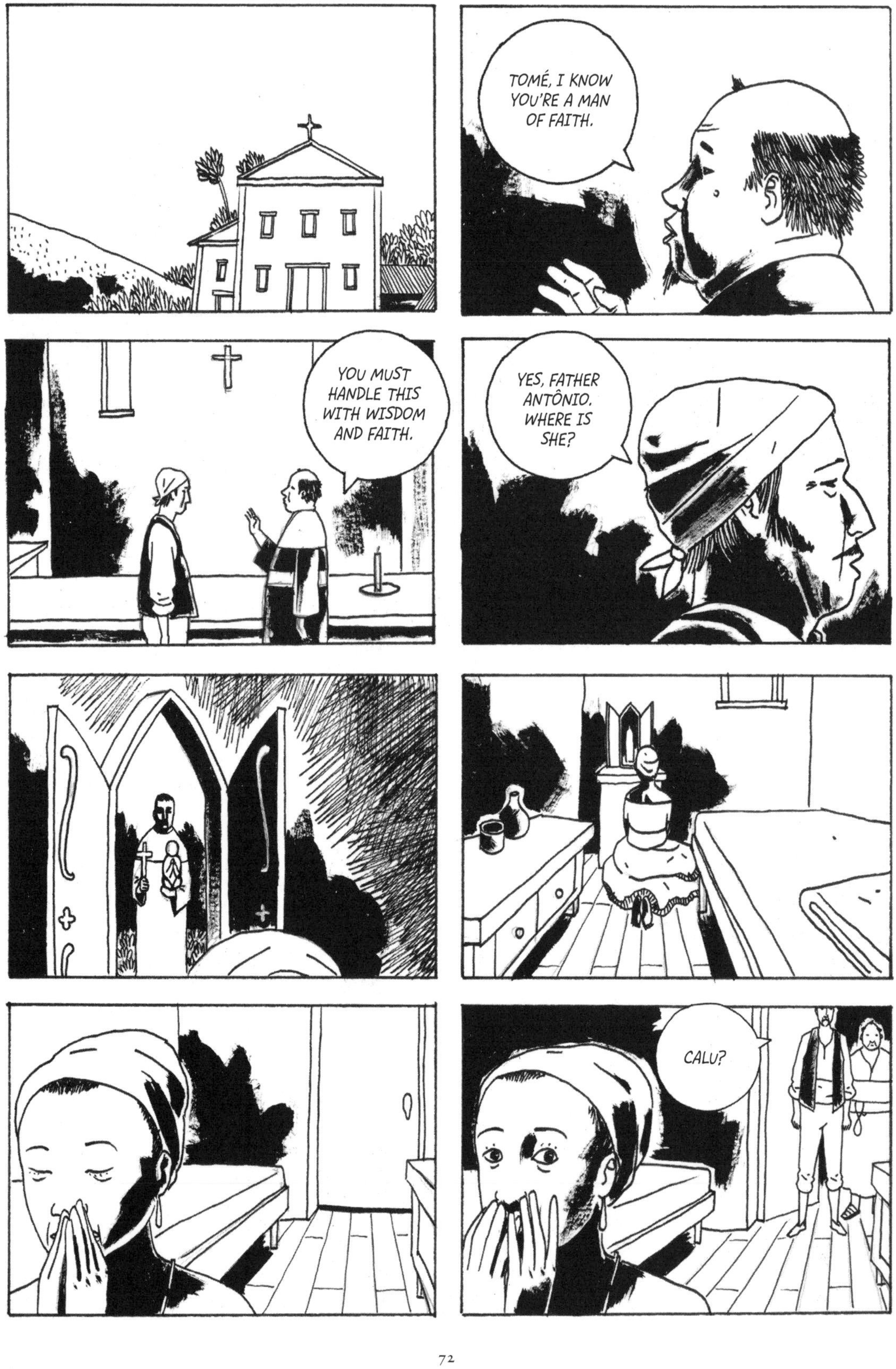
TOMÉ, I KNOW YOU'RE A MAN OF FAITH.
YOU MUST HANDLE THIS WITH WISDOM AND FAITH.
YES, FATHER ANTÔNIO. WHERE IS SHE?
CALU?

YOU SHOULDN'T HAVE TALKED TO THE PRIEST, CALU.

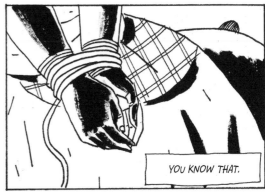

YOU KNOW THAT.

IT WON'T DO. THE PRIEST MUSTN'T FIND OUT.

NOBODY CAN.

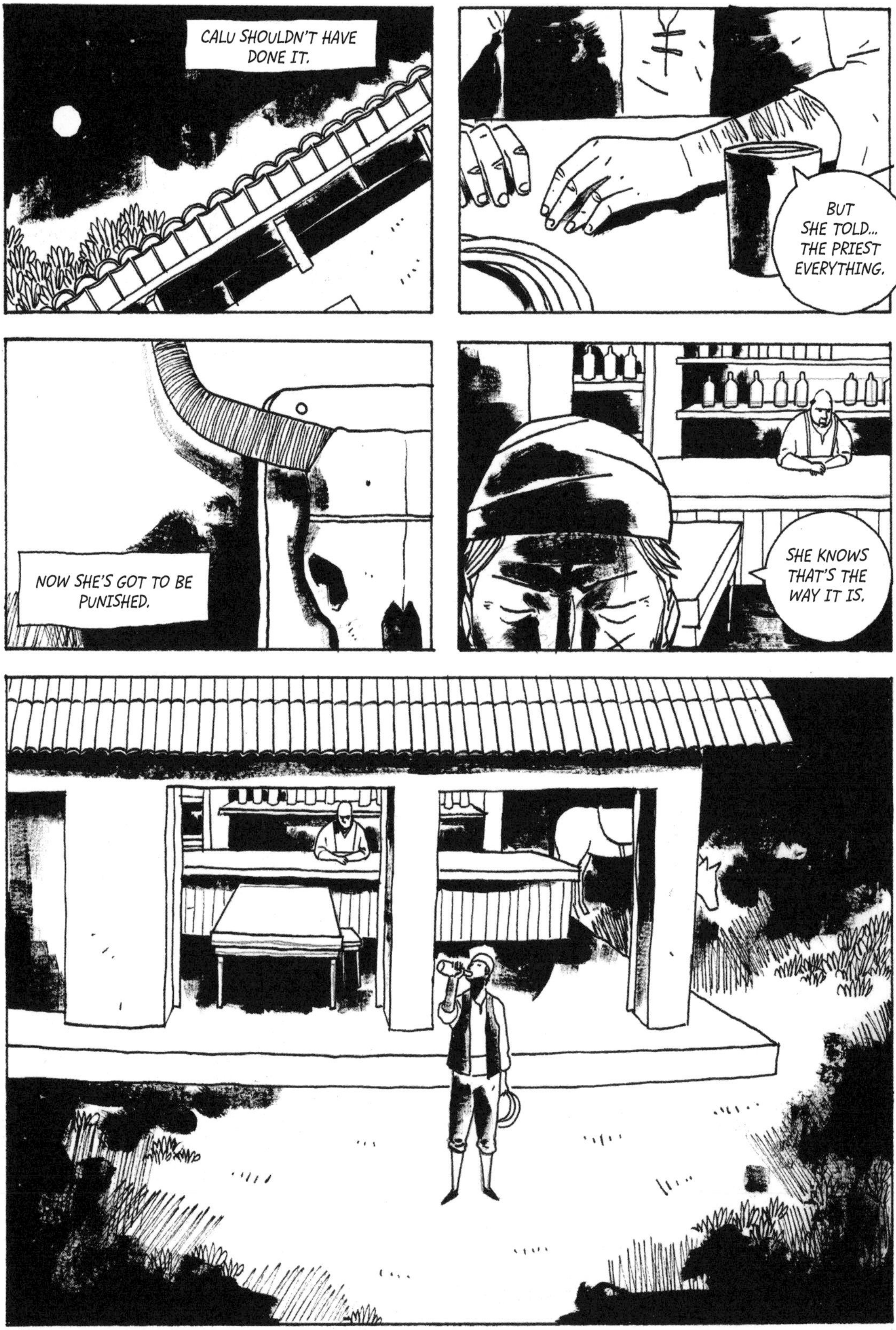
CALU SHOULDN'T HAVE DONE IT.
BUT SHE TOLD... THE PRIEST EVERYTHING.
NOW SHE'S GOT TO BE PUNISHED.
SHE KNOWS THAT'S THE WAY IT IS.

HE'S COMING. YOU'LL SEE.

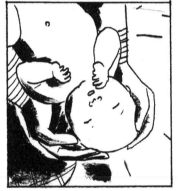

YOU SHOULDN'T HAVE TOLD, CALU.

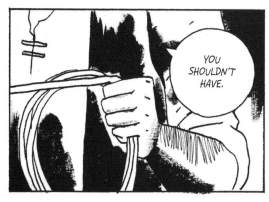

YOU SHOULDN'T HAVE.

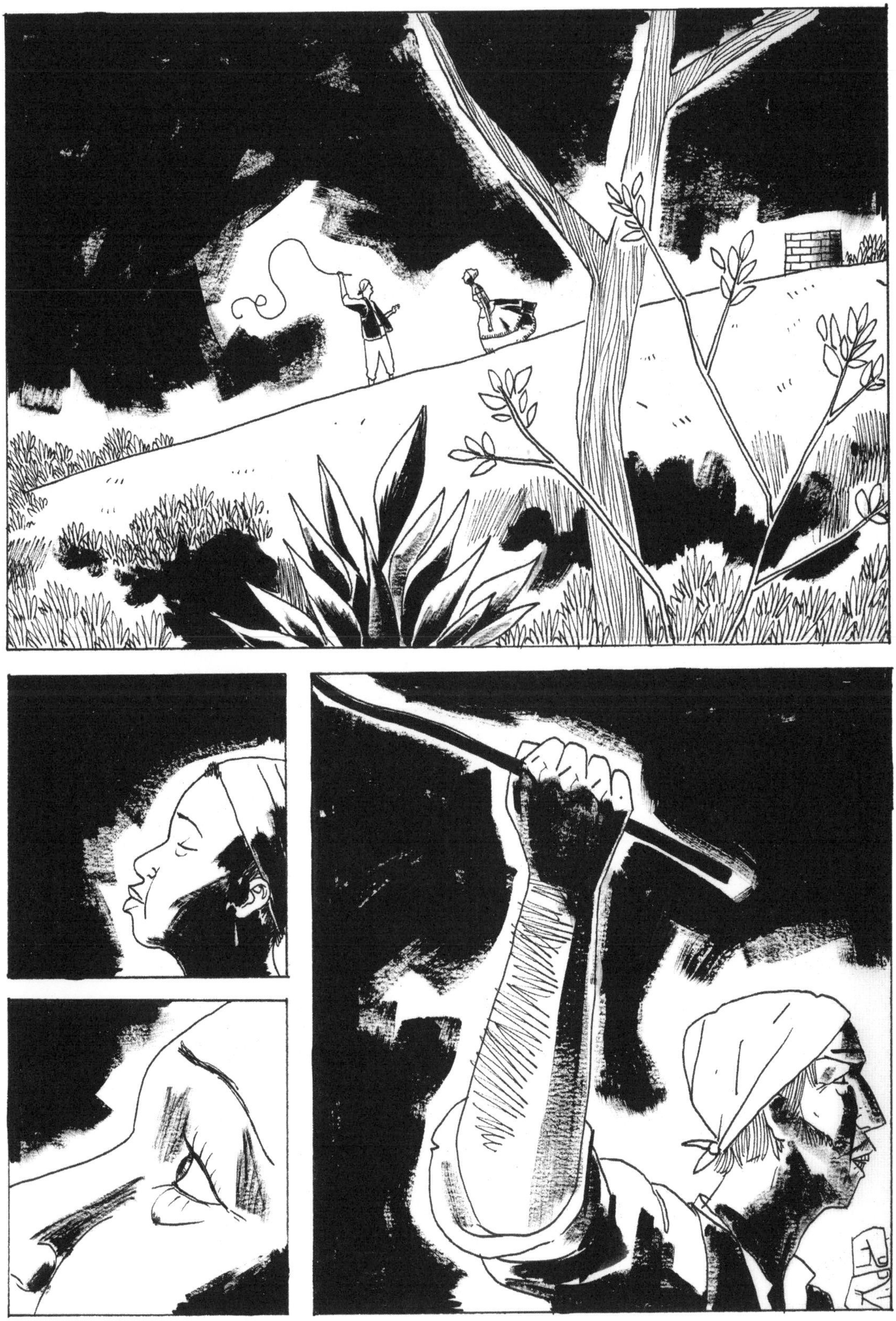

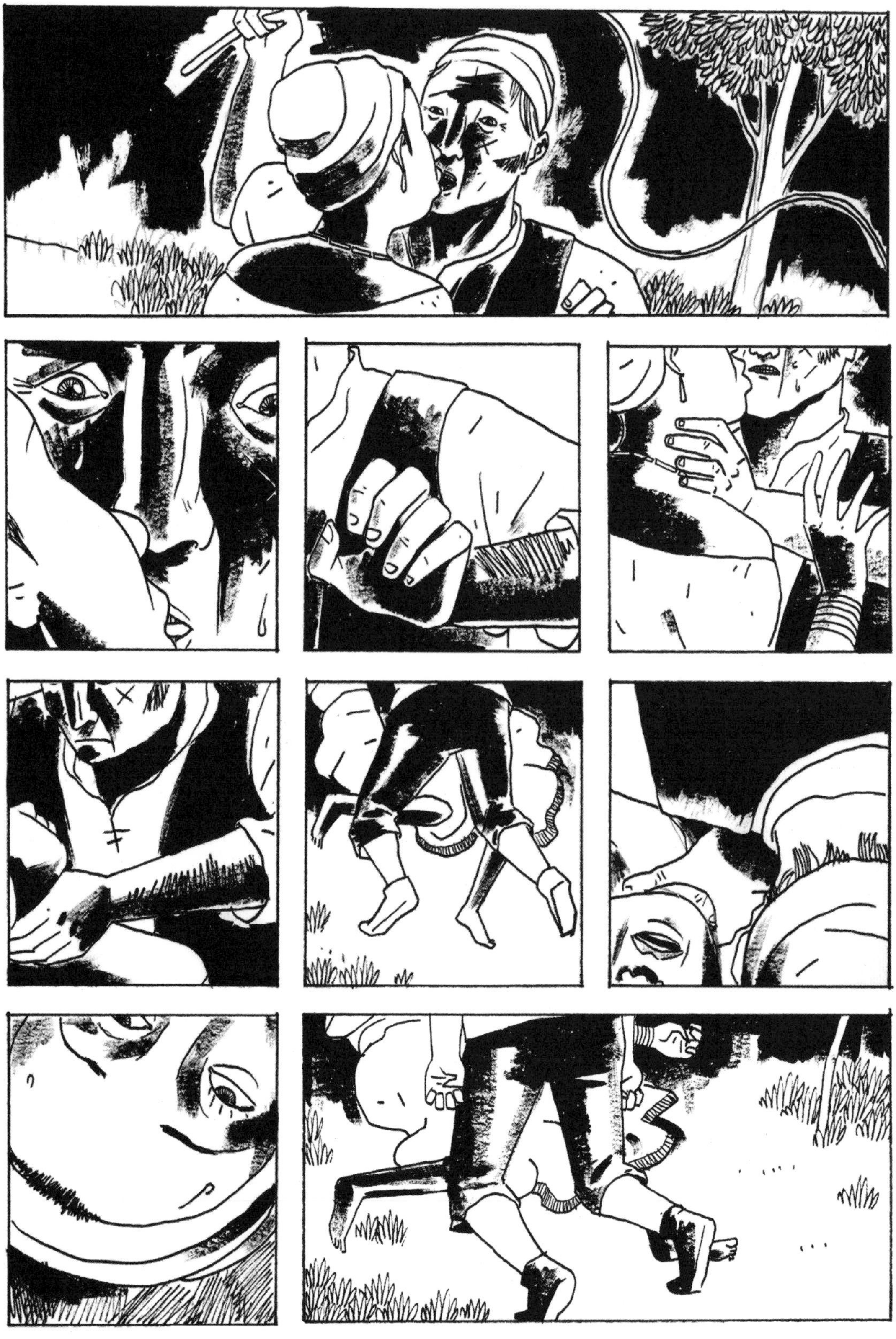
...
...

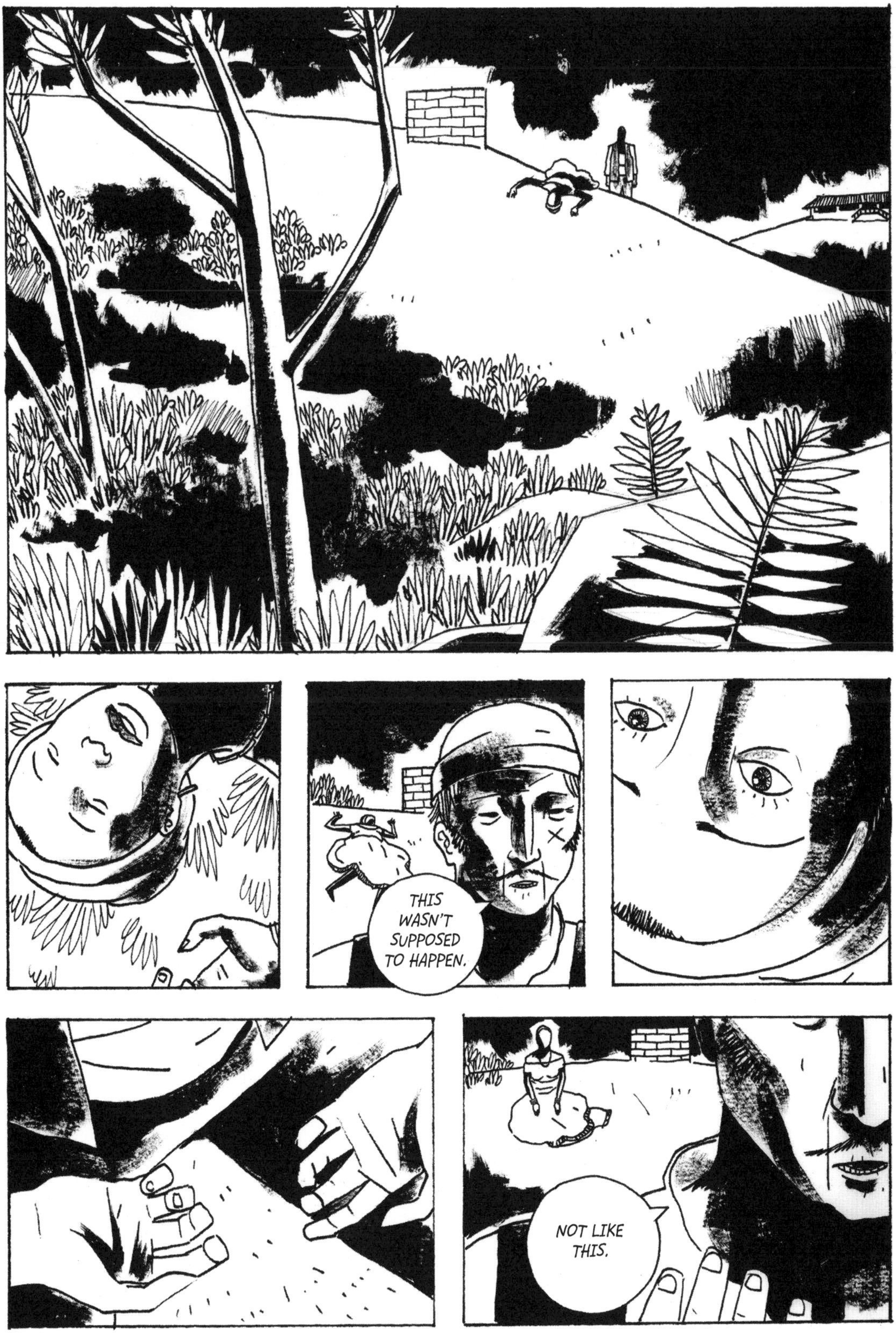
THIS WASN'T SUPPOSED TO HAPPEN.
NOT LIKE THIS.

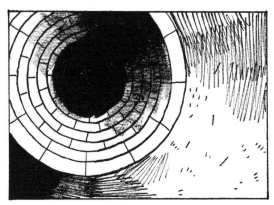

NO...

IT WASN'T...

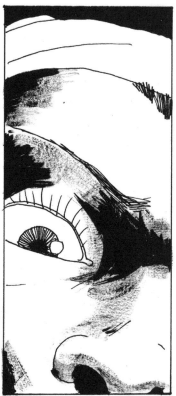

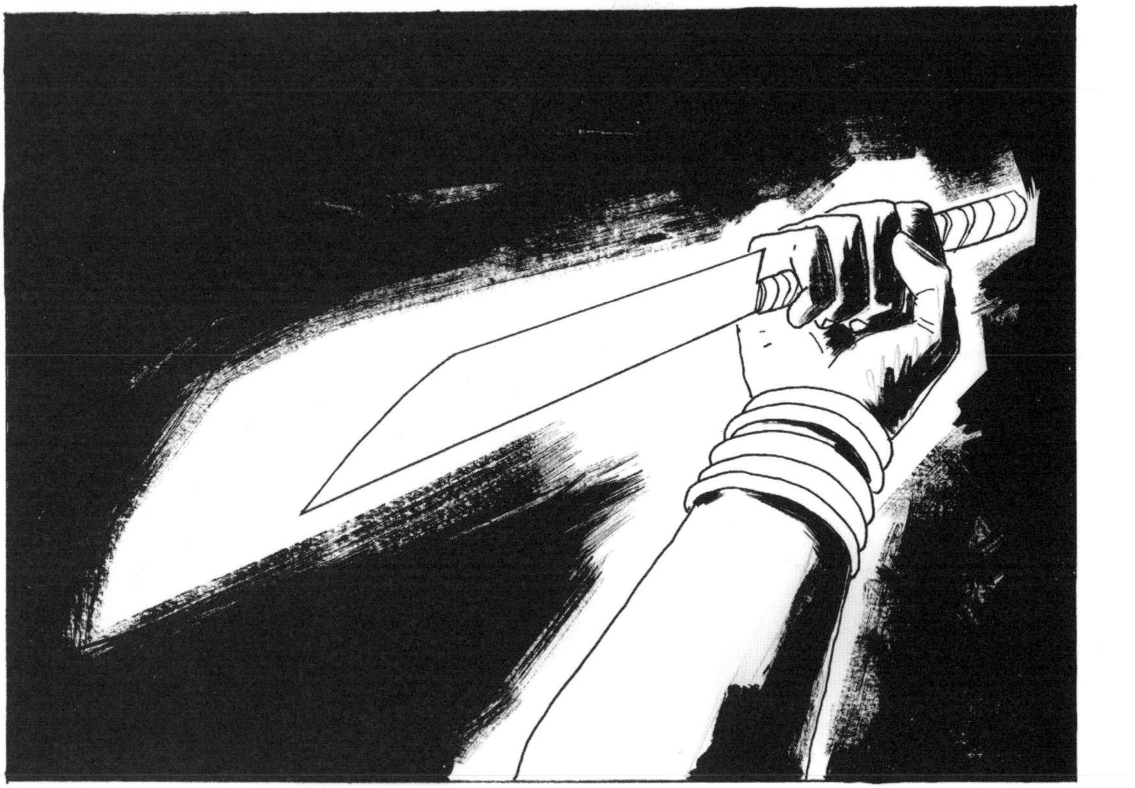

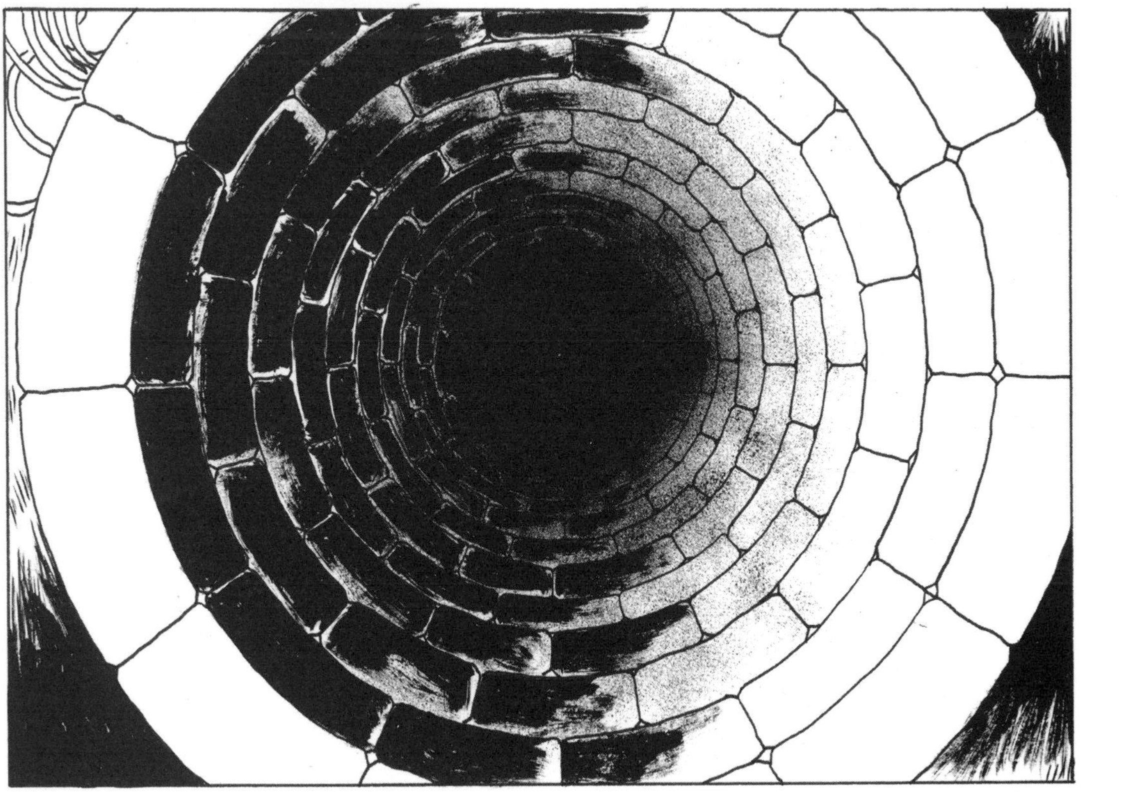

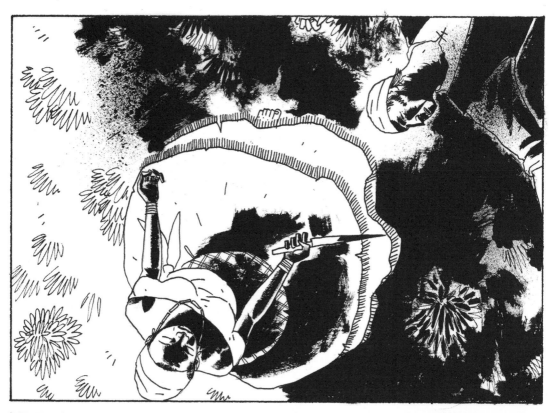

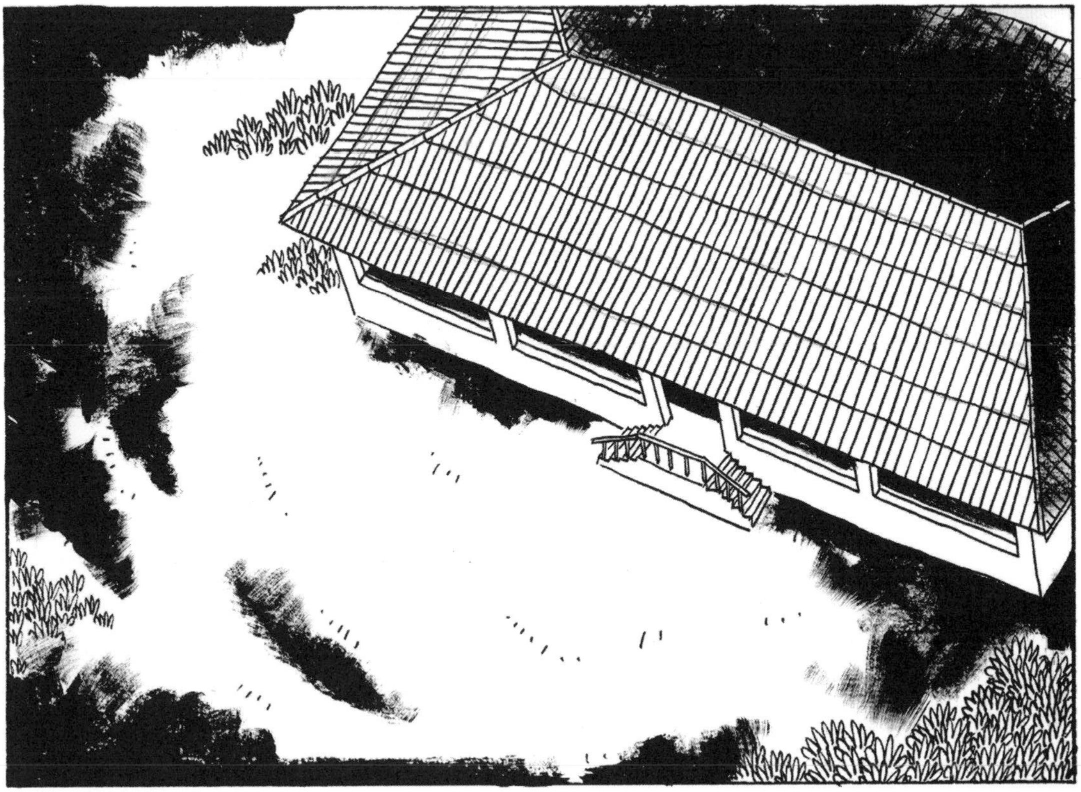

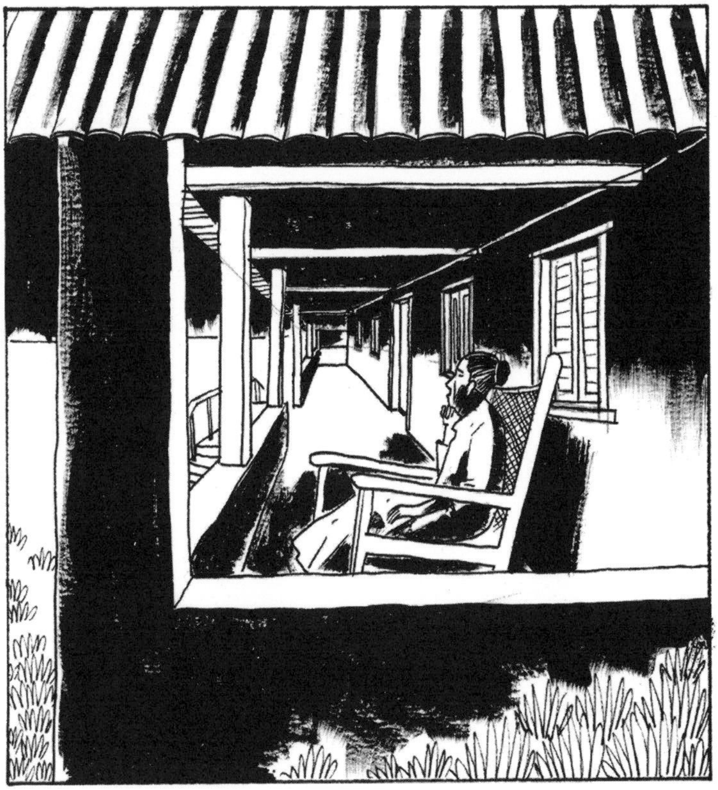

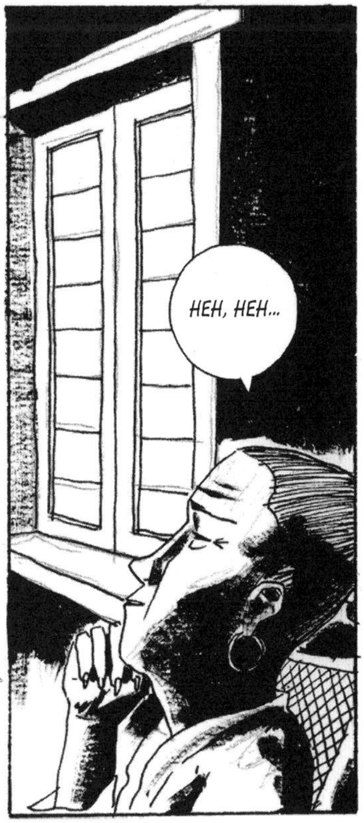
HEH, HEH...

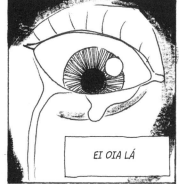

EI OIA LÁ

Ô MININO MANÉ NO UANDÁ

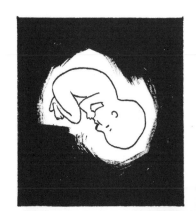

OIA LÁ!

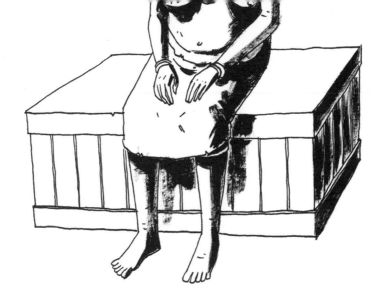

cumbe

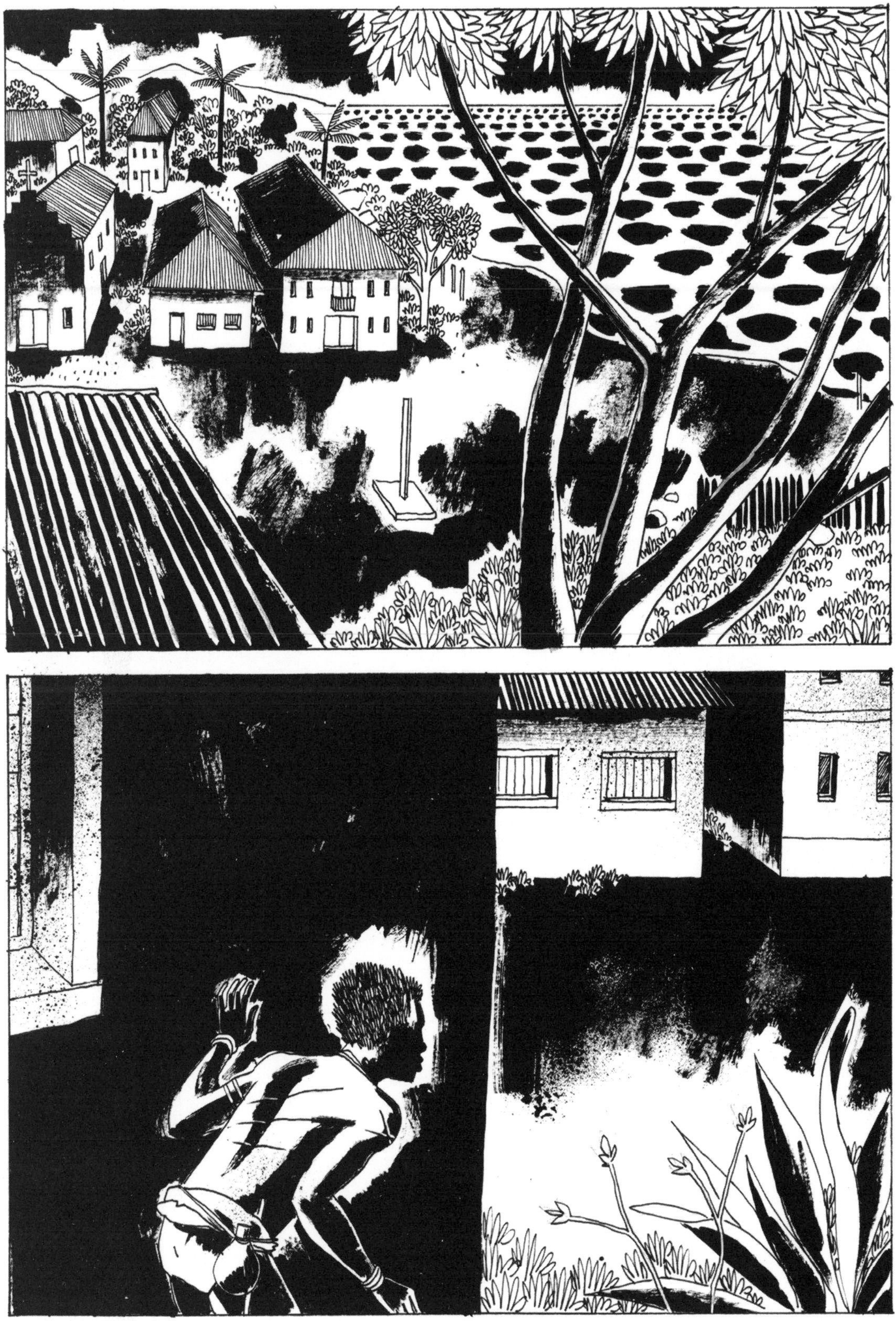

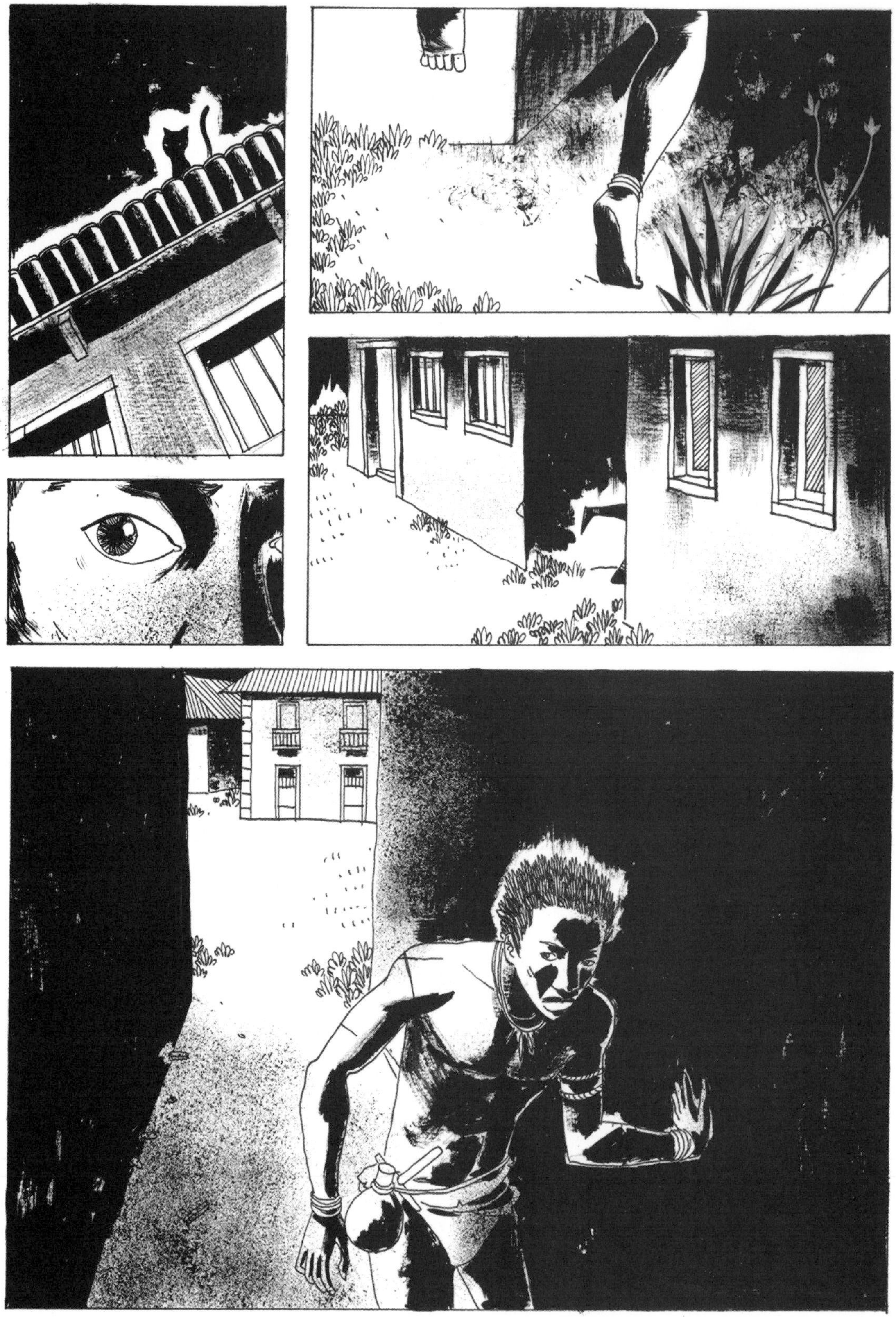

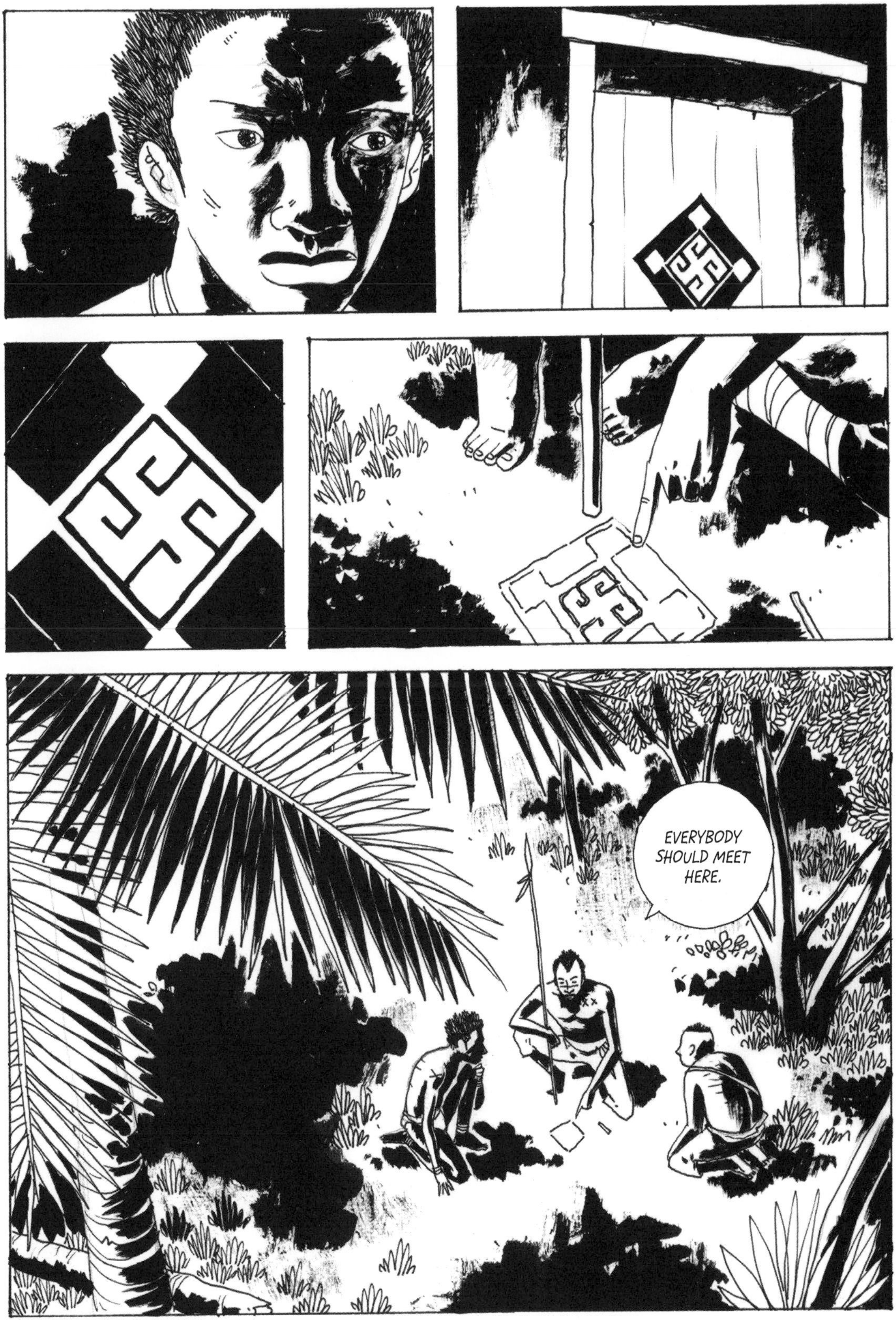
EVERYBODY SHOULD MEET HERE.

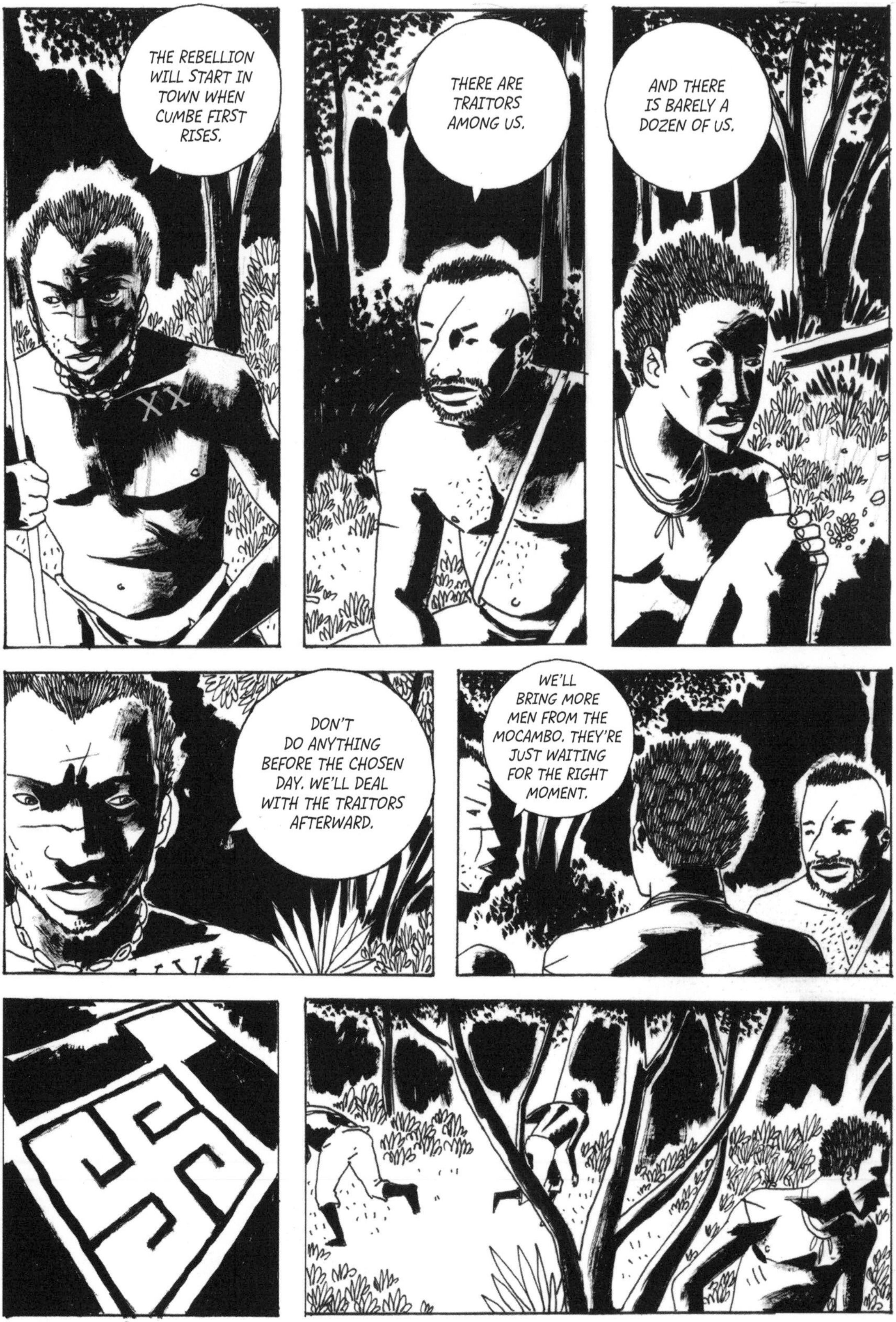
THE REBELLION WILL START IN TOWN WHEN CUMBE FIRST RISES.
THERE ARE TRAITORS AMONG US.
AND THERE IS BARELY A DOZEN OF US.
DON'T DO ANYTHING BEFORE THE CHOSEN DAY. WE'LL DEAL WITH THE TRAITORS AFTERWARD.
WE'LL BRING MORE MEN FROM THE MOCAMBO. THEY'RE JUST WAITING FOR THE RIGHT MOMENT.

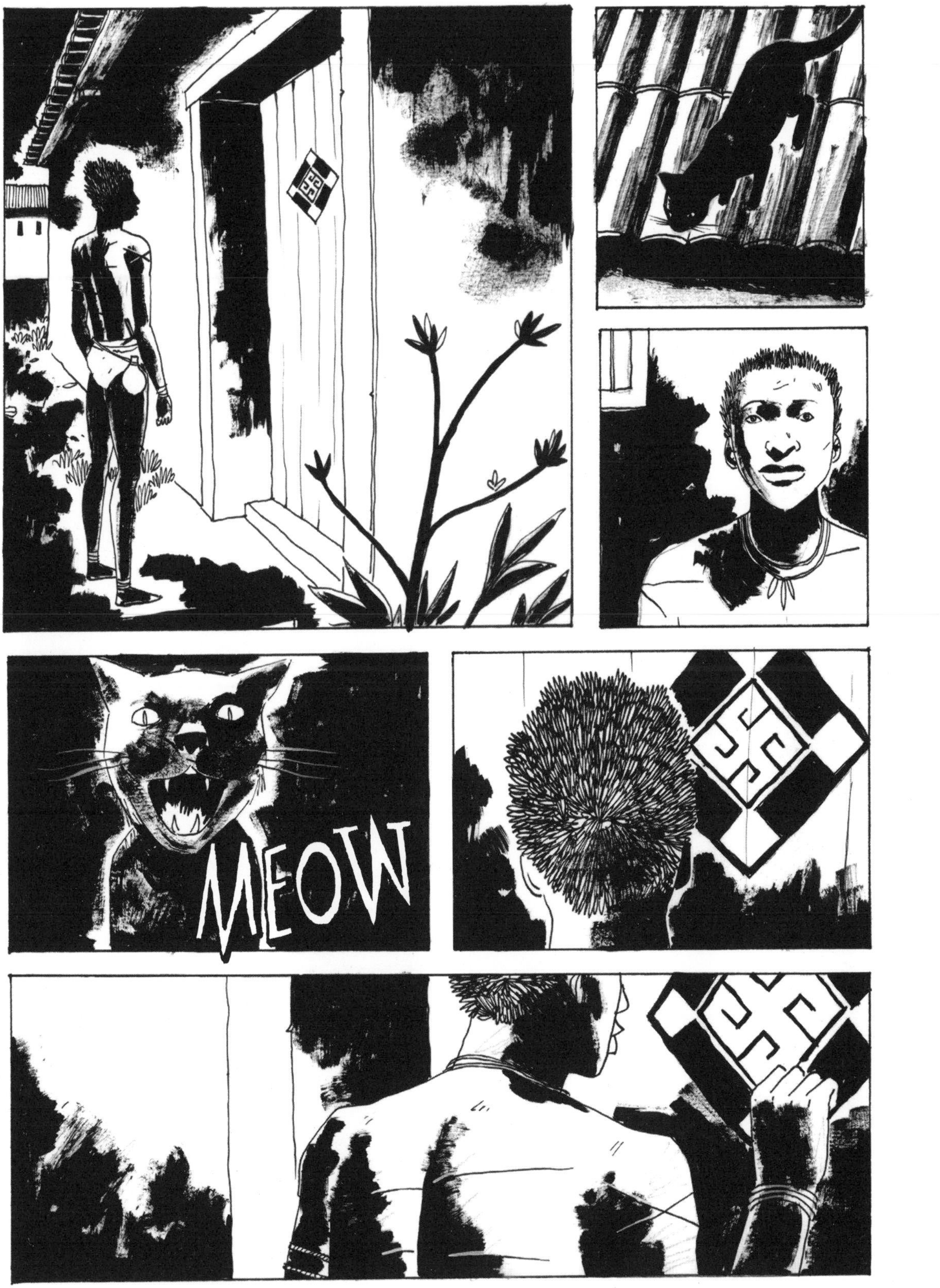
MEOW

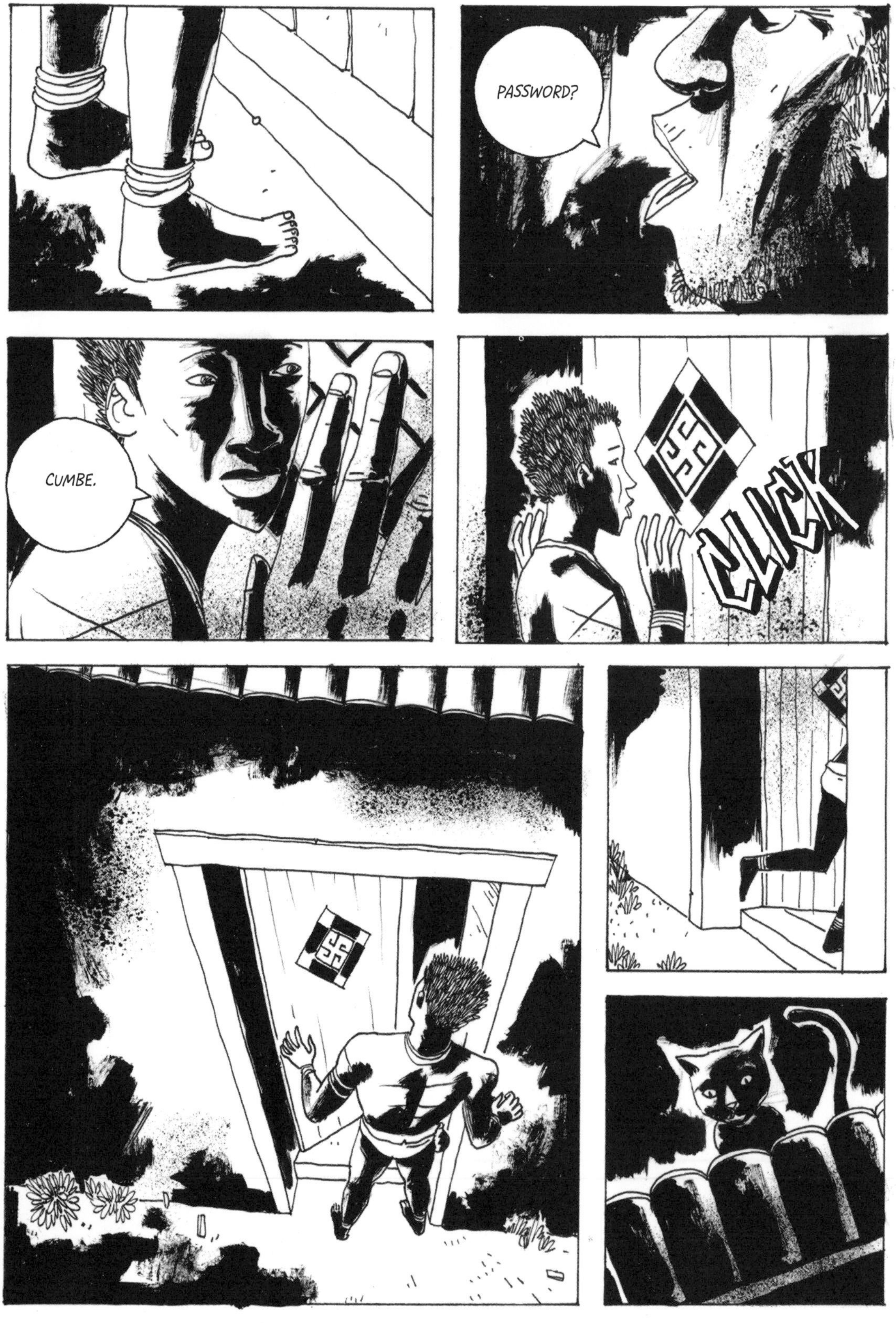
PASSWORD?
CUMBE.
CLICK

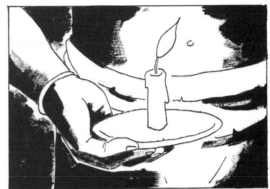

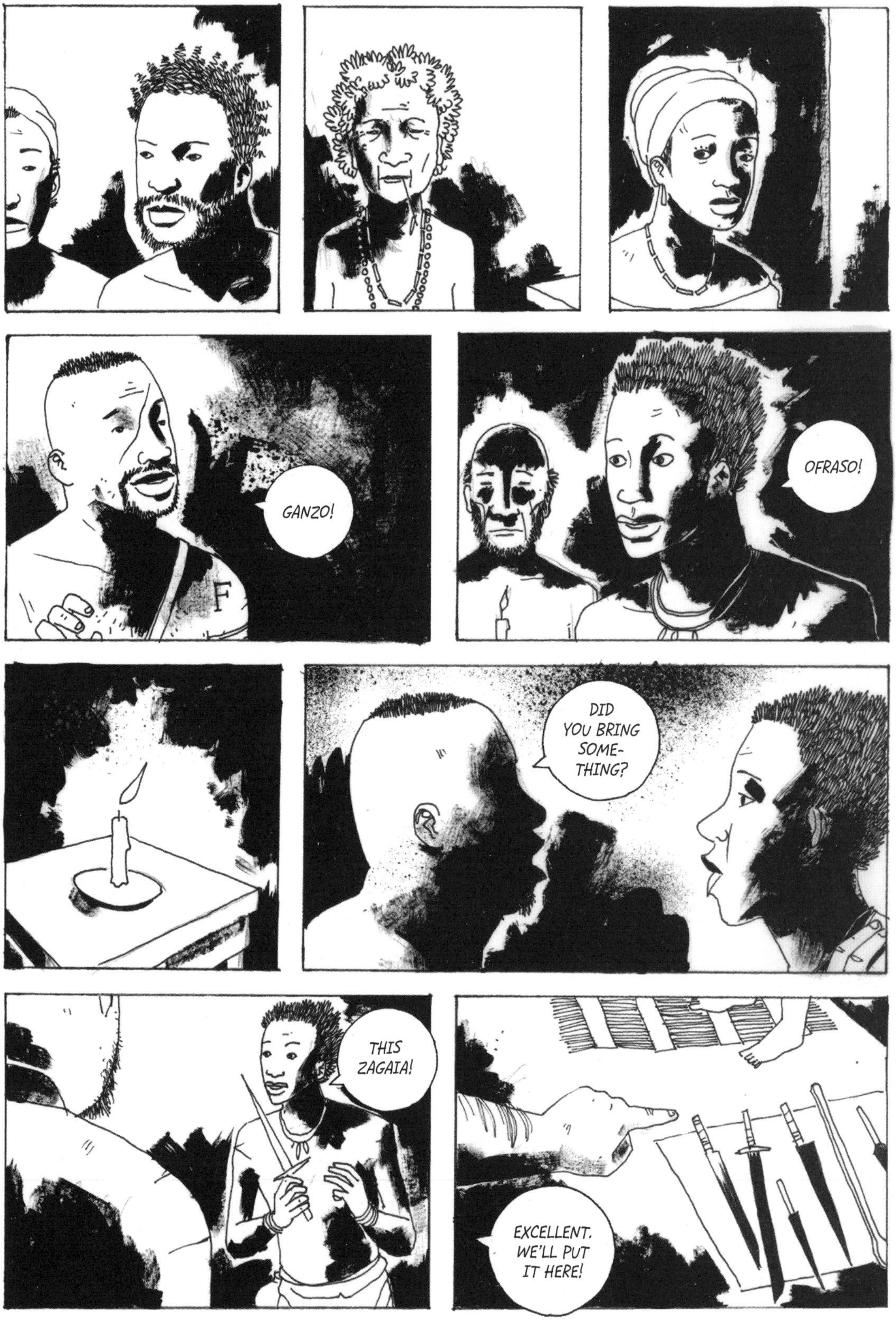
GANZO!
OFRASO!
DID YOU BRING SOME-THING?
THIS ZAGAIA!
EXCELLENT. WE'LL PUT IT HERE!

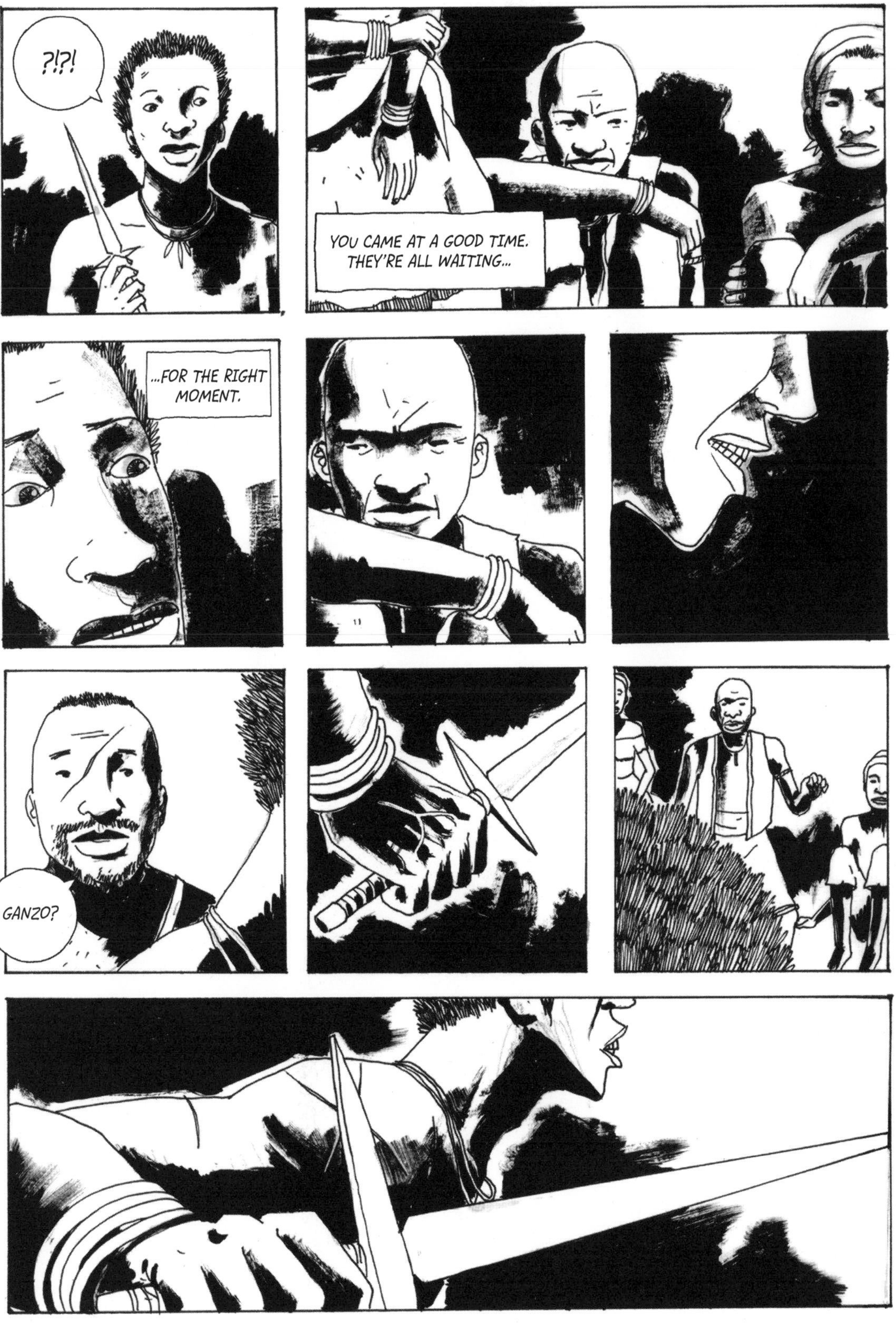
?!?!
YOU CAME AT A GOOD TIME. THEY'RE ALL WAITING...
...FOR THE RIGHT MOMENT.
GANZO?

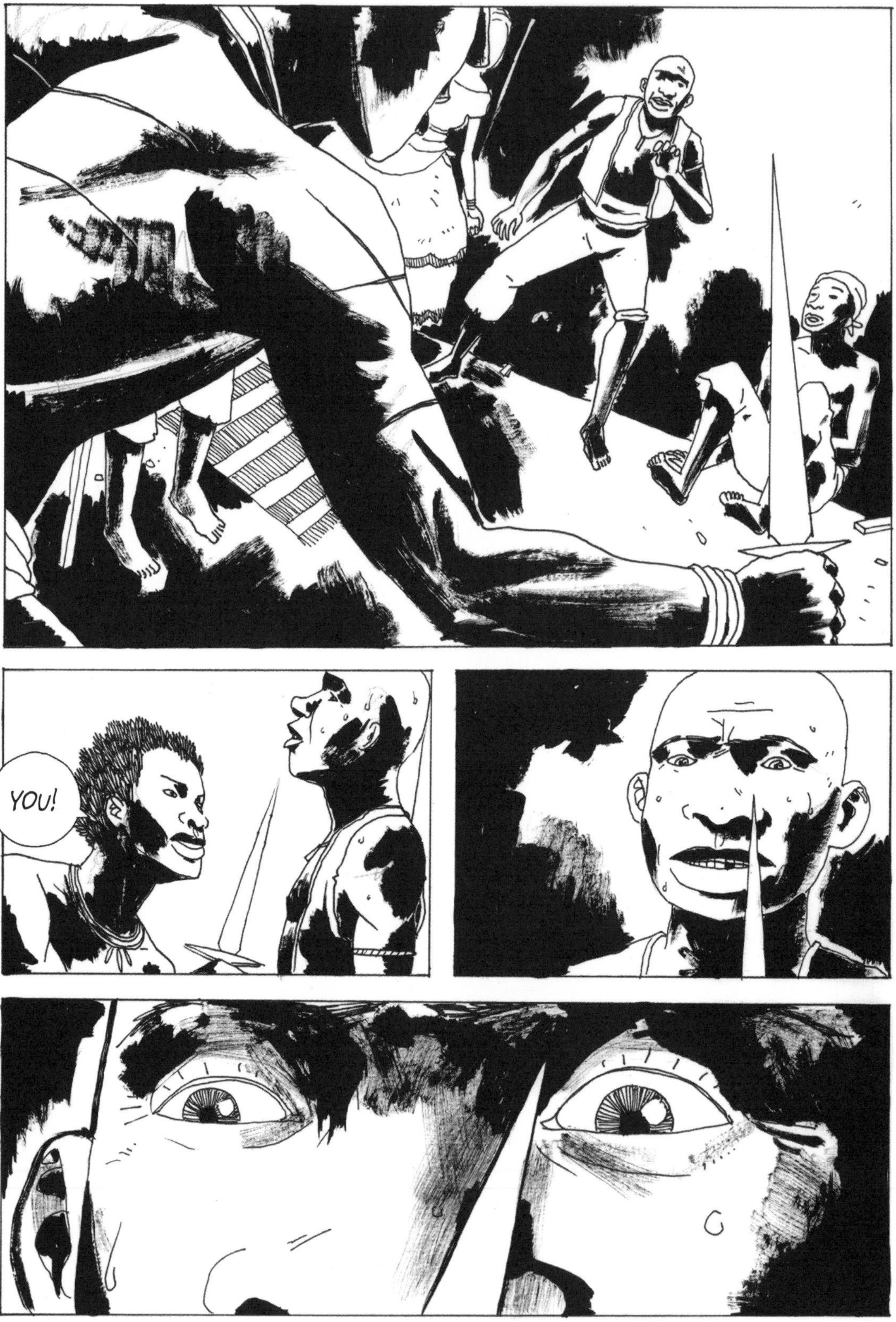
YOU!

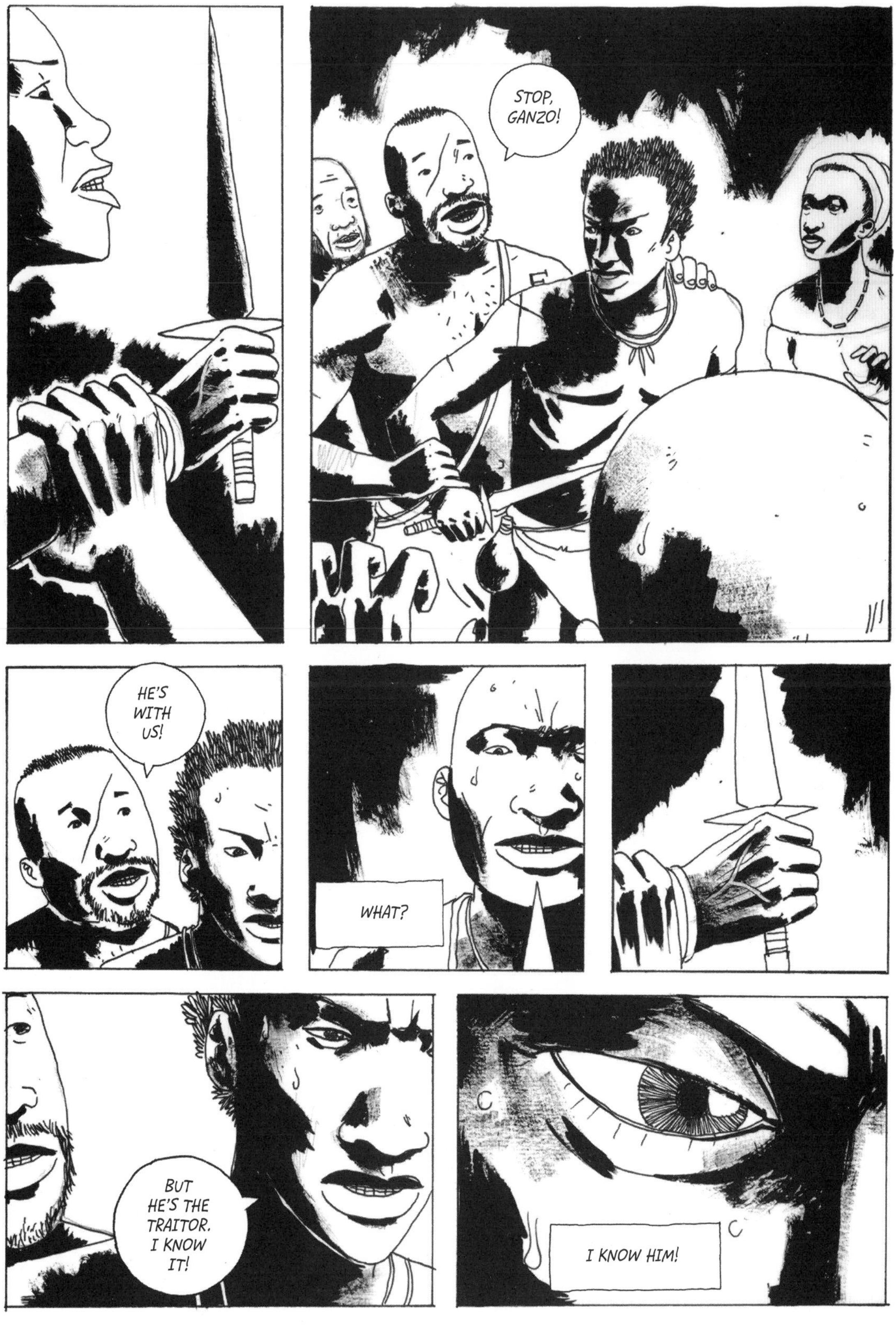
STOP, GANZO!
HE'S WITH US!
WHAT?
BUT HE'S THE TRAITOR. I KNOW IT!
I KNOW HIM!

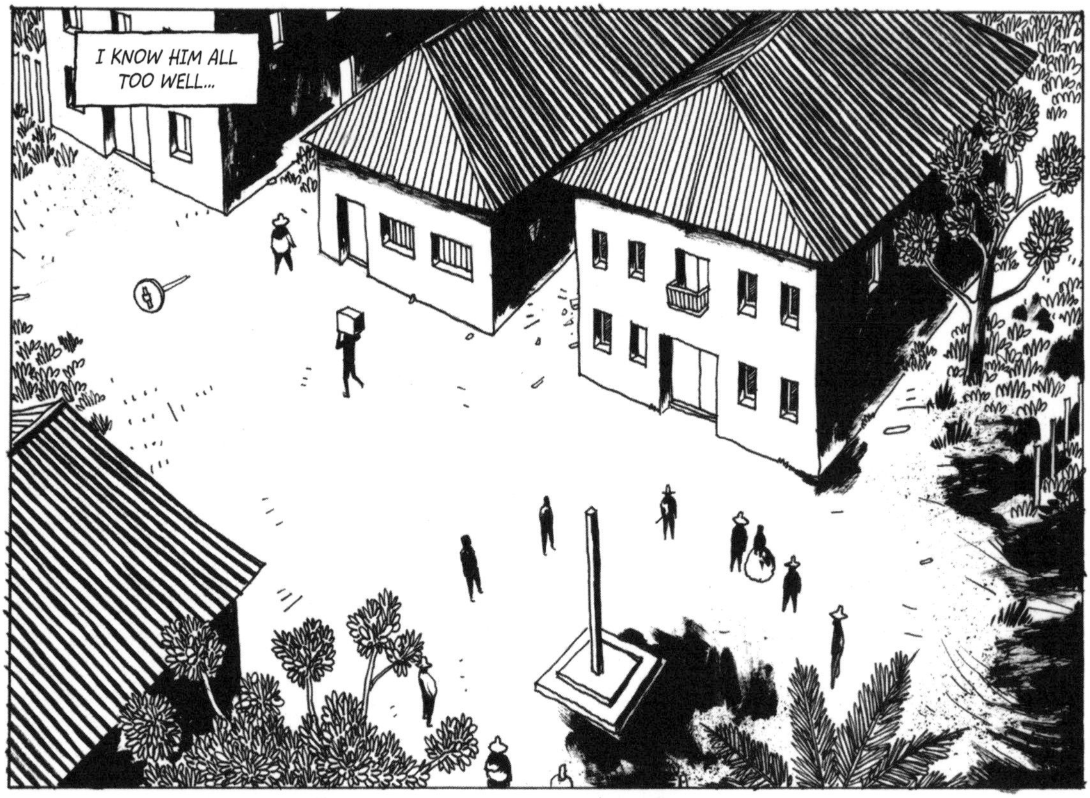
I KNOW HIM ALL TOO WELL...

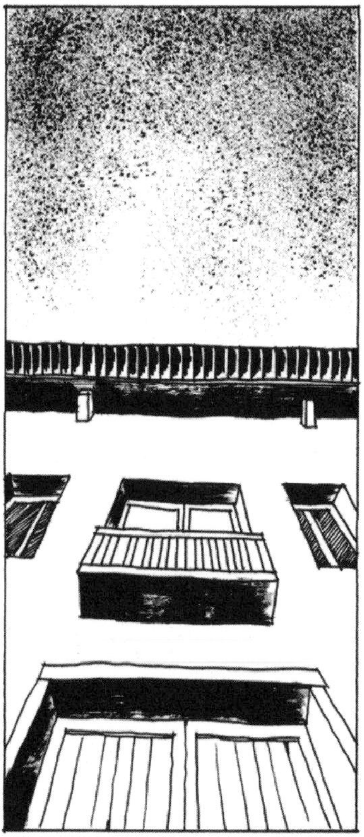

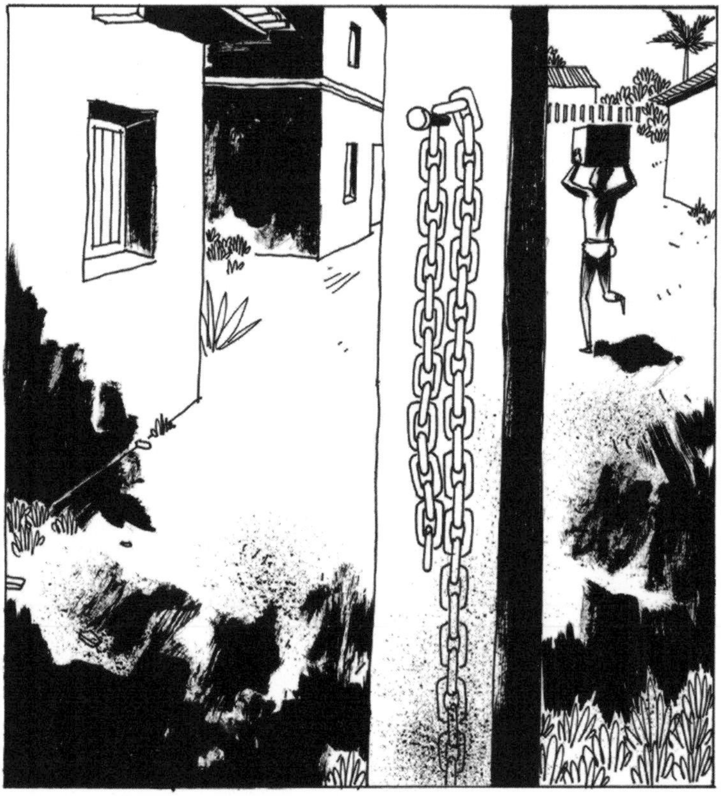

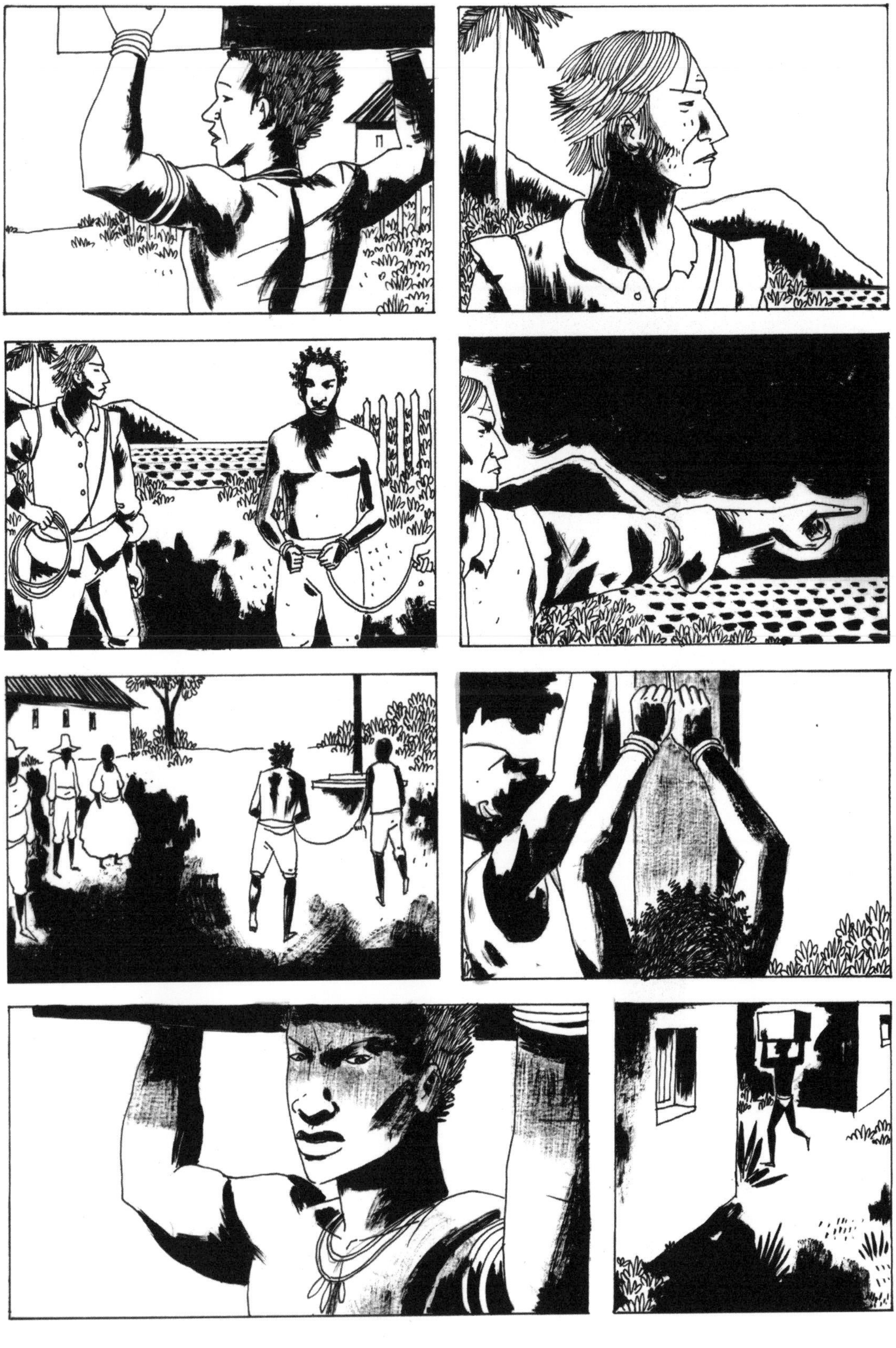

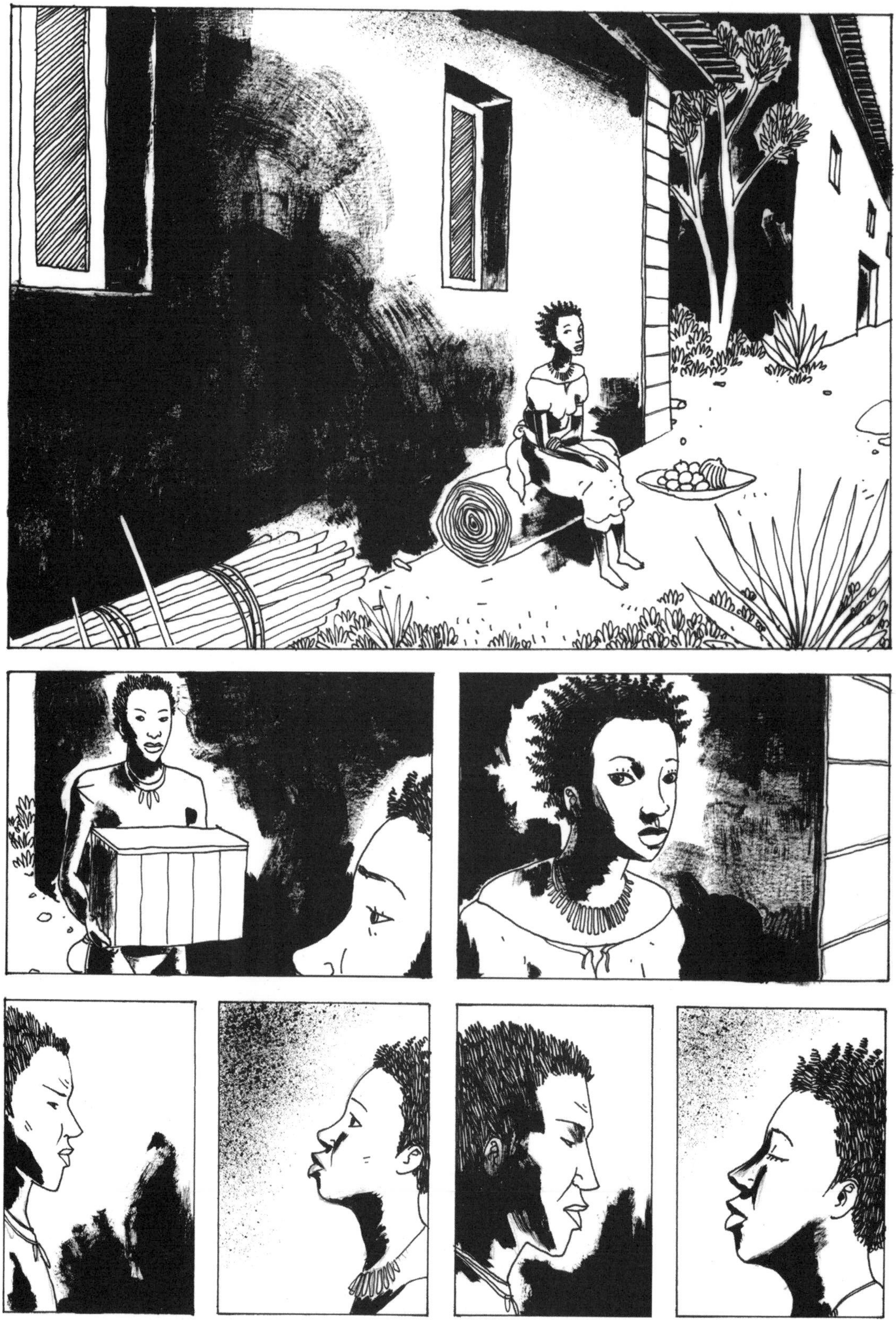

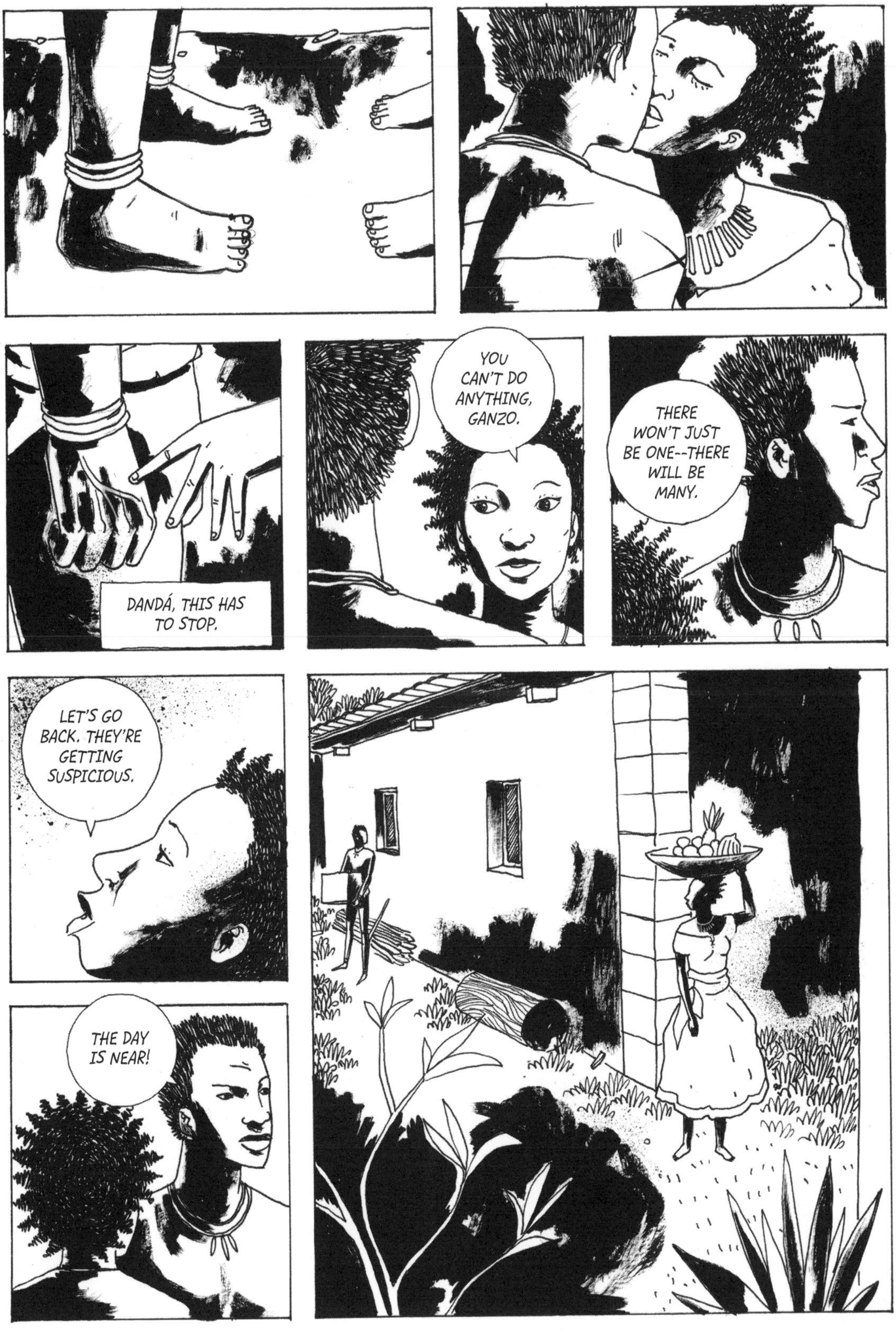
DANDÁ, THIS HAS TO STOP.
YOU CAN'T DO ANYTHING, GANZO.
THERE WON'T JUST BE ONE--THERE WILL BE MANY.
LET'S GO BACK. THEY'RE GETTING SUSPICIOUS.
THE DAY IS NEAR!

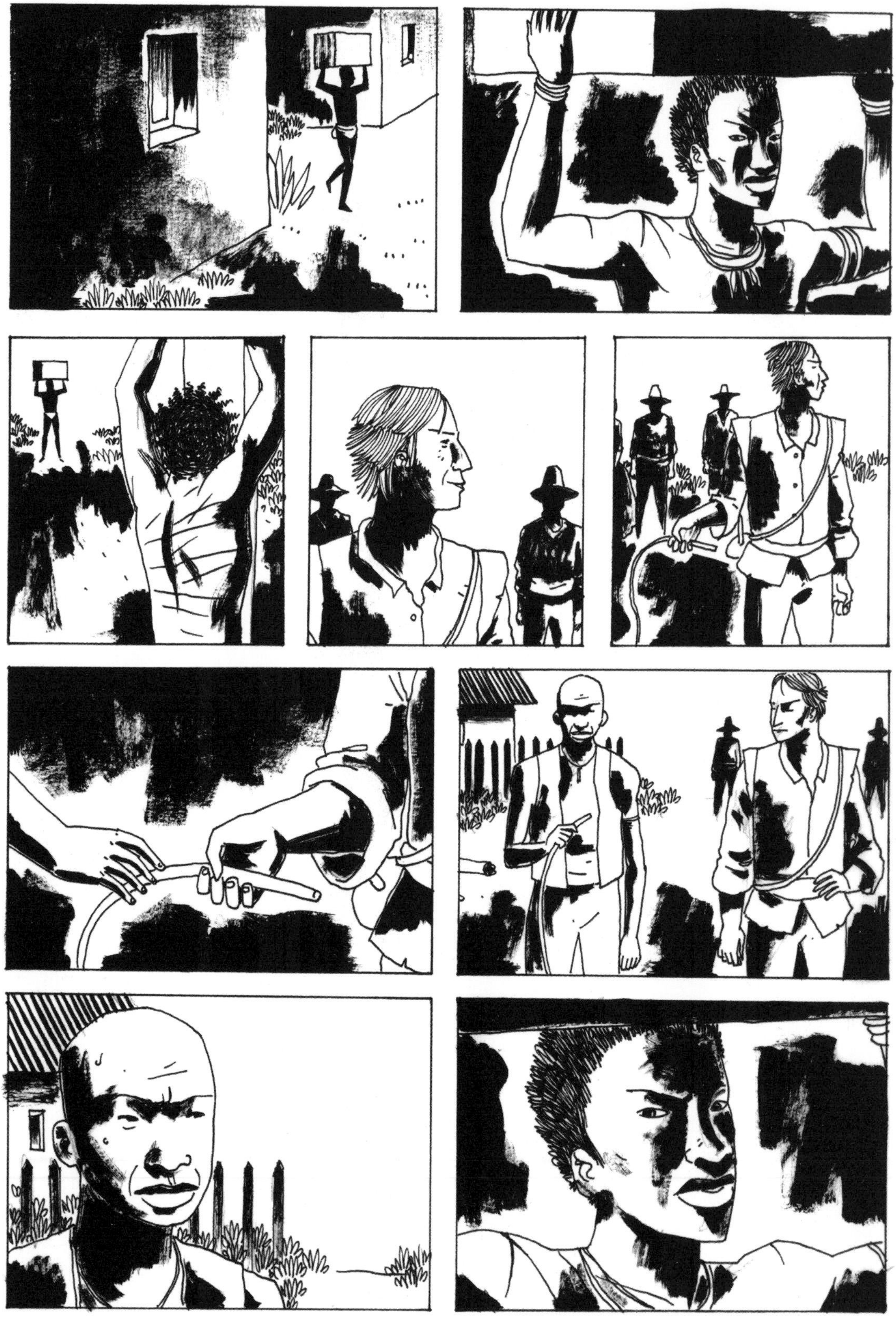

TRAITORS CAN'T STAY.

YOU DON'T KNOW ME!

STOP, GANZO!

EVERYBODY HERE HAS RITUAL SCARS. YOU DON'T HAVE ANY.

YOU DON'T KNOW WHAT YOU'RE TALKING ABOUT.

HE DOESN'T HAVE ANY BECAUSE HE'S ONE OF THEM! HE'S WITH THE WHITES!

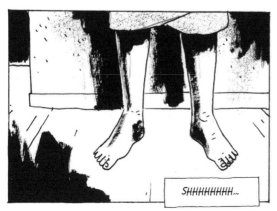

SHHHHHHHH...

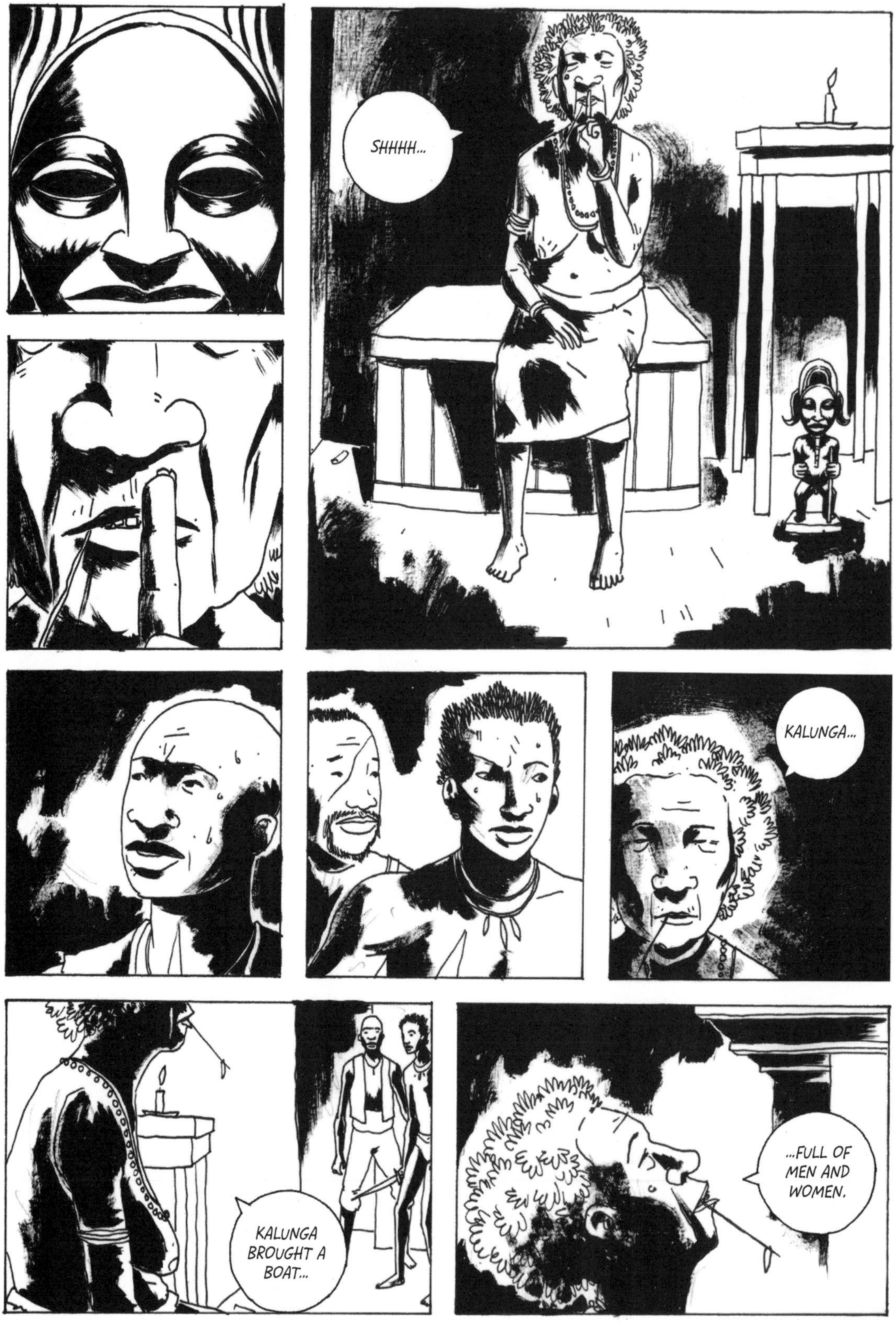
SHHHH...
KALUNGA...
KALUNGA BROUGHT A BOAT...
...FULL OF MEN AND WOMEN.

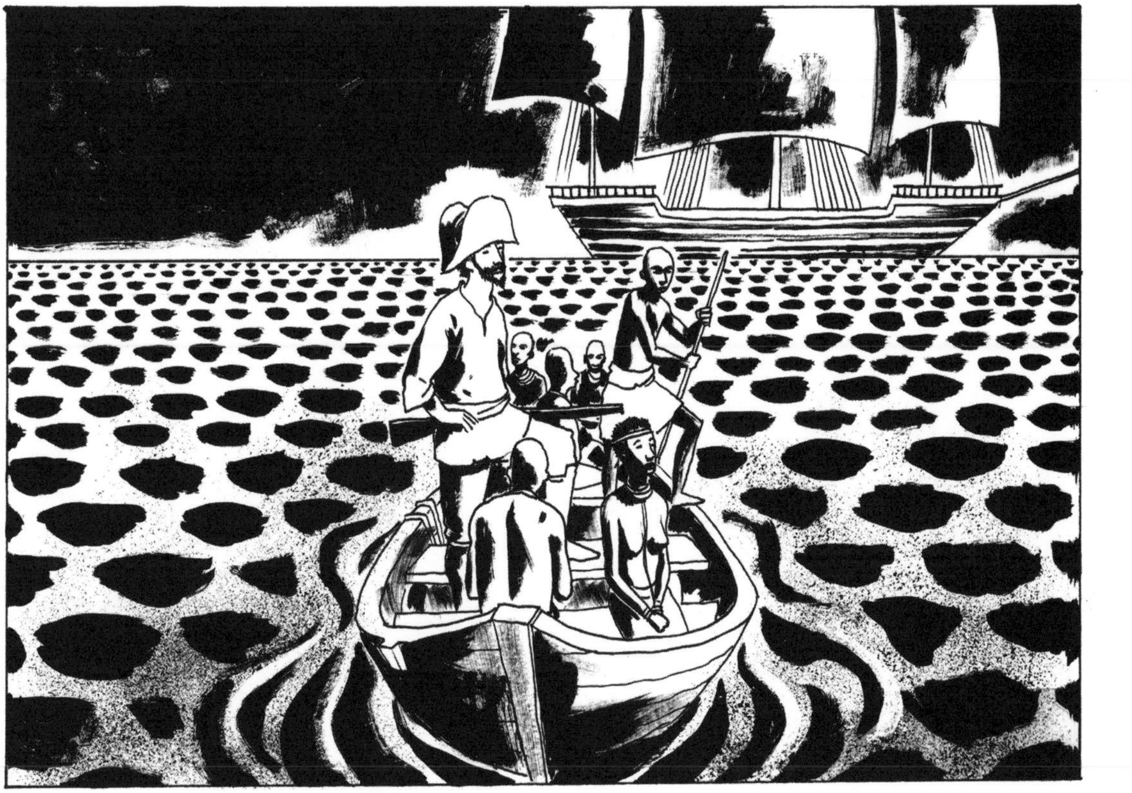

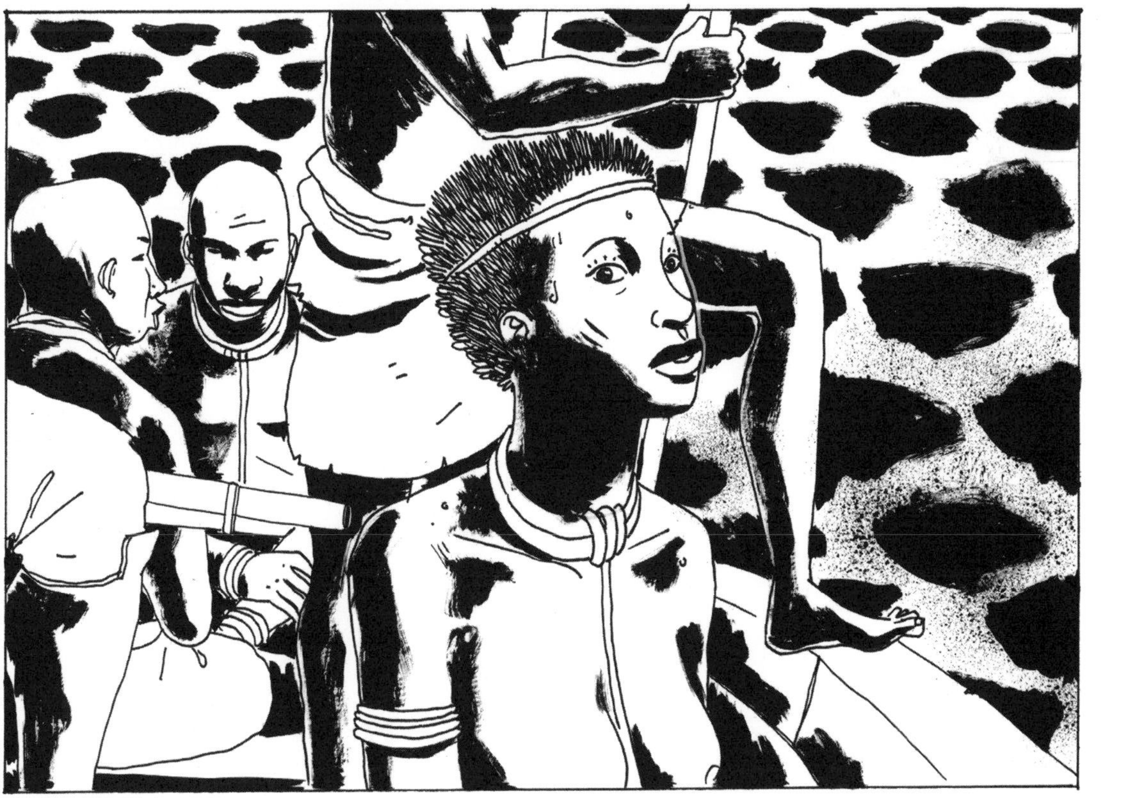

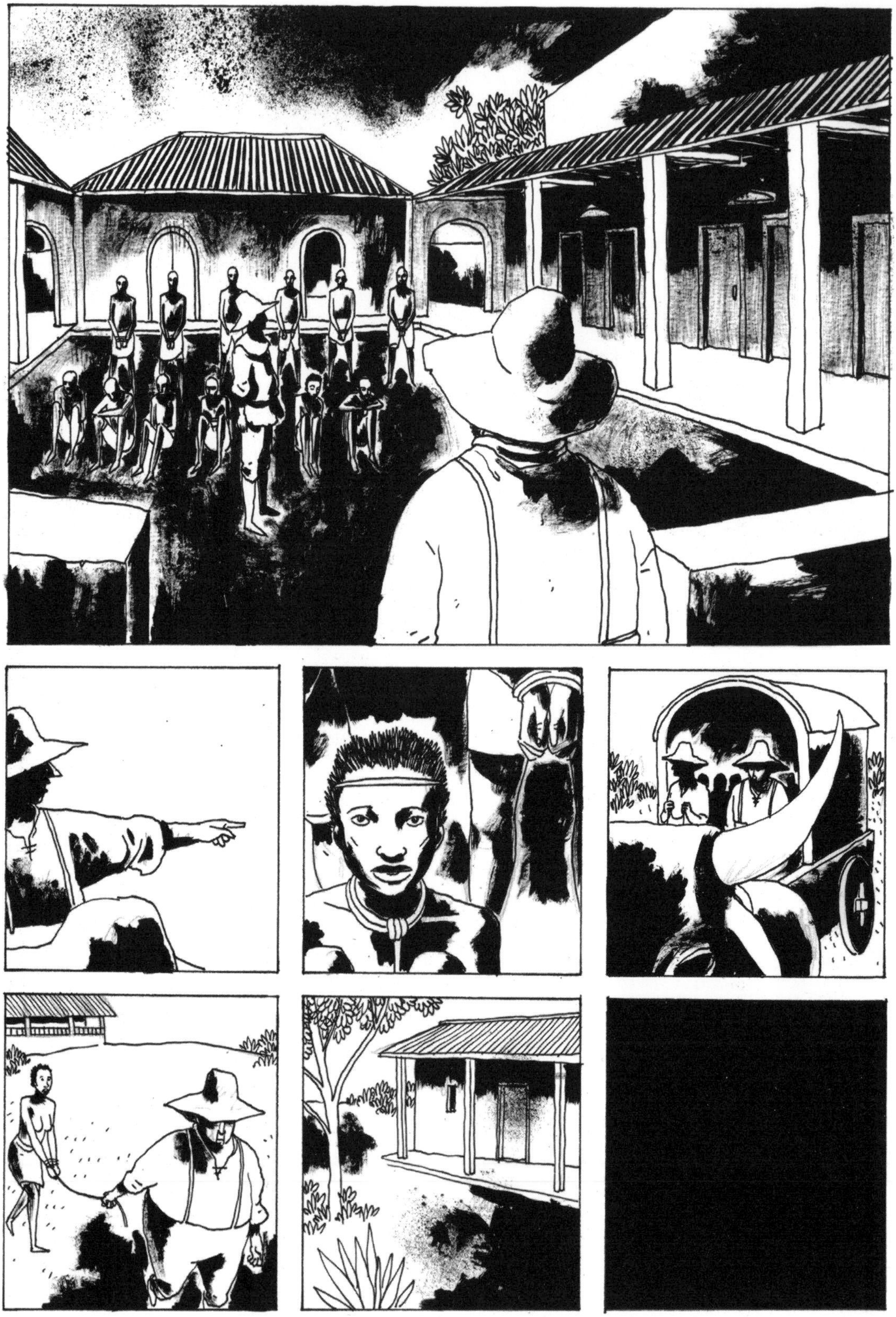

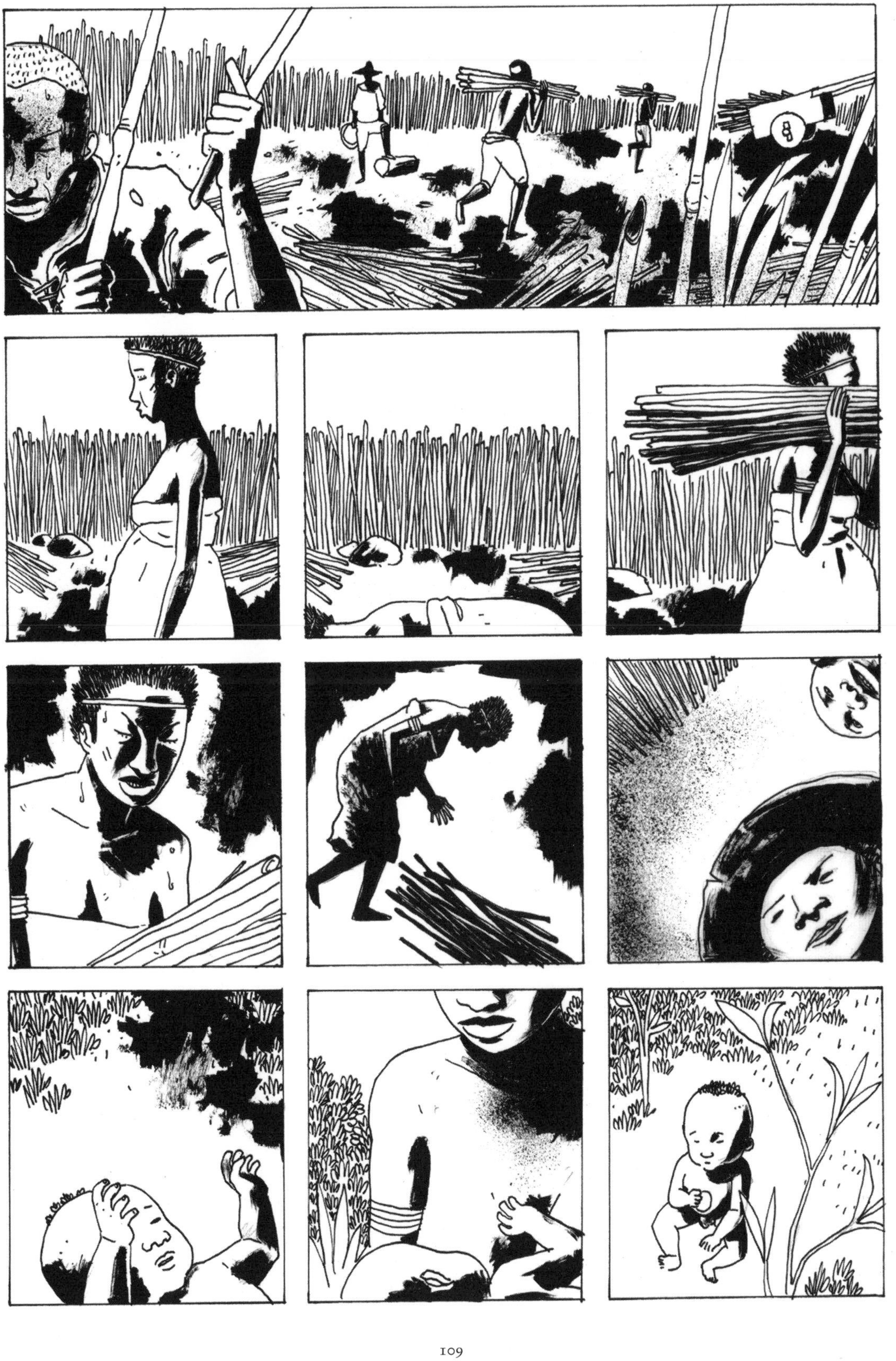

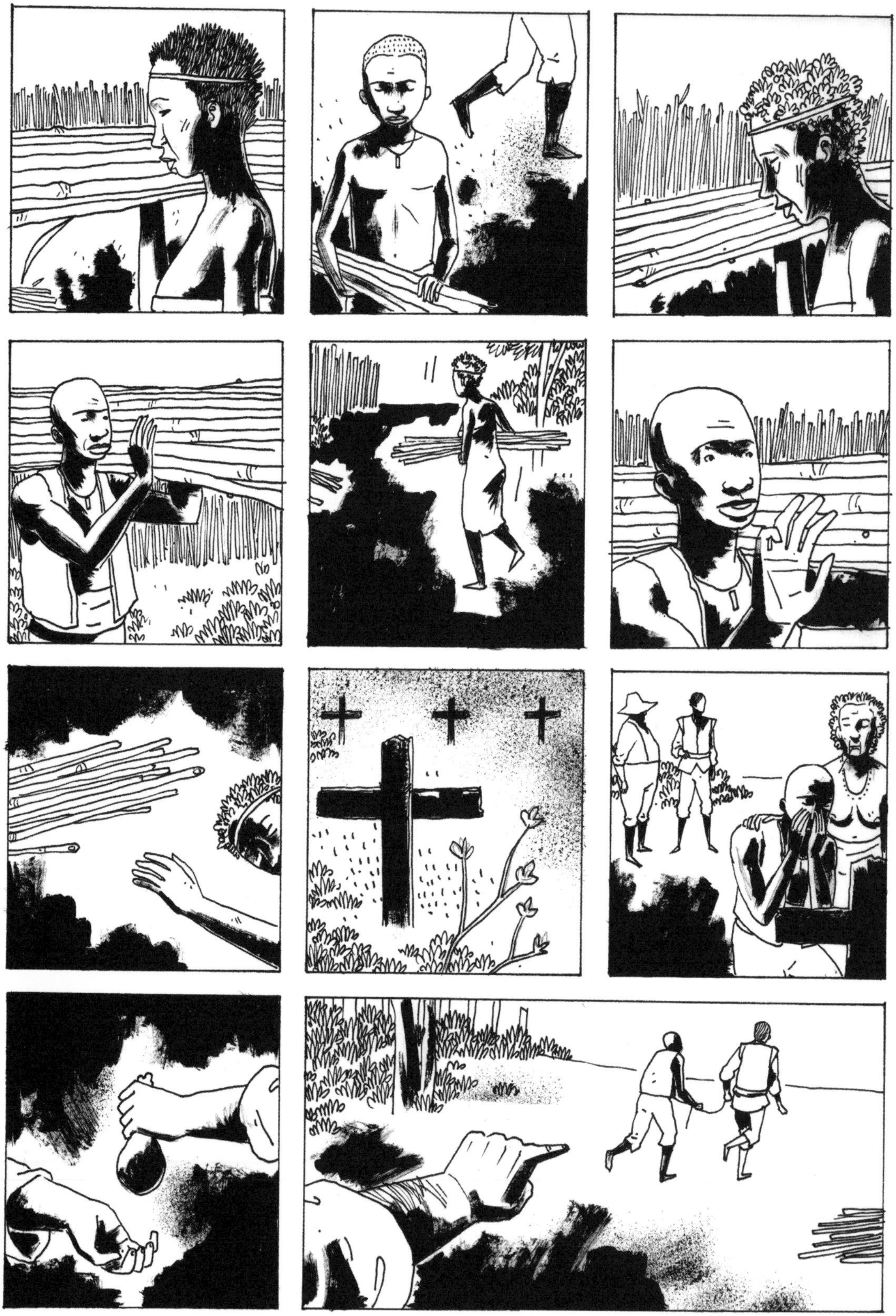

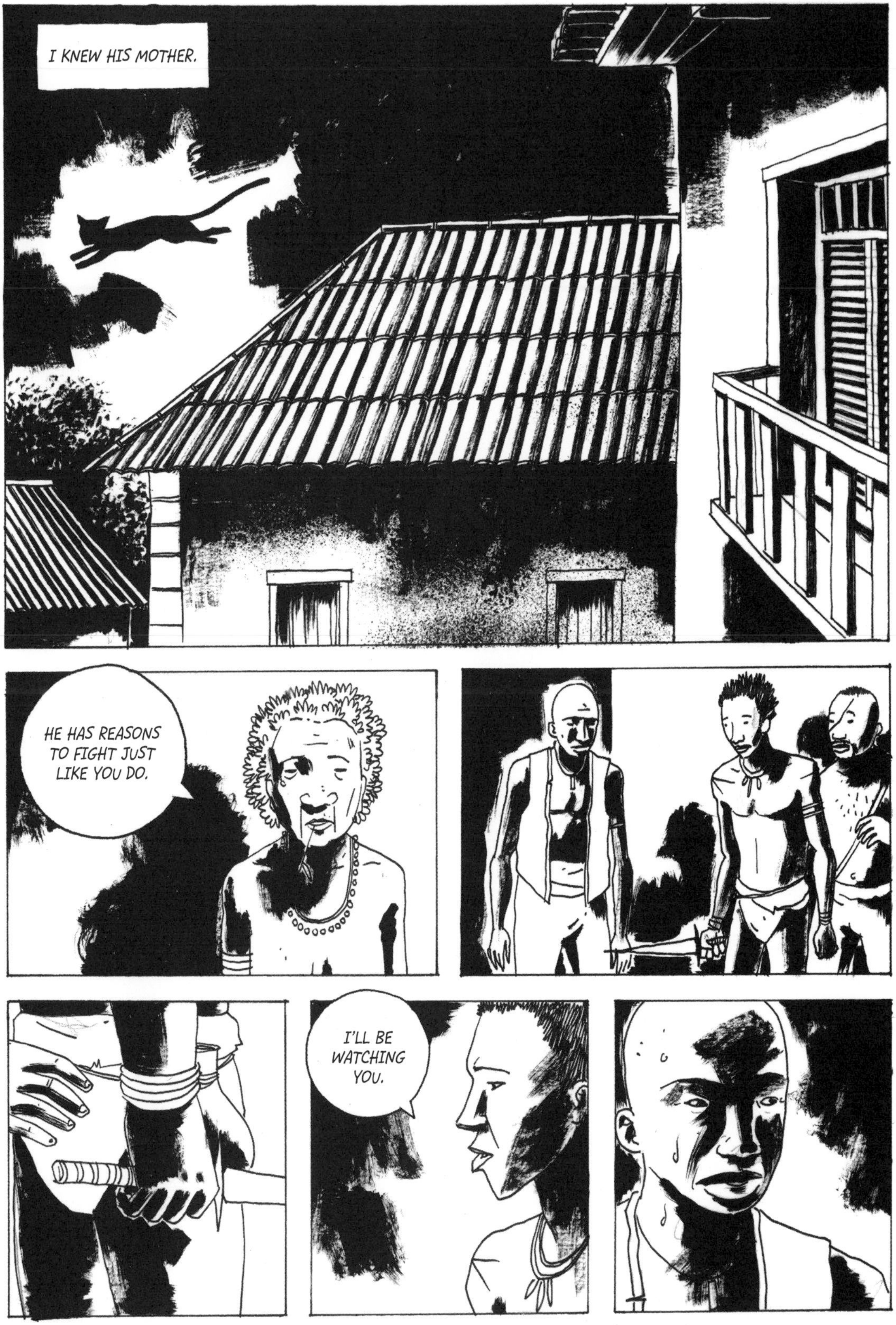
I KNEW HIS MOTHER.
HE HAS REASONS TO FIGHT JUST LIKE YOU DO.
I'LL BE WATCHING YOU.

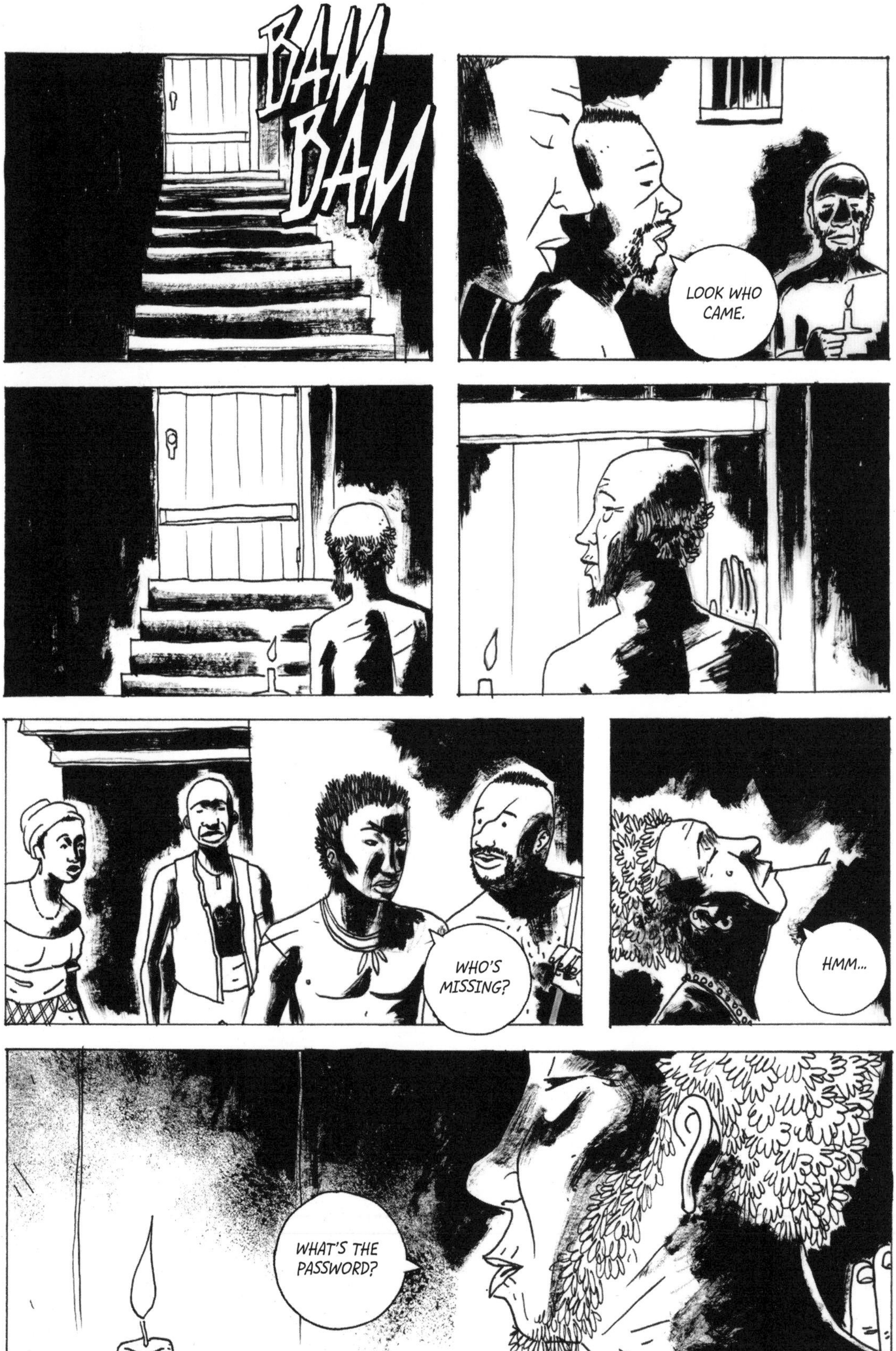
BAM
BAM
LOOK WHO CAME.
WHO'S MISSING?
HMM...
WHAT'S THE PASSWORD?

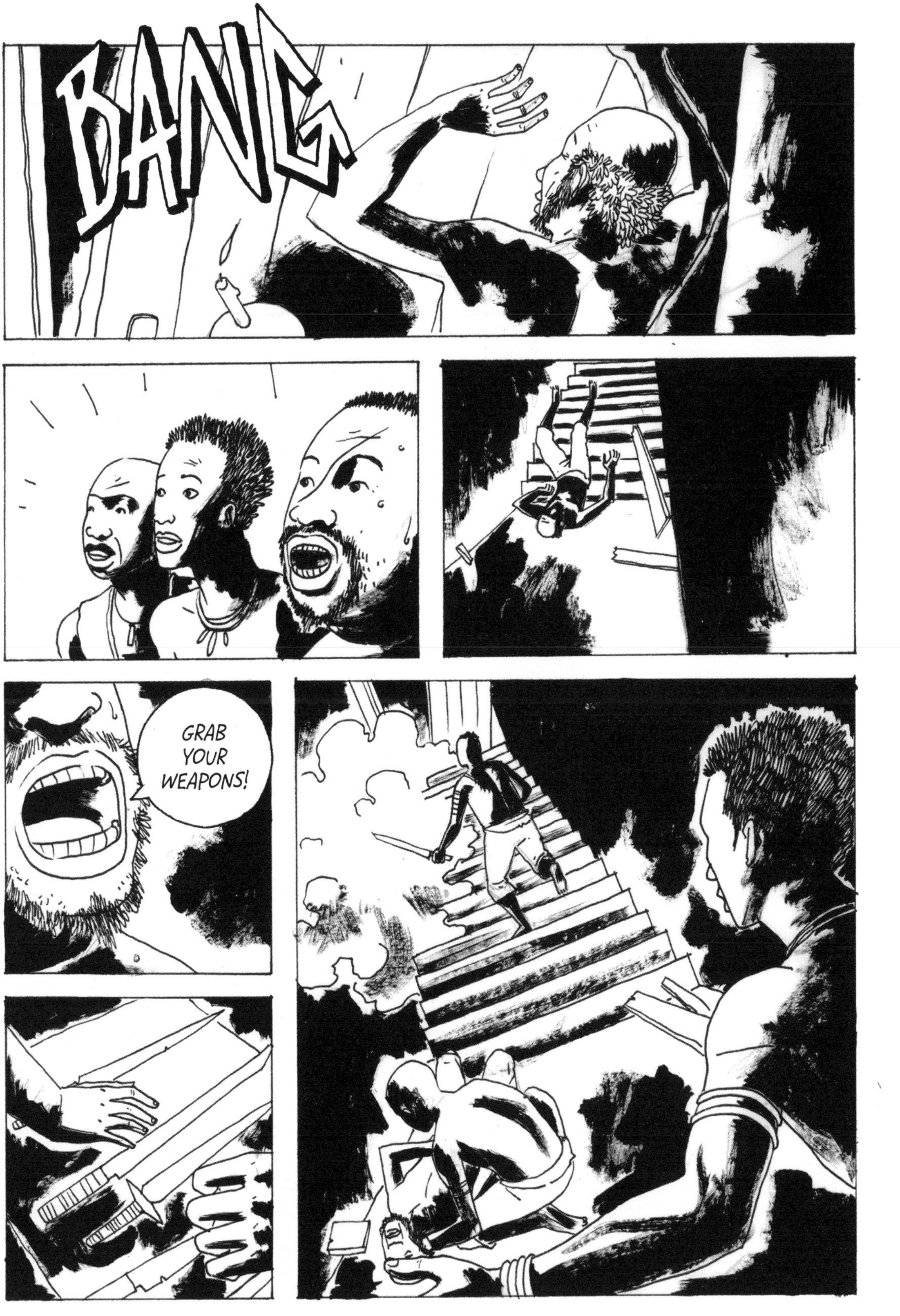
BANG
GRAB YOUR WEAPONS!

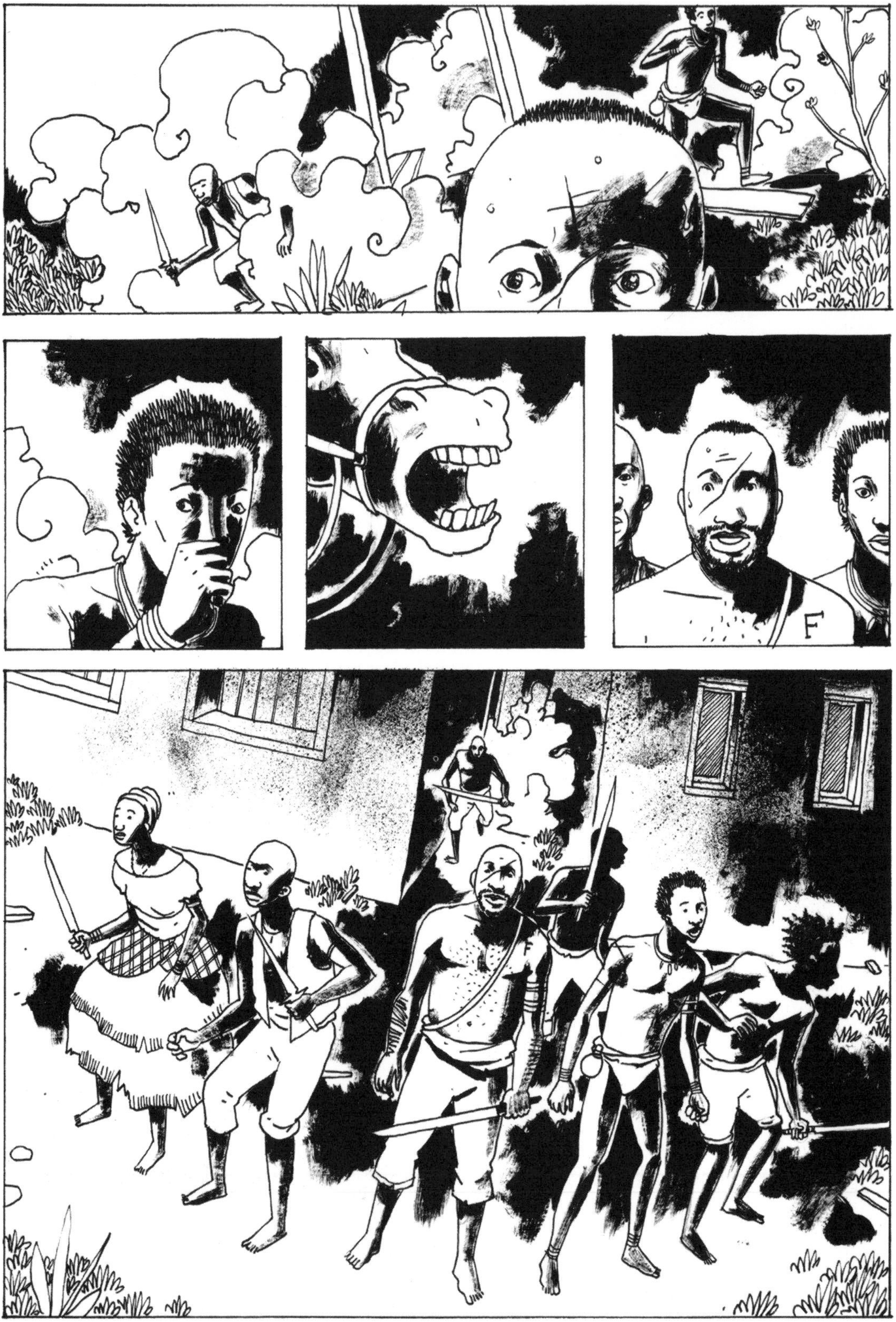

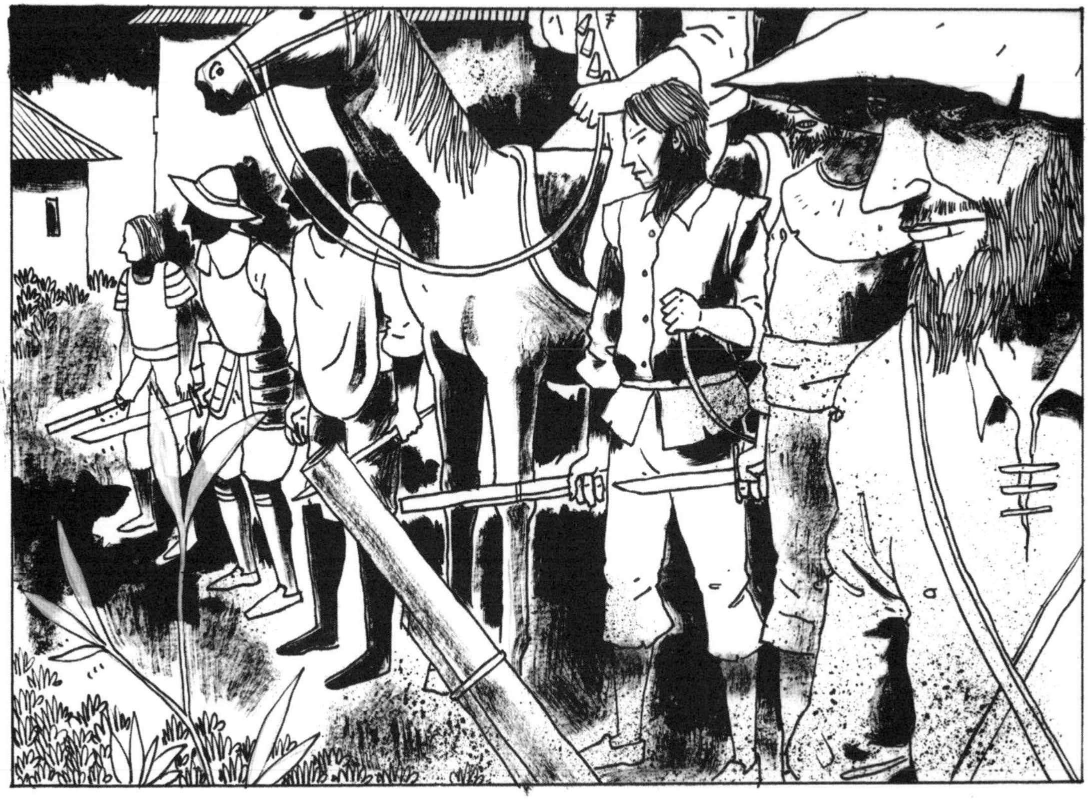

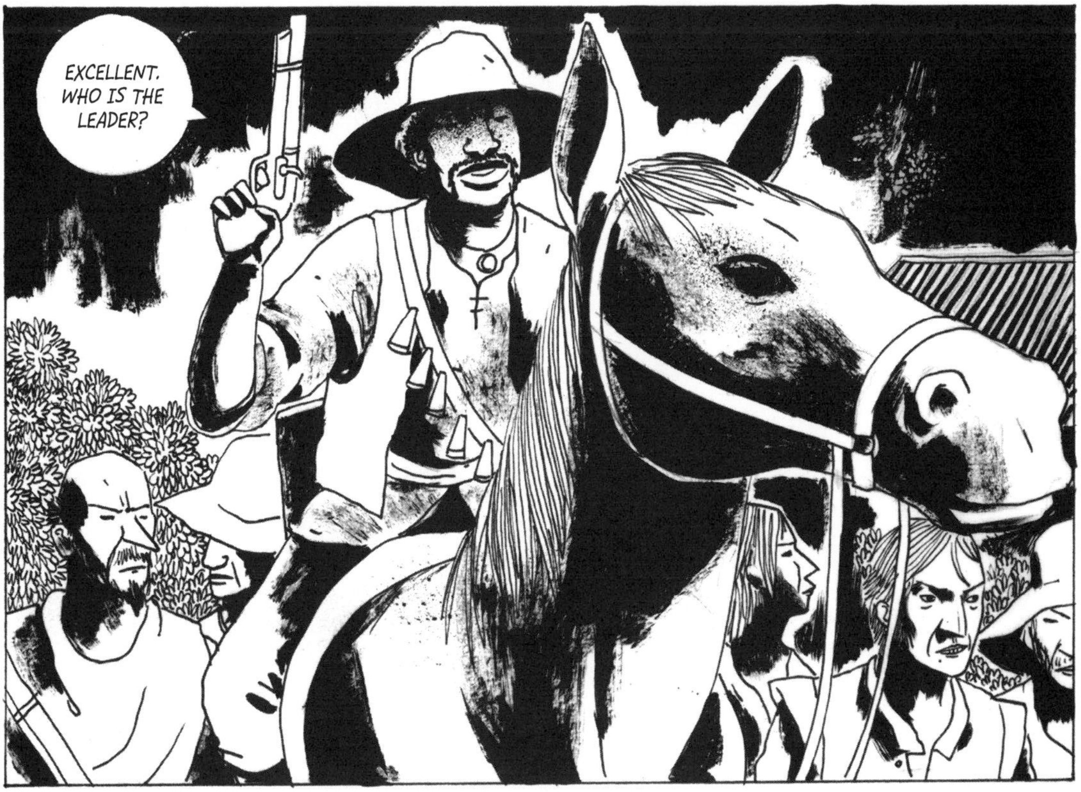
EXCELLENT. WHO IS THE LEADER?

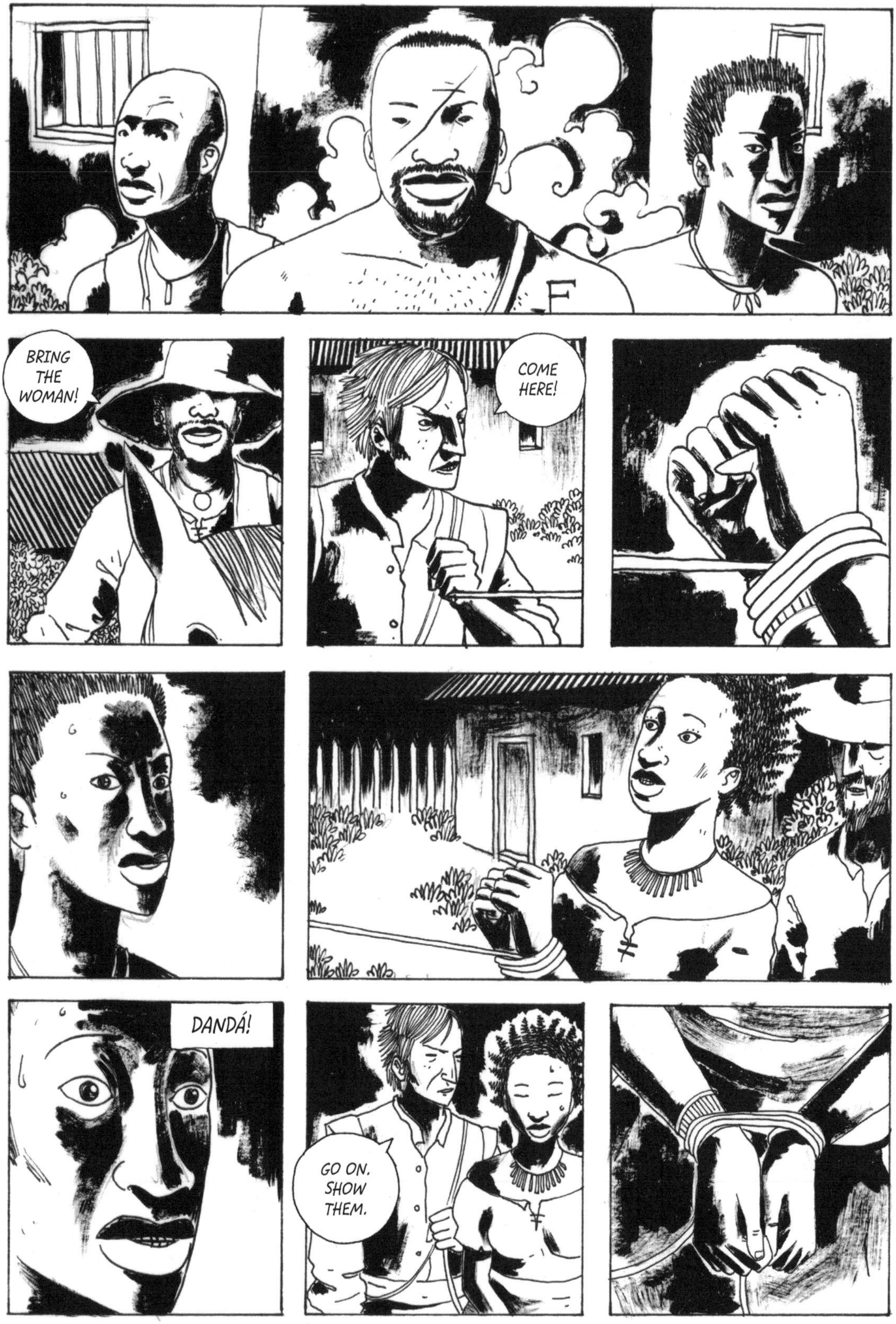
BRING THE WOMAN!
COME HERE!
DANDÁ!
GO ON. SHOW THEM.

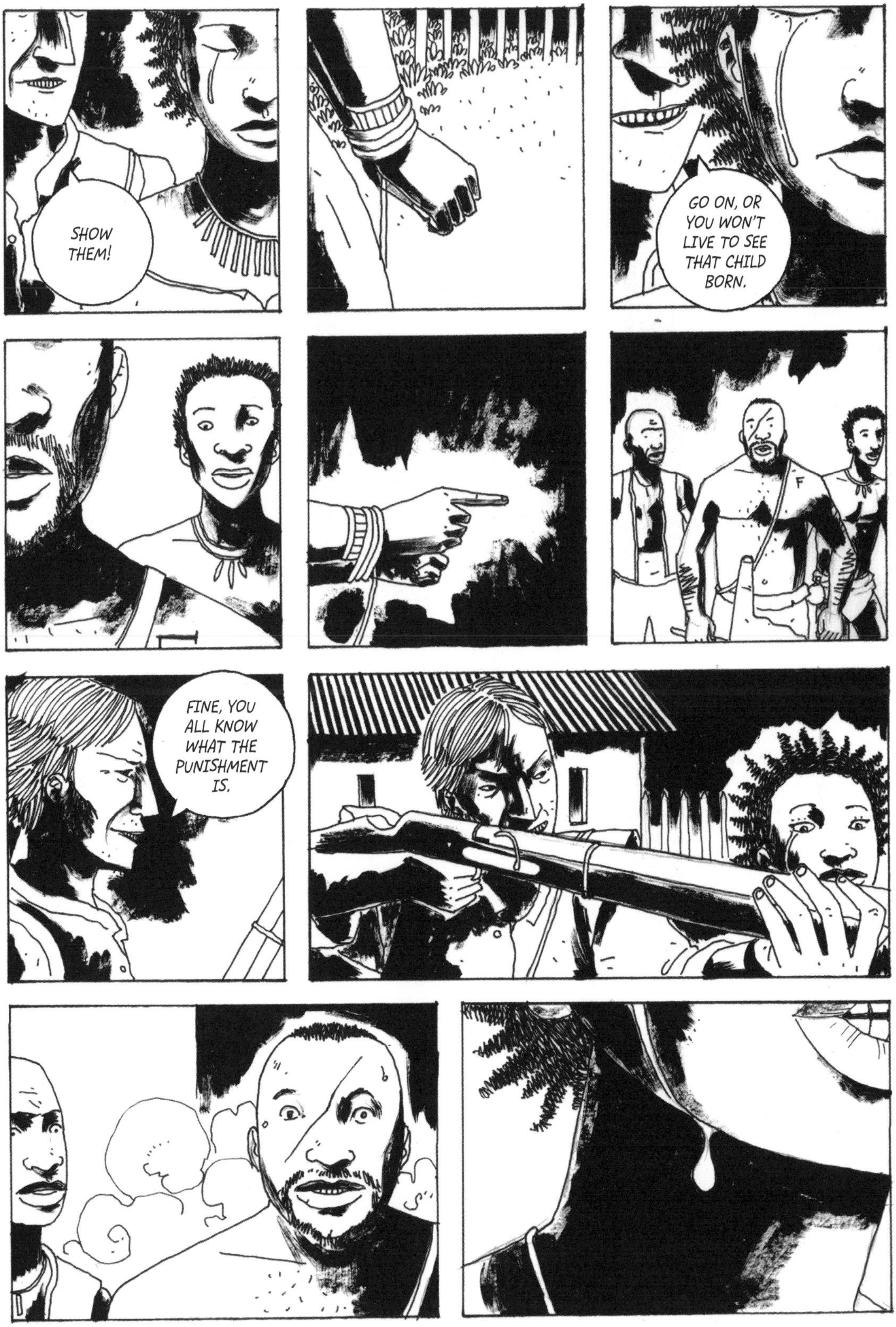
SHOW THEM!
GO ON, OR YOU WON'T LIVE TO SEE THAT CHILD BORN.
FINE, YOU ALL KNOW WHAT THE PUNISHMENT IS.

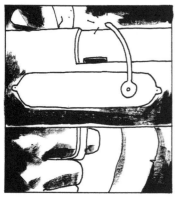

BANG

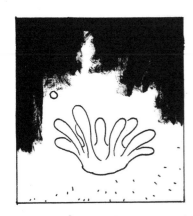

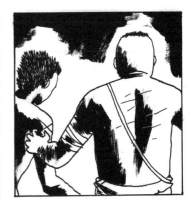

A REBELLIOUS SLAVE ISN'T WORTH ANYTHING.

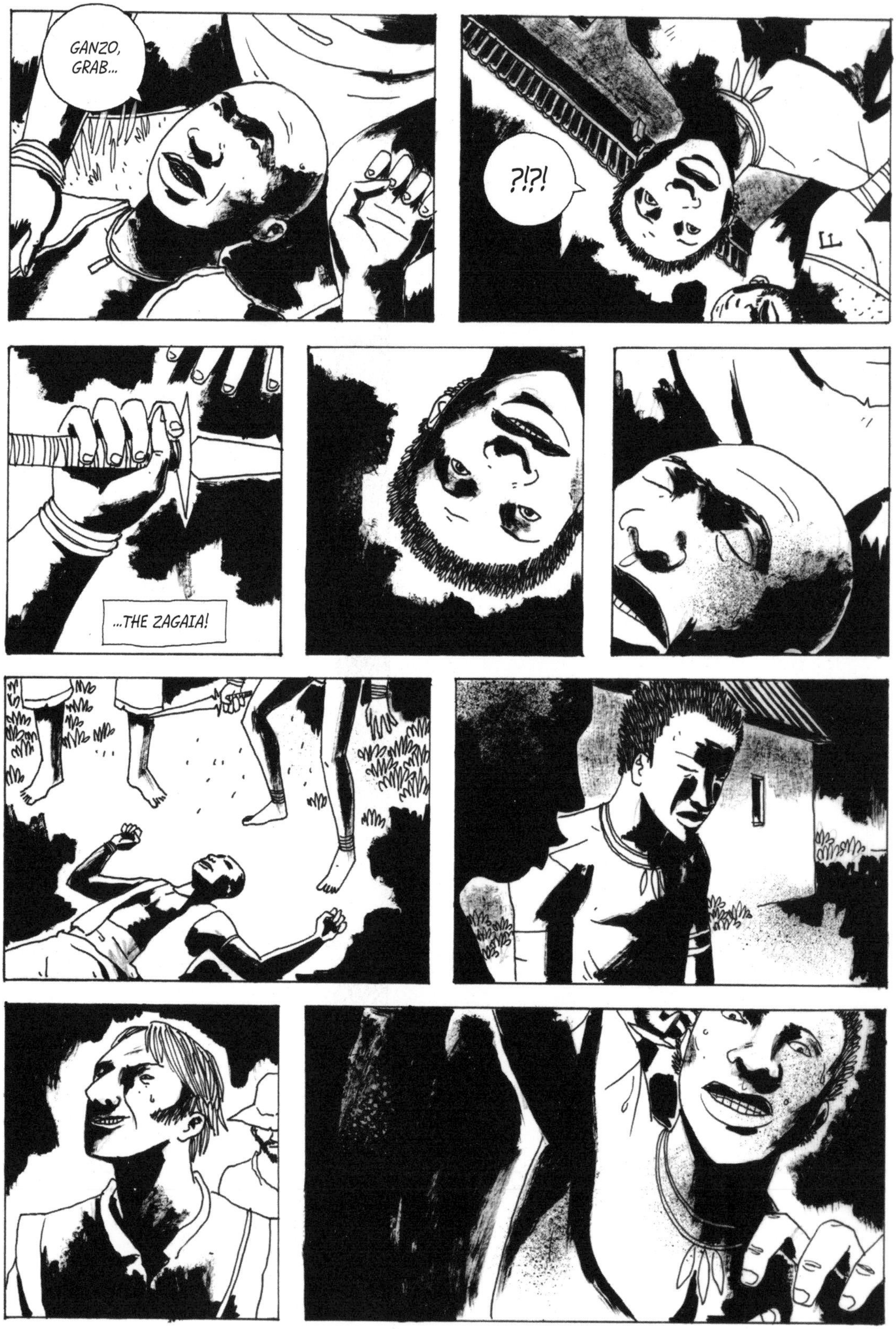
GANZO, GRAB...
?!?!
...THE ZAGAIA!

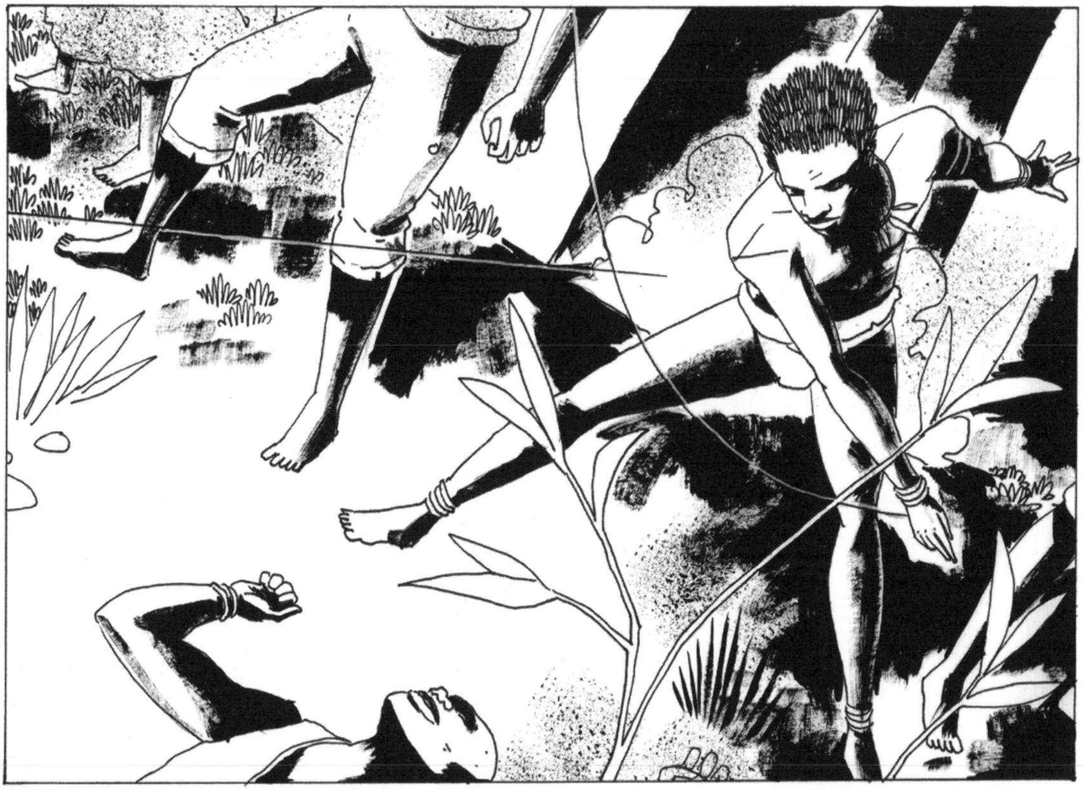

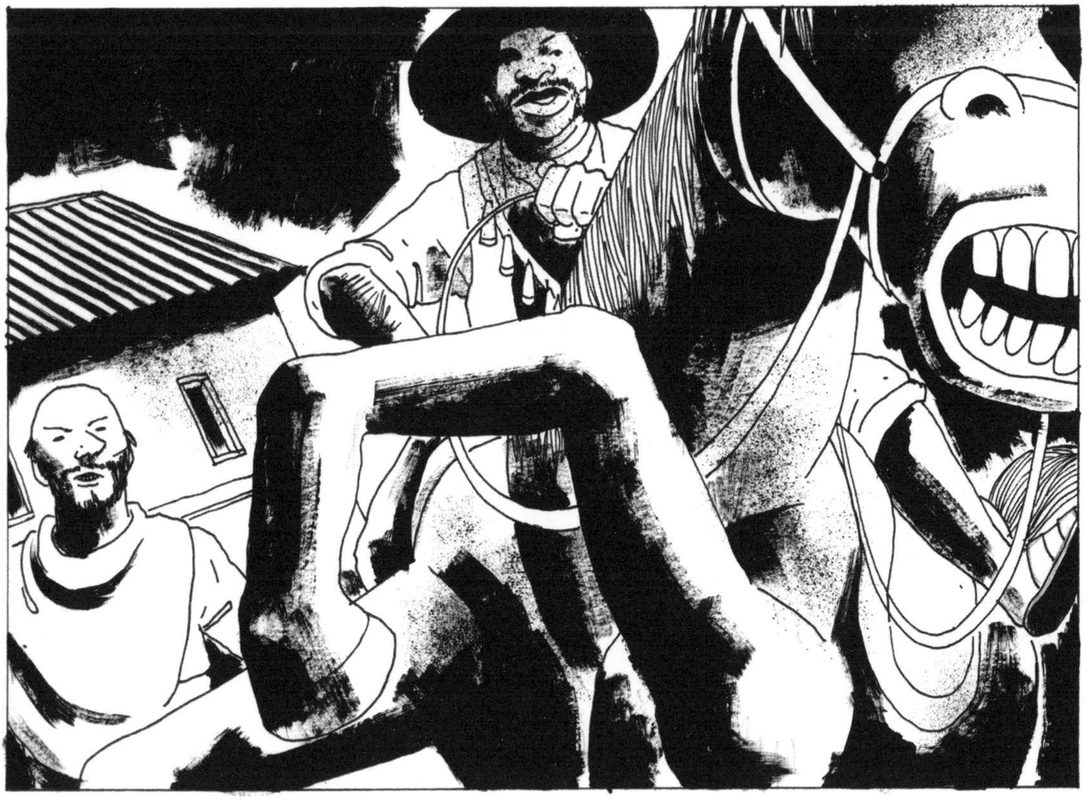

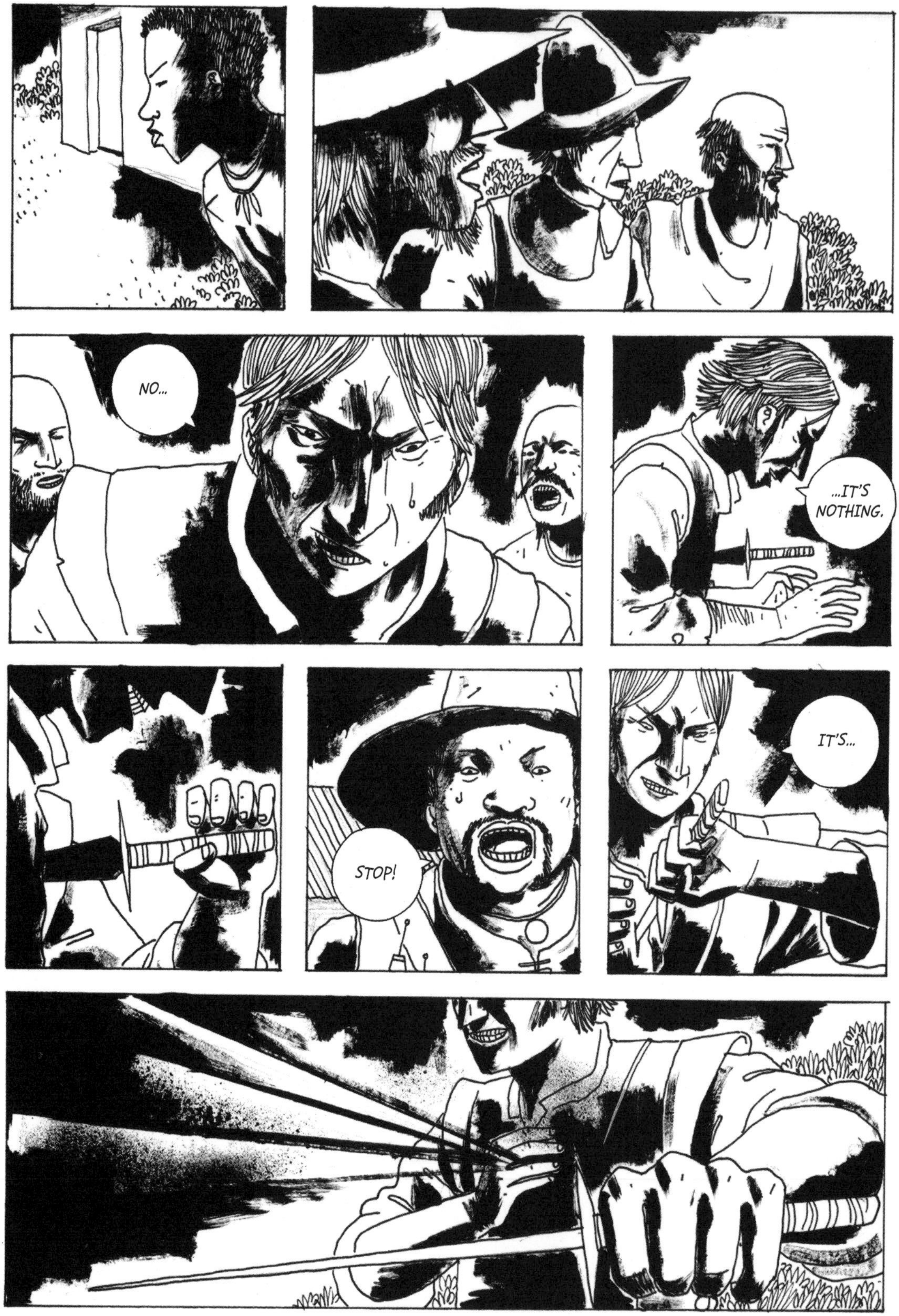
NO...
...IT'S NOTHING.
STOP!
IT'S...

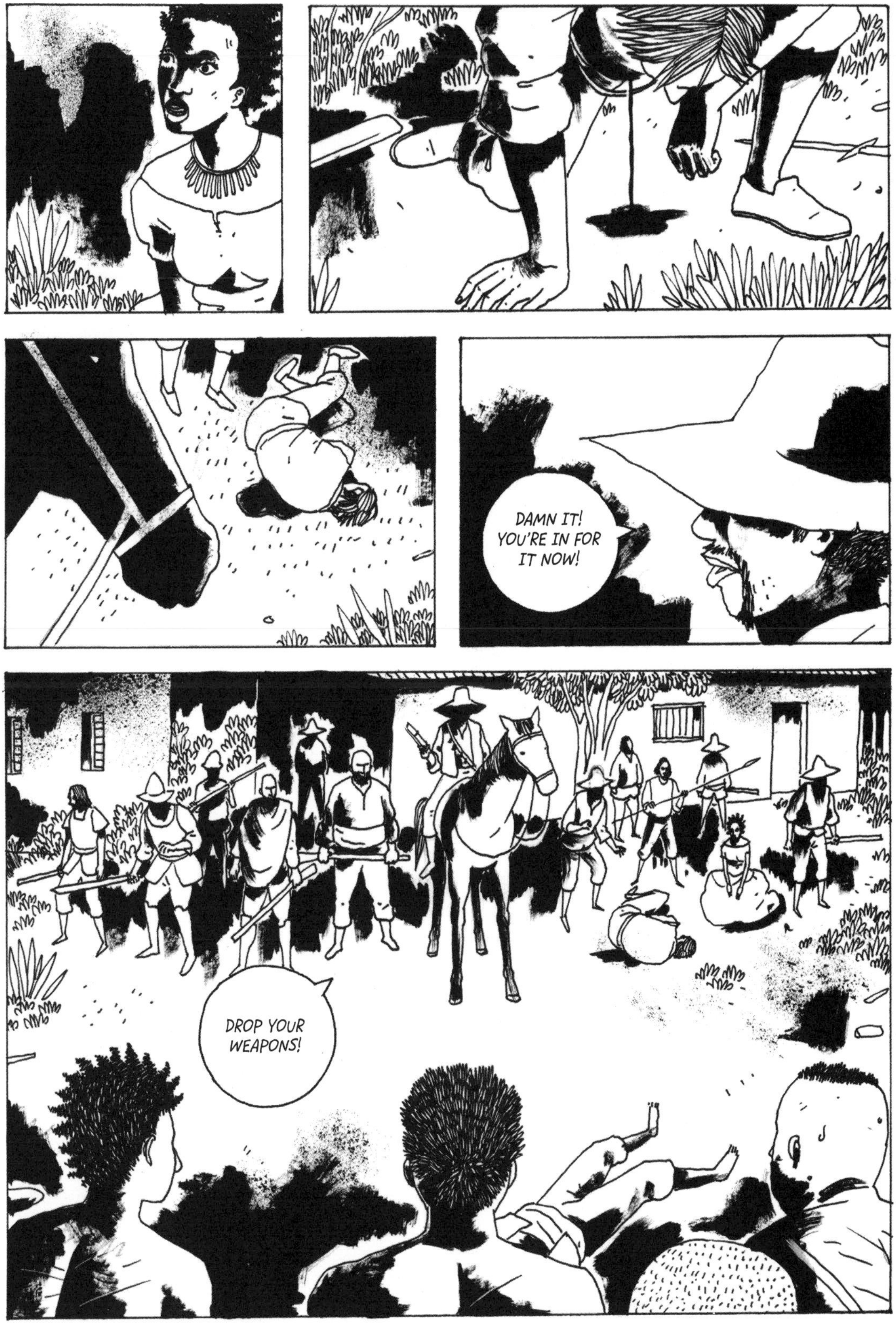
DAMN IT!
YOU'RE IN FOR IT NOW!
DROP YOUR WEAPONS!

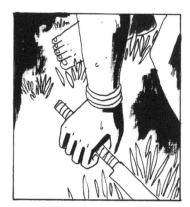

FIRE!

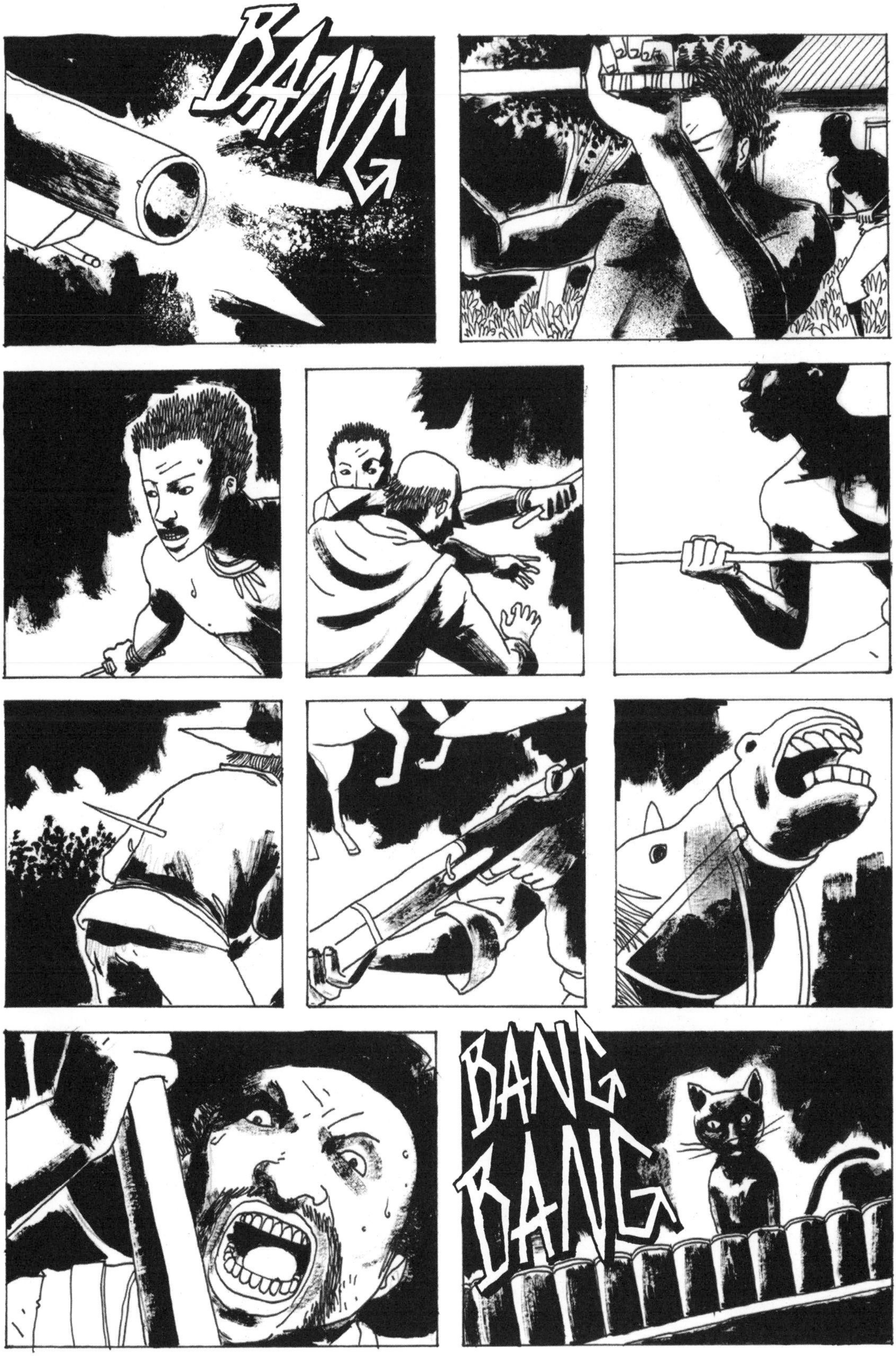
BANG
BANG
BANG

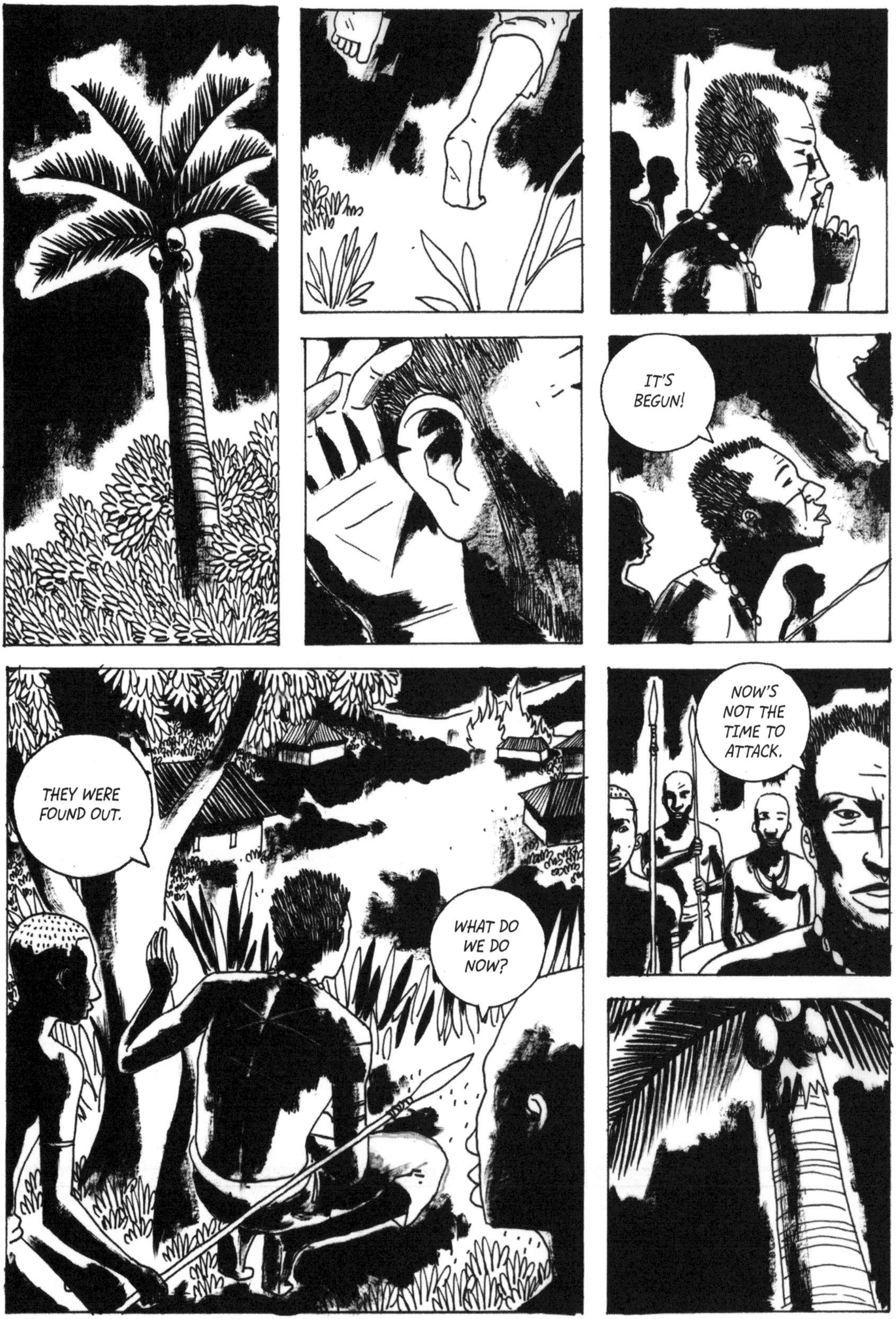
IT'S BEGUN!
THEY WERE FOUND OUT.
WHAT DO WE DO NOW?
NOW'S NOT THE TIME TO ATTACK.

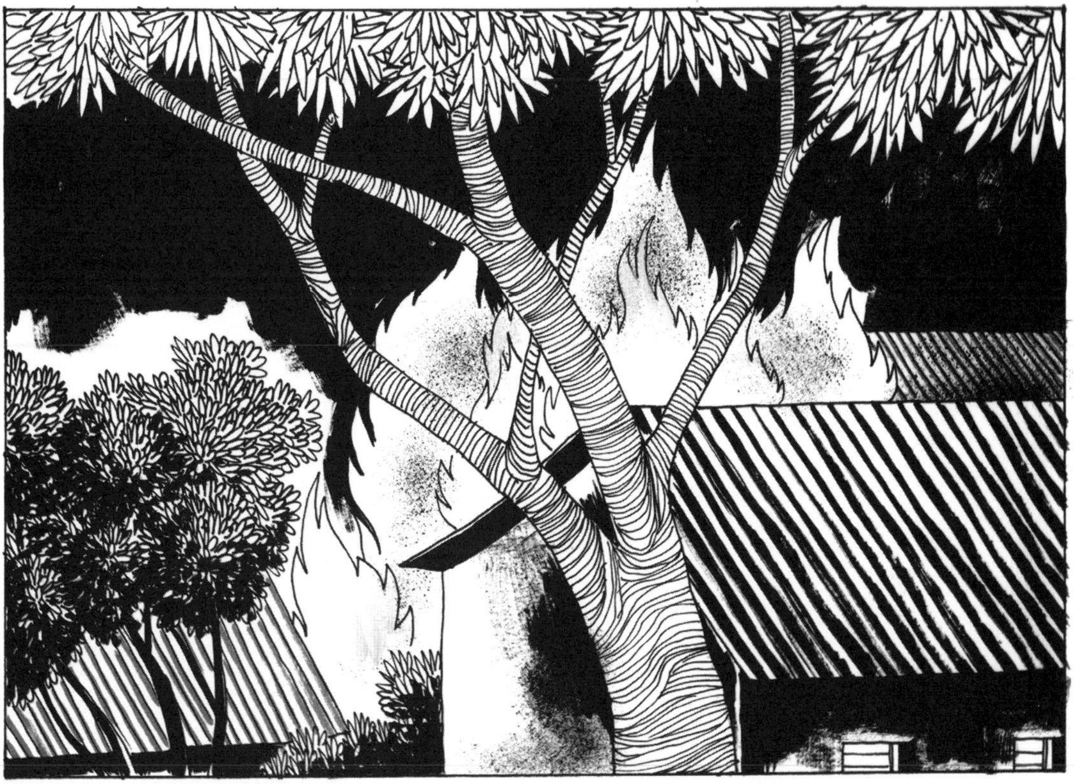

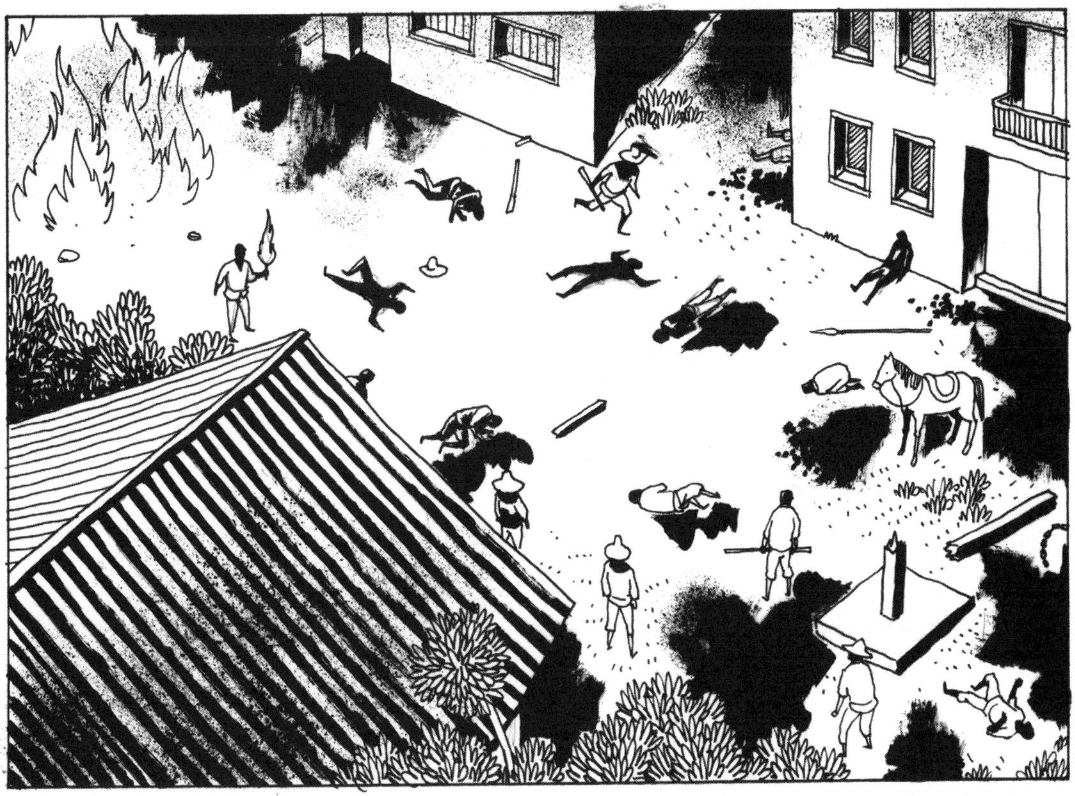

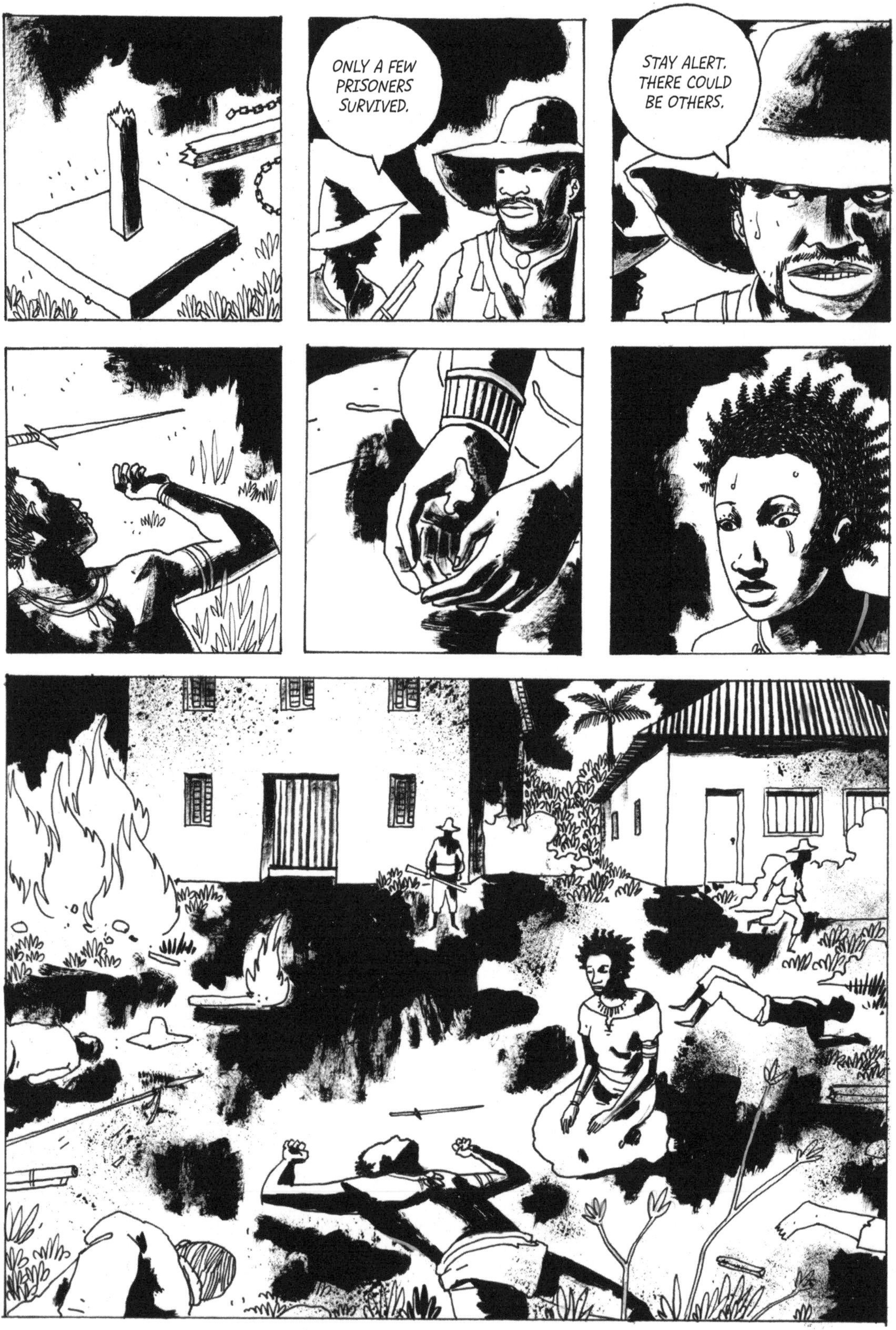

ONLY A FEW PRISONERS SURVIVED.
STAY ALERT. THERE COULD BE OTHERS.

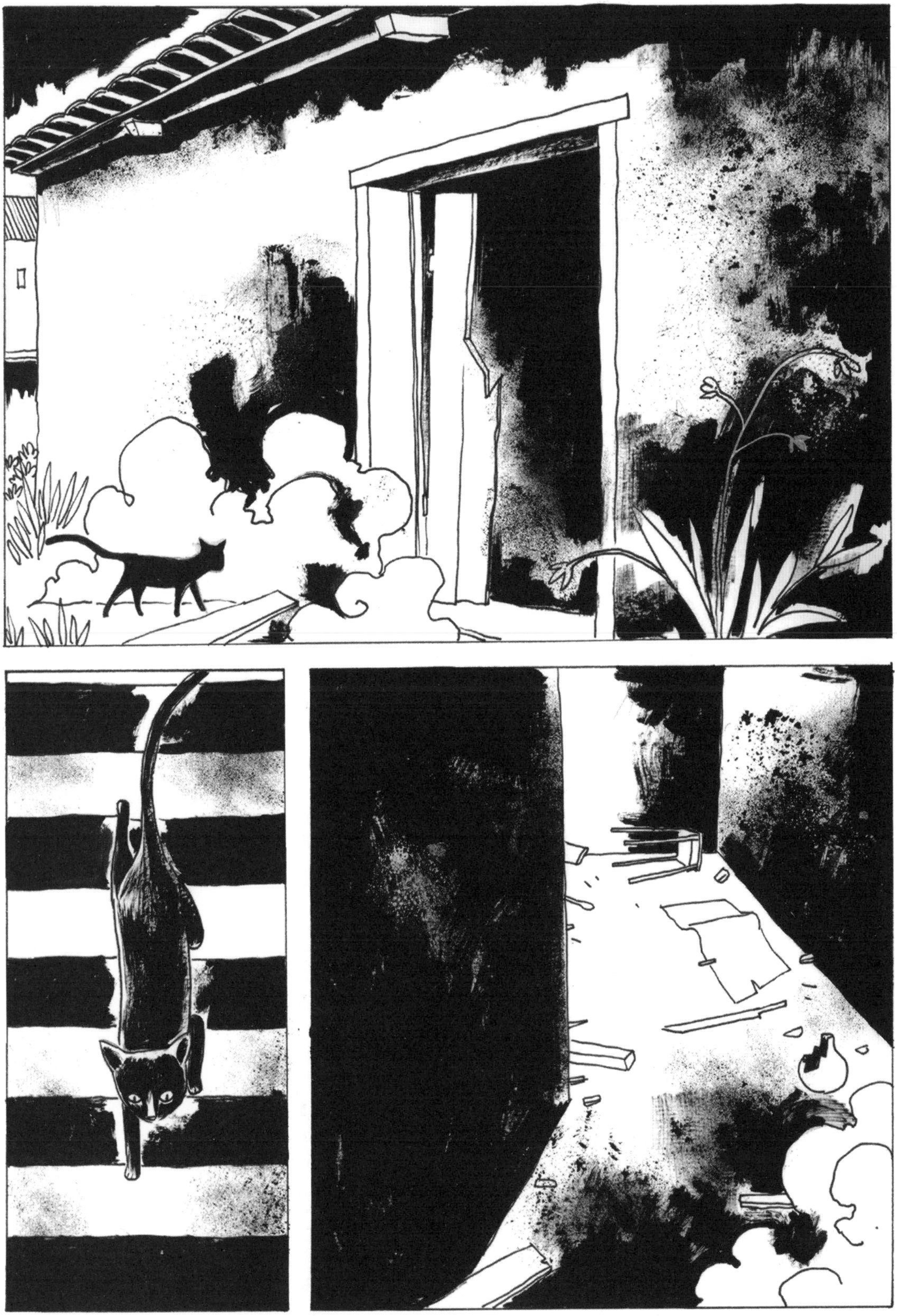

CUMBE WILL COME AGAIN.

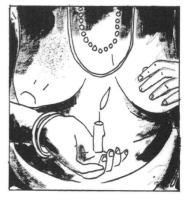

CUMBE IS STRENGTH. IT ALWAYS COMES BACK.

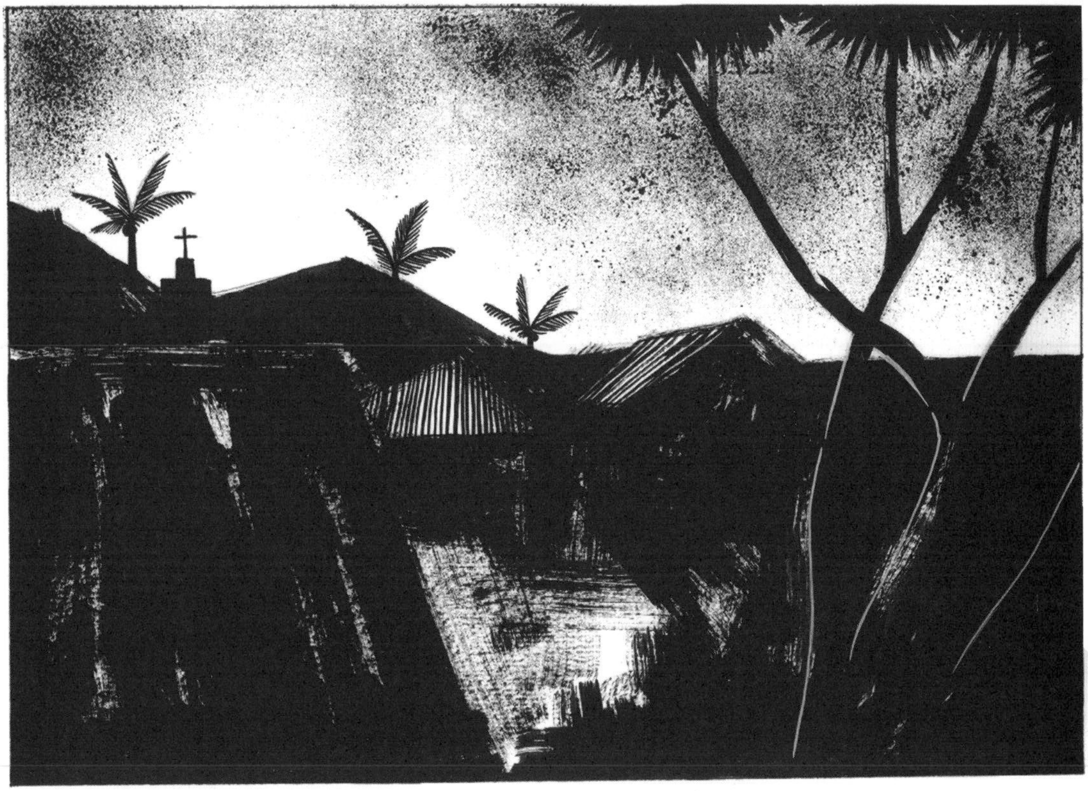

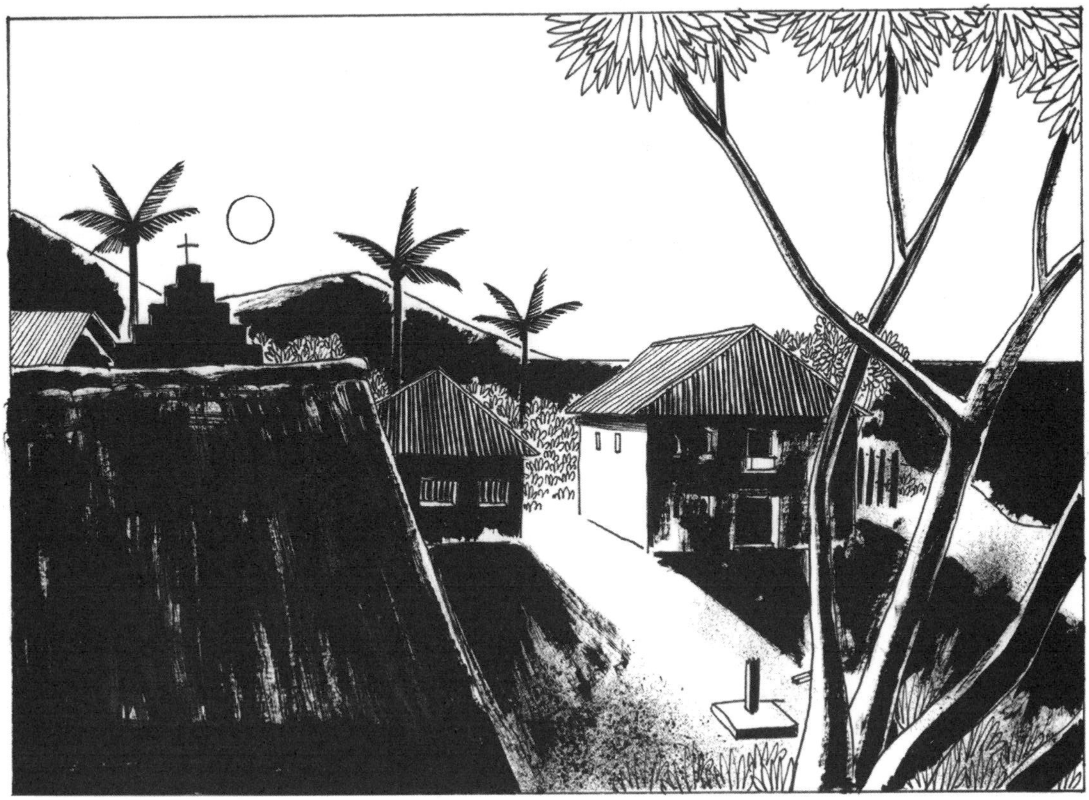

malungo

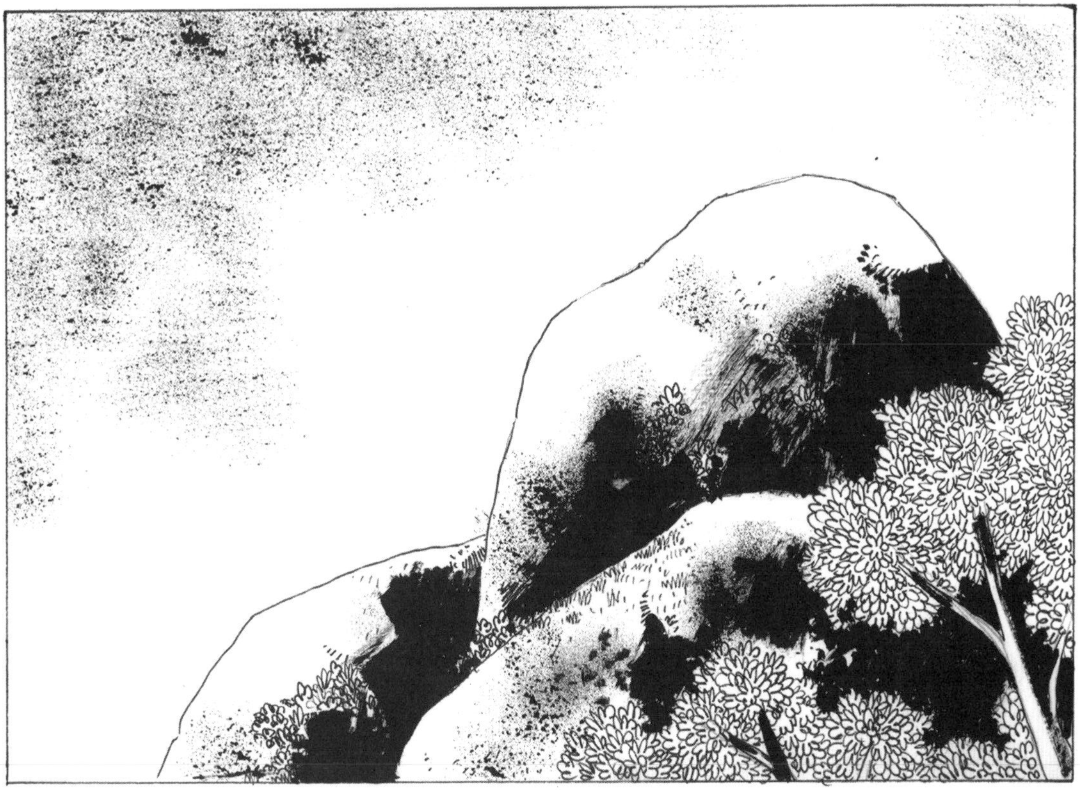
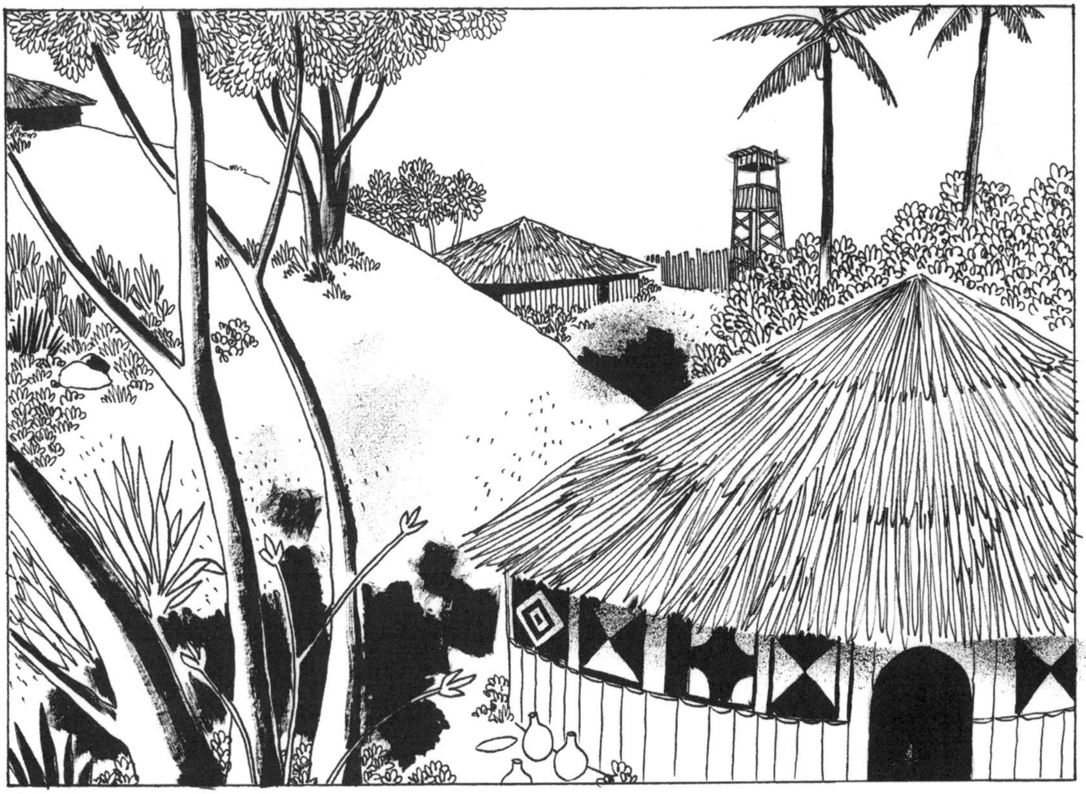

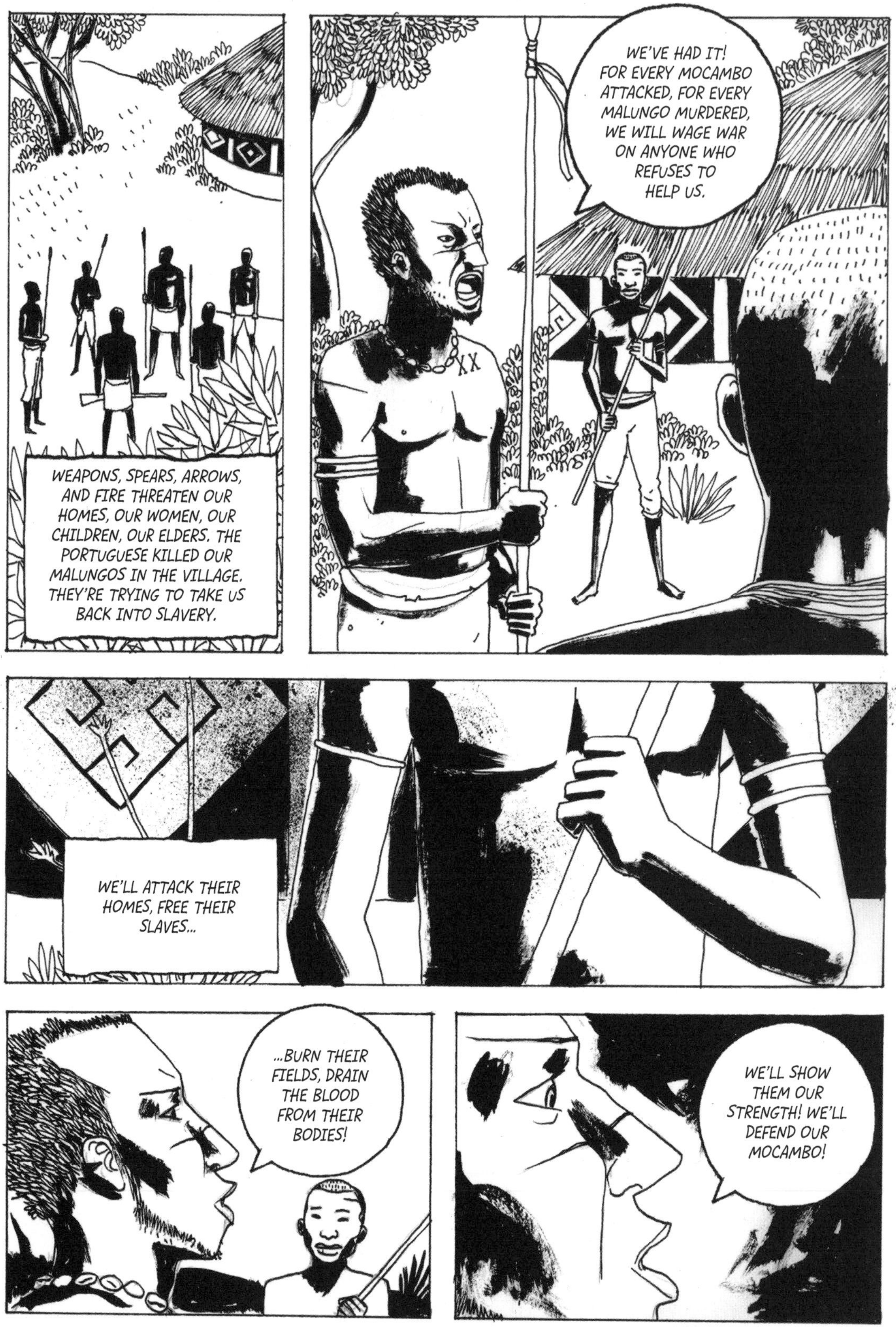
WEAPONS, SPEARS, ARROWS, AND FIRE THREATEN OUR HOMES, OUR WOMEN, OUR CHILDREN, OUR ELDERS. THE PORTUGUESE KILLED OUR MALUNGOS IN THE VILLAGE. THEY'RE TRYING TO TAKE US BACK INTO SLAVERY.
WE'VE HAD IT! FOR EVERY MOCAMBO ATTACKED, FOR EVERY MALUNGO MURDERED, WE WILL WAGE WAR ON ANYONE WHO REFUSES TO HELP US.
WE'LL ATTACK THEIR HOMES, FREE THEIR SLAVES...
...BURN THEIR FIELDS, DRAIN THE BLOOD FROM THEIR BODIES!
WE'LL SHOW THEM OUR STRENGTH! WE'LL DEFEND OUR MOCAMBO!

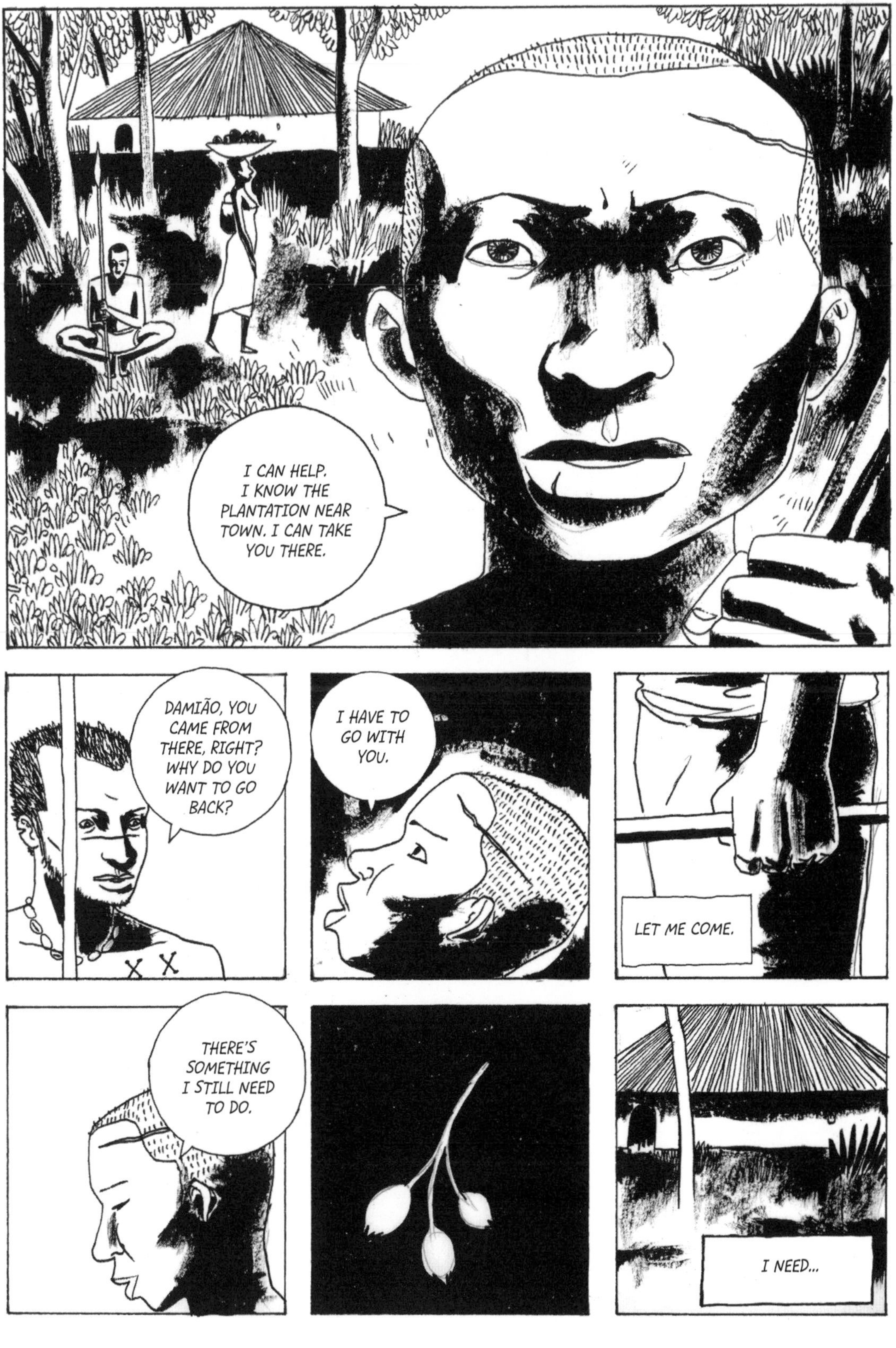
I CAN HELP. I KNOW THE PLANTATION NEAR TOWN. I CAN TAKE YOU THERE.
DAMIÃO, YOU CAME FROM THERE, RIGHT? WHY DO YOU WANT TO GO BACK?
I HAVE TO GO WITH YOU.
LET ME COME.
THERE'S SOMETHING I STILL NEED TO DO.
I NEED...

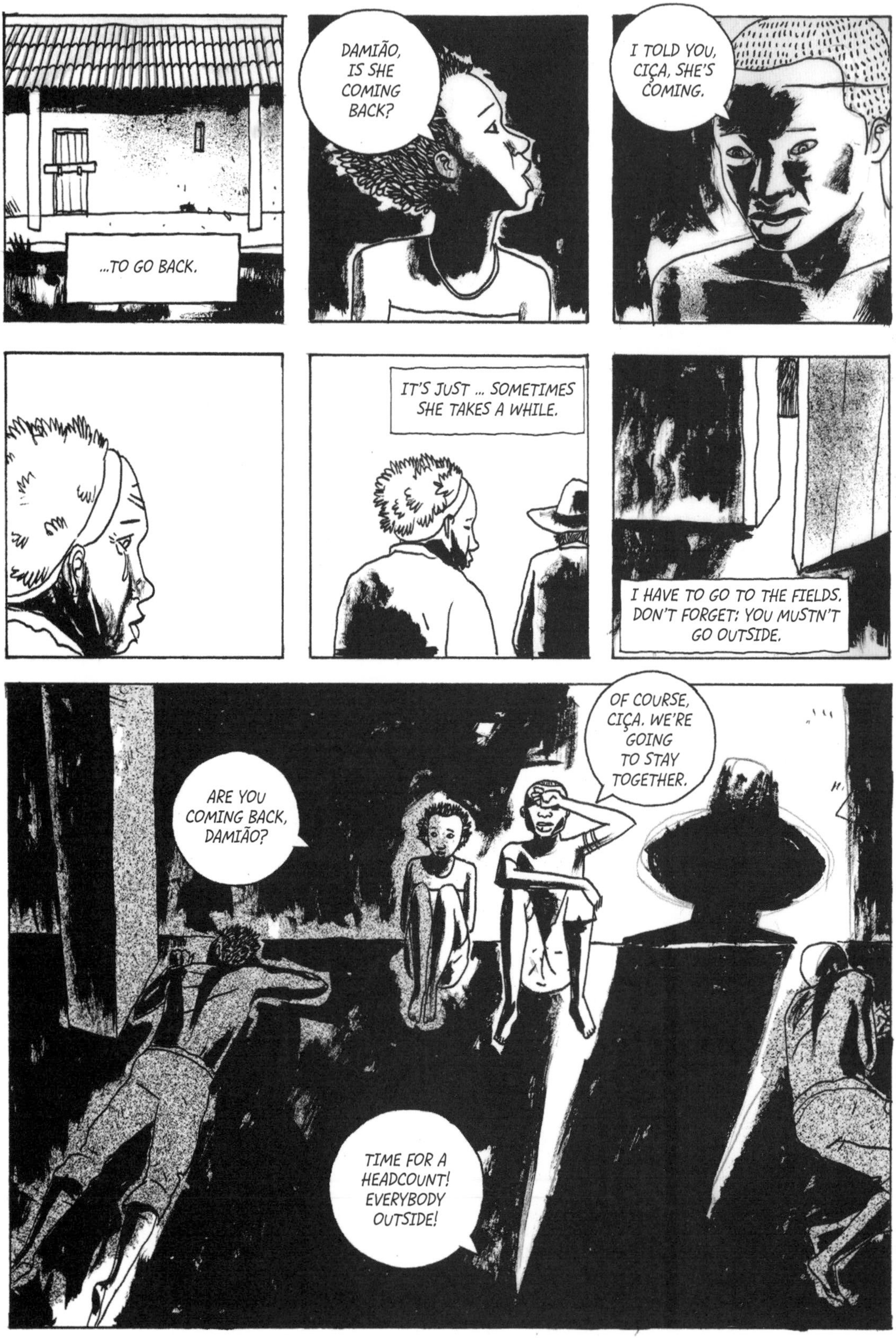
...TO GO BACK.
DAMIÃO, IS SHE COMING BACK?
I TOLD YOU, CIÇA, SHE'S COMING.
IT'S JUST ... SOMETIMES SHE TAKES A WHILE.
I HAVE TO GO TO THE FIELDS. DON'T FORGET: YOU MUSTN'T GO OUTSIDE.
ARE YOU COMING BACK, DAMIÃO?
OF COURSE, CIÇA. WE'RE GOING TO STAY TOGETHER.
TIME FOR A HEADCOUNT! EVERYBODY OUTSIDE!

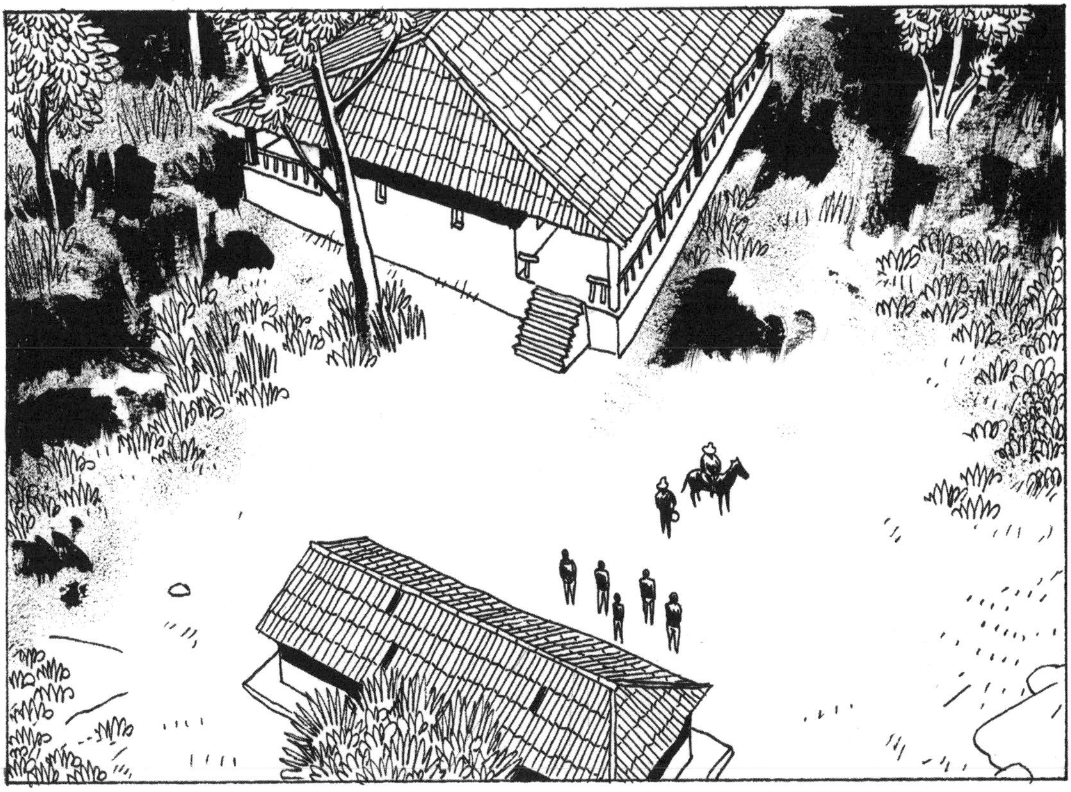

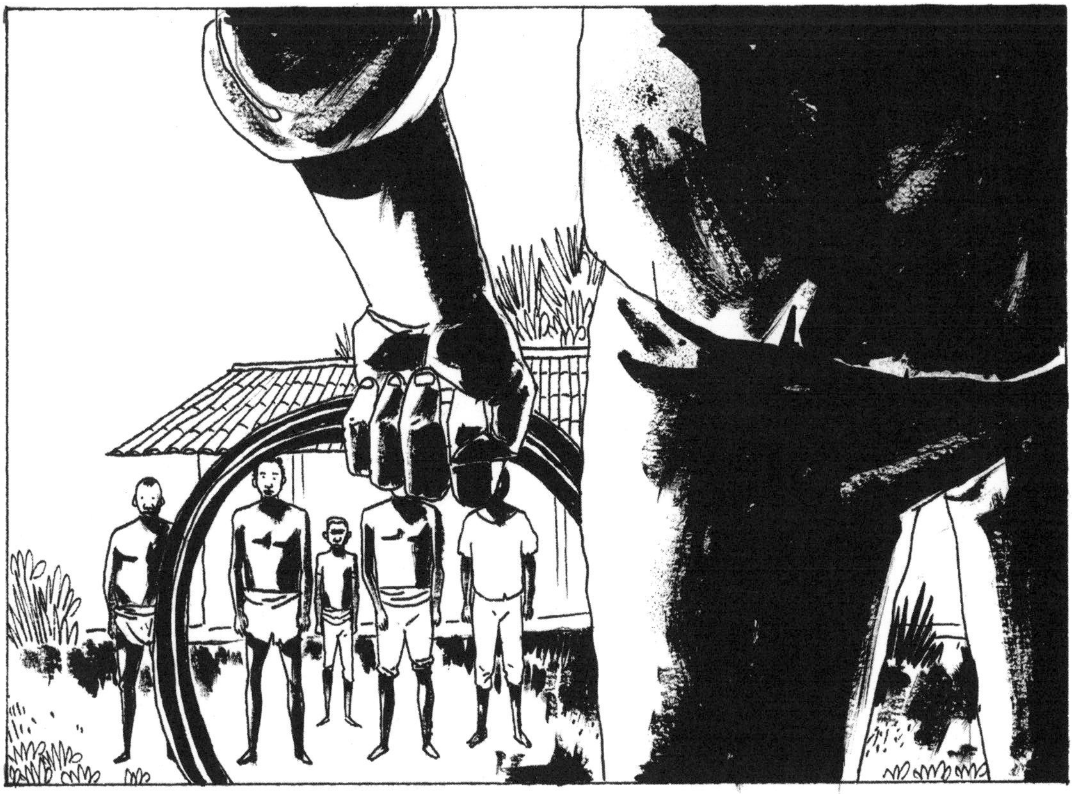

THREE, FOUR, FIVE...

THERE ARE STILL PEOPLE THERE...

WHO'S MISSING?

SIR, MY SISTER CAN'T WORK YET. SHE'S LITTLE ... AND SHE'S SICK...

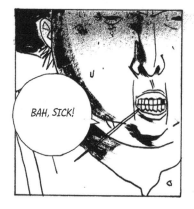

BAH, SICK!

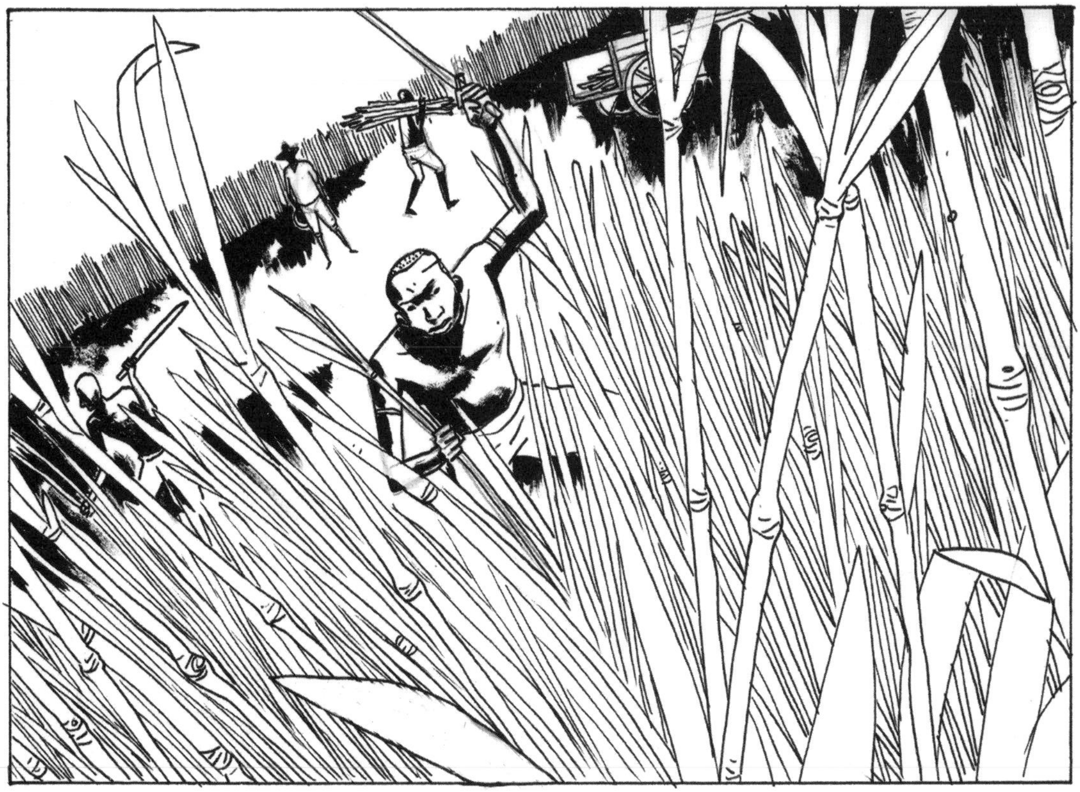

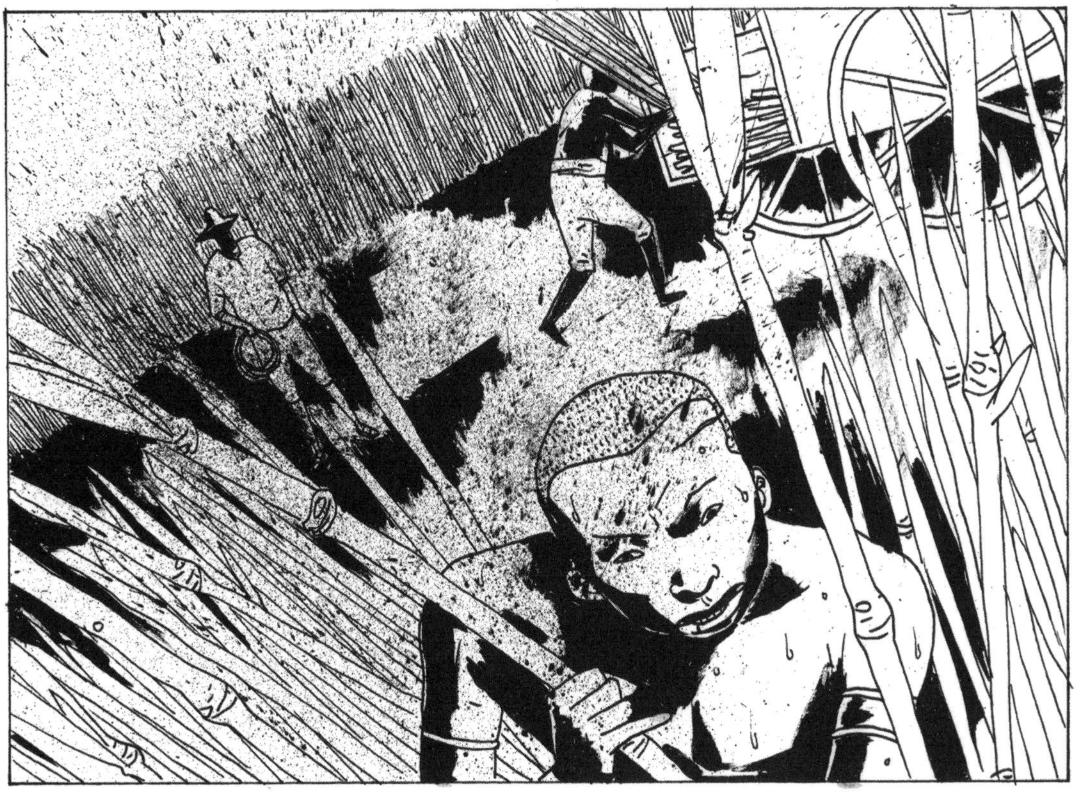

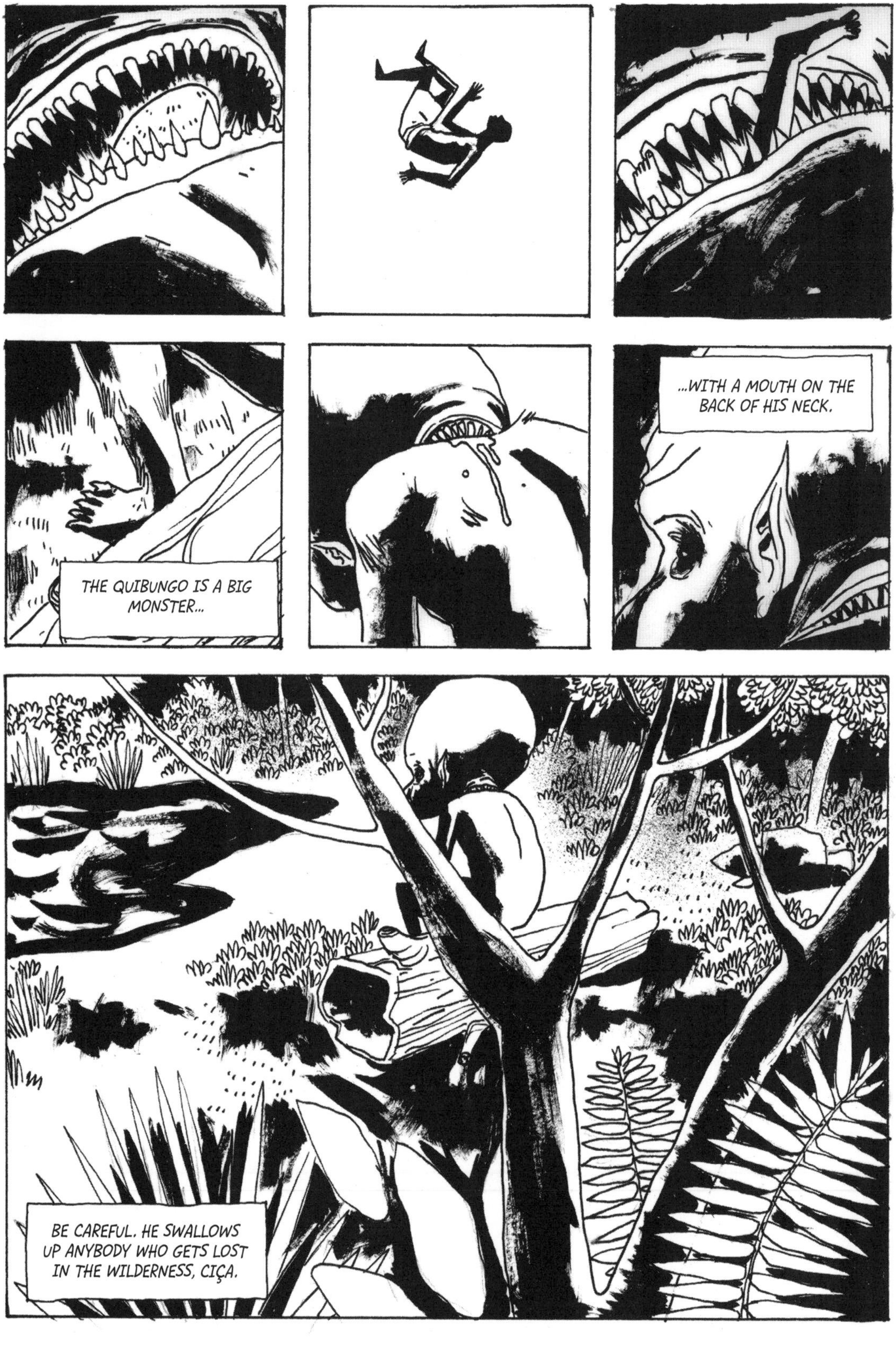
THE QUIBUNGO IS A BIG MONSTER...
...WITH A MOUTH ON THE BACK OF HIS NECK.
BE CAREFUL. HE SWALLOWS UP ANYBODY WHO GETS LOST IN THE WILDERNESS, CIÇA.

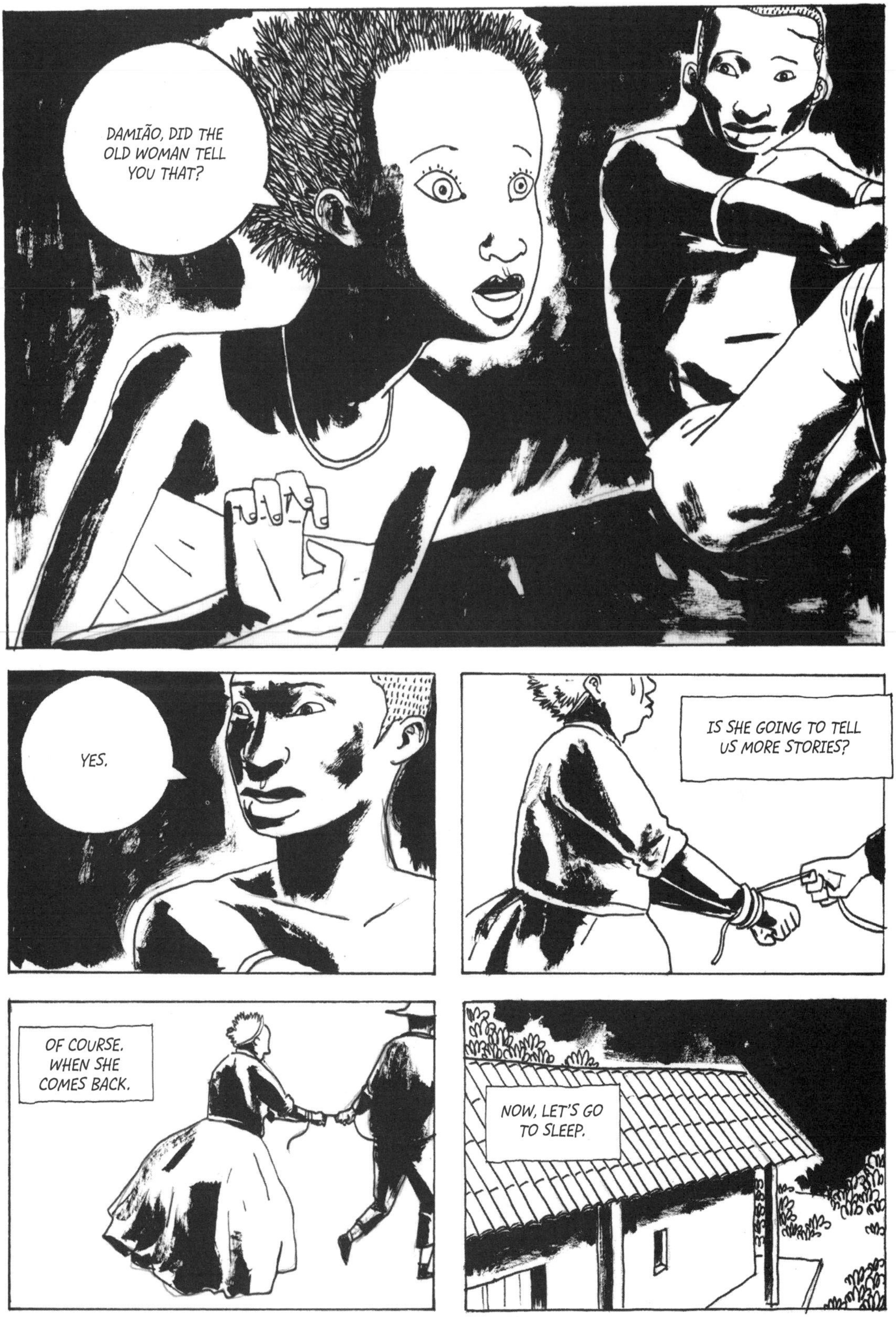
DAMIÃO, DID THE OLD WOMAN TELL YOU THAT?
YES.
IS SHE GOING TO TELL US MORE STORIES?
OF COURSE. WHEN SHE COMES BACK.
NOW, LET'S GO TO SLEEP.

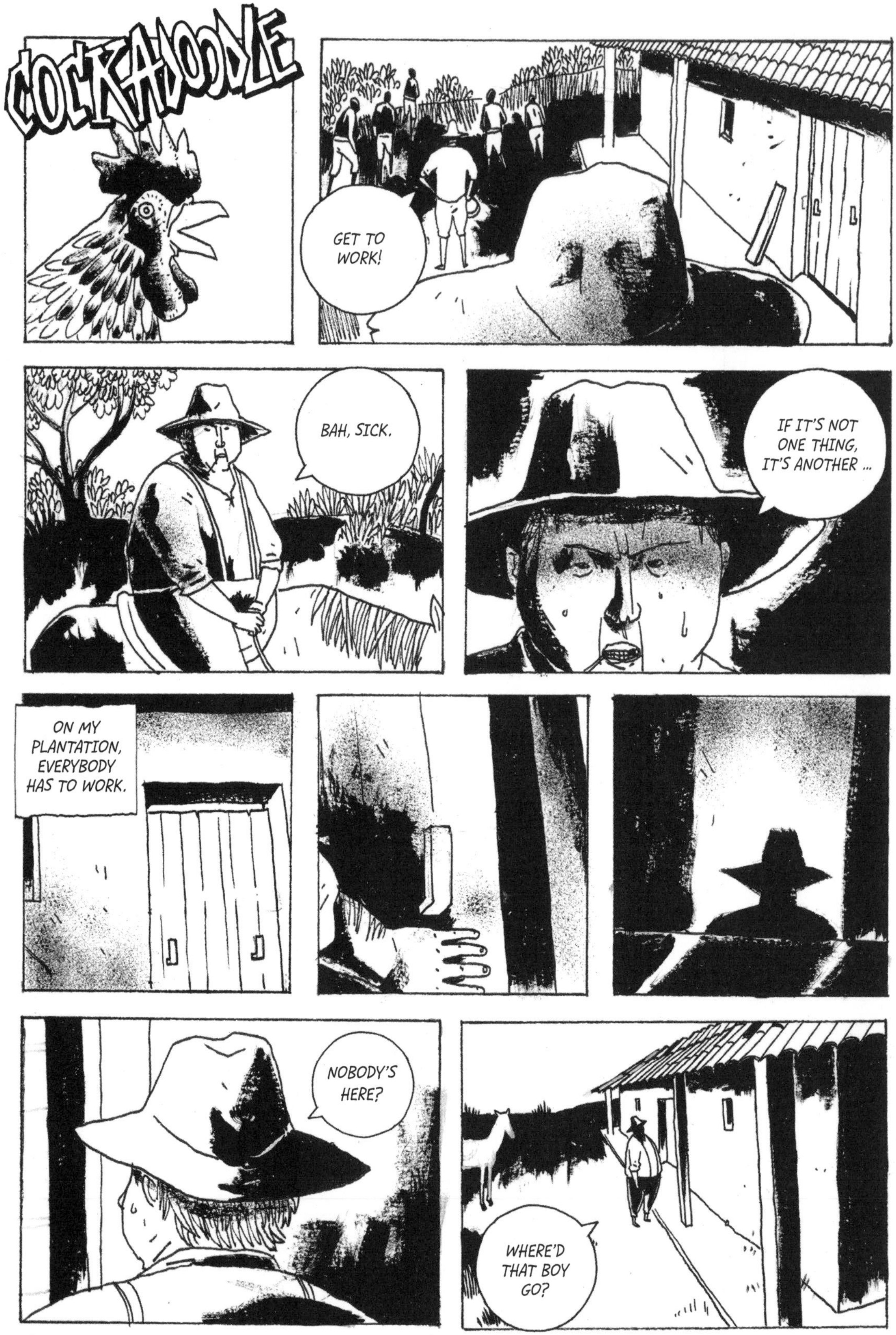
COCKADOODLE
GET TO WORK!
BAH, SICK.
IF IT'S NOT ONE THING, IT'S ANOTHER ...
ON MY PLANTATION, EVERYBODY HAS TO WORK.
NOBODY'S HERE?
WHERE'D THAT BOY GO?

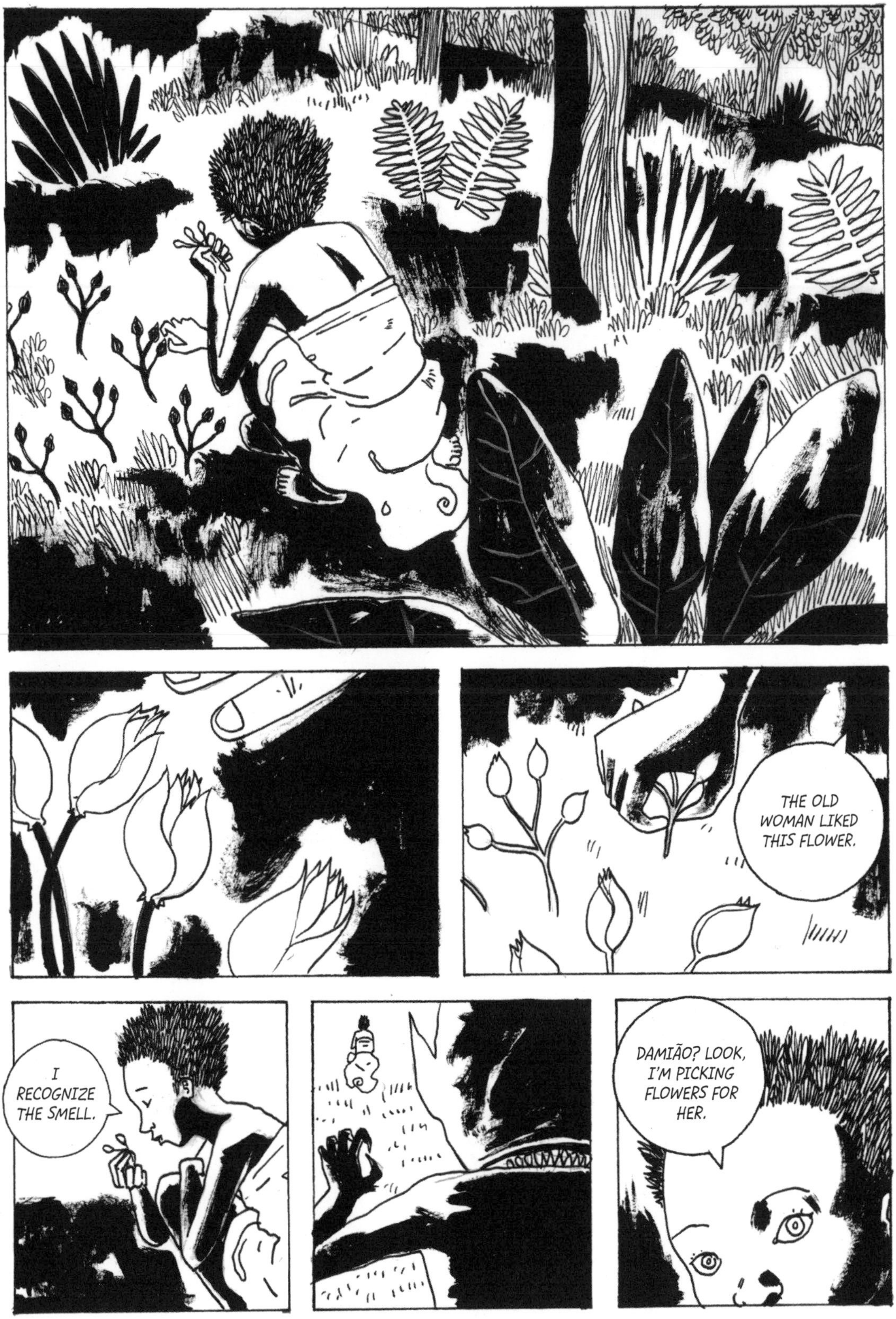
THE OLD WOMAN LIKED THIS FLOWER.
I RECOGNIZE THE SMELL.
DAMIÃO? LOOK, I'M PICKING FLOWERS FOR HER.

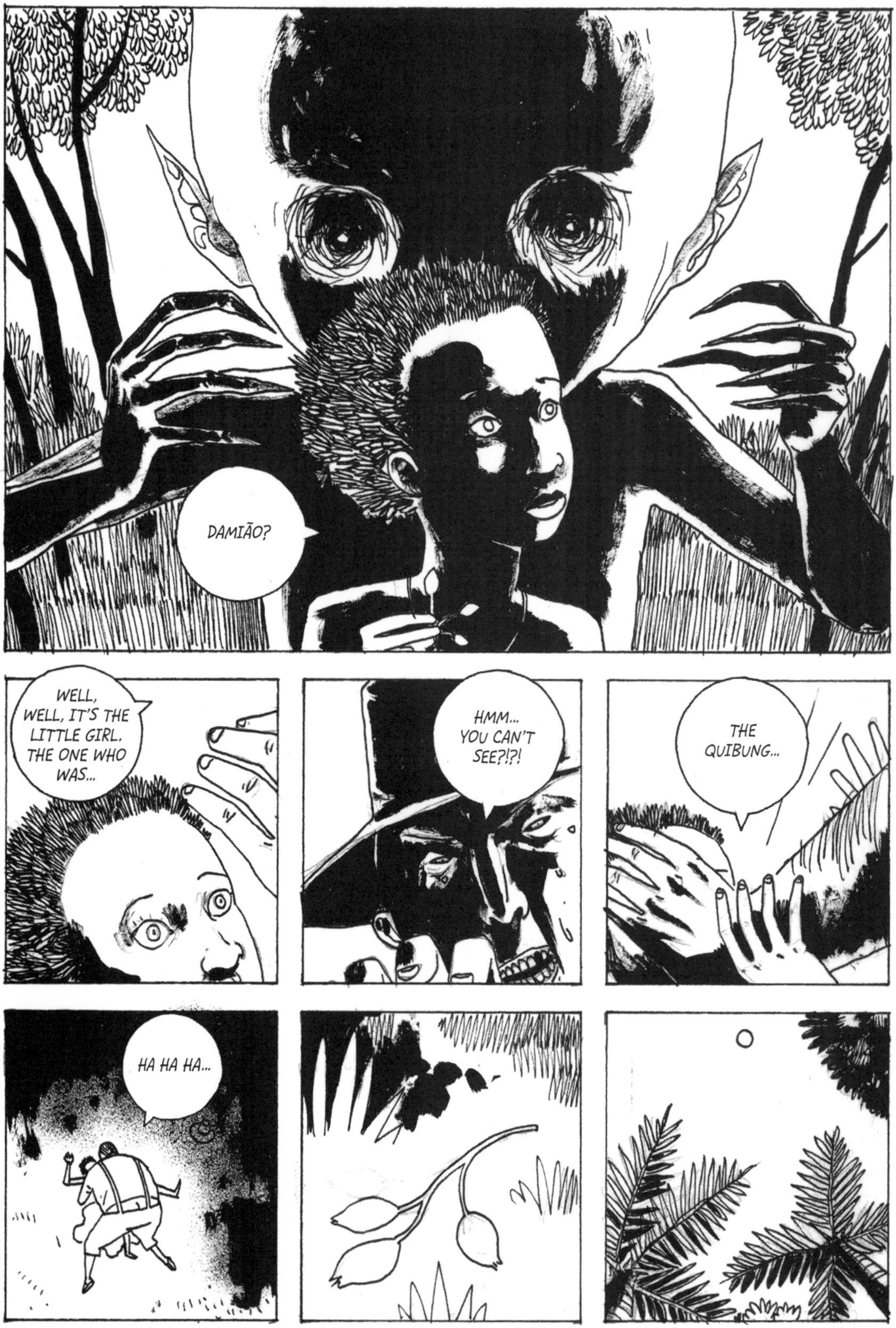
DAMIÃO?
WELL, WELL, IT'S THE LITTLE GIRL. THE ONE WHO WAS...
HMM... YOU CAN'T SEE?!?!
THE QUIBUNG...
HA HA HA...

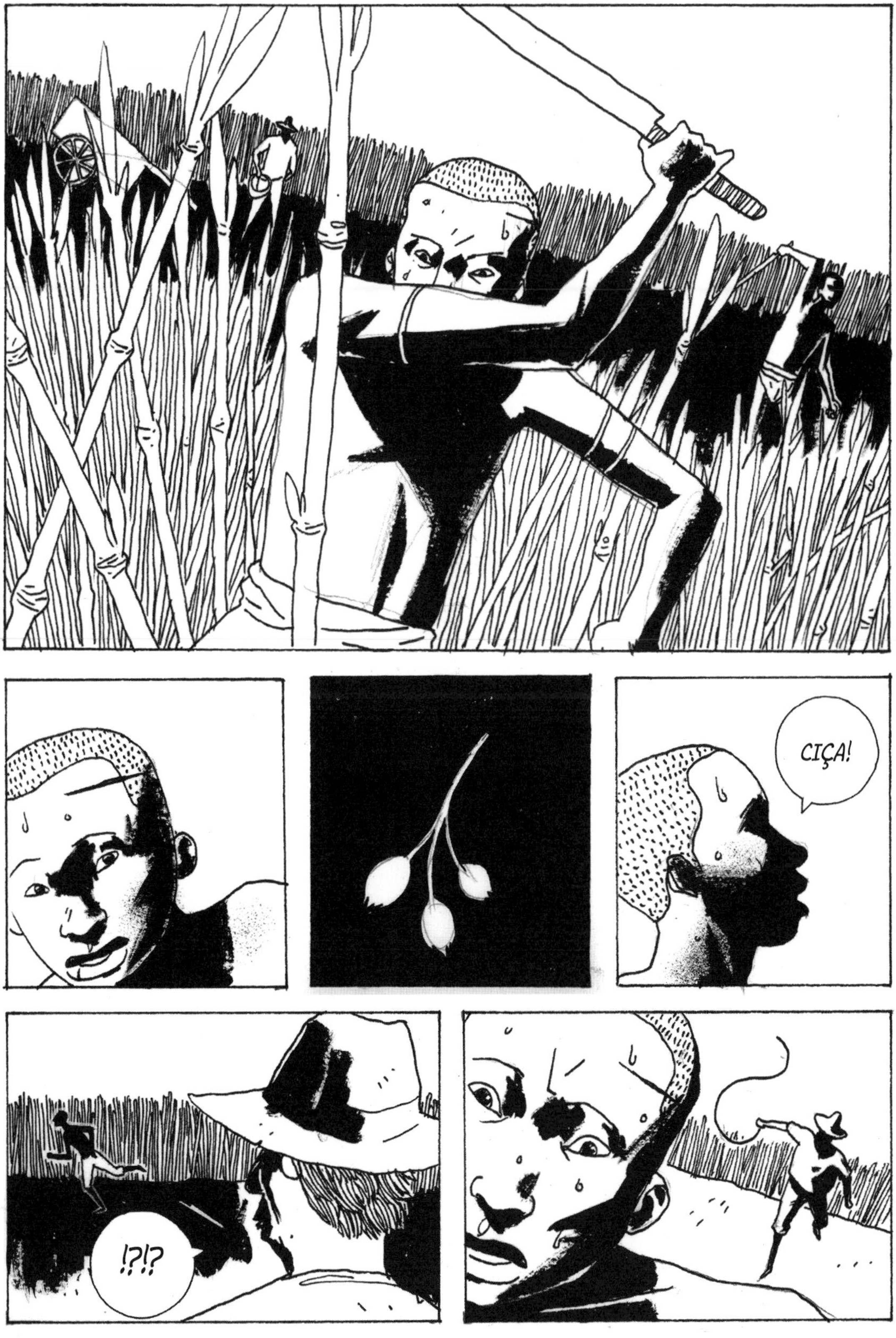
CIÇA!
!?!?

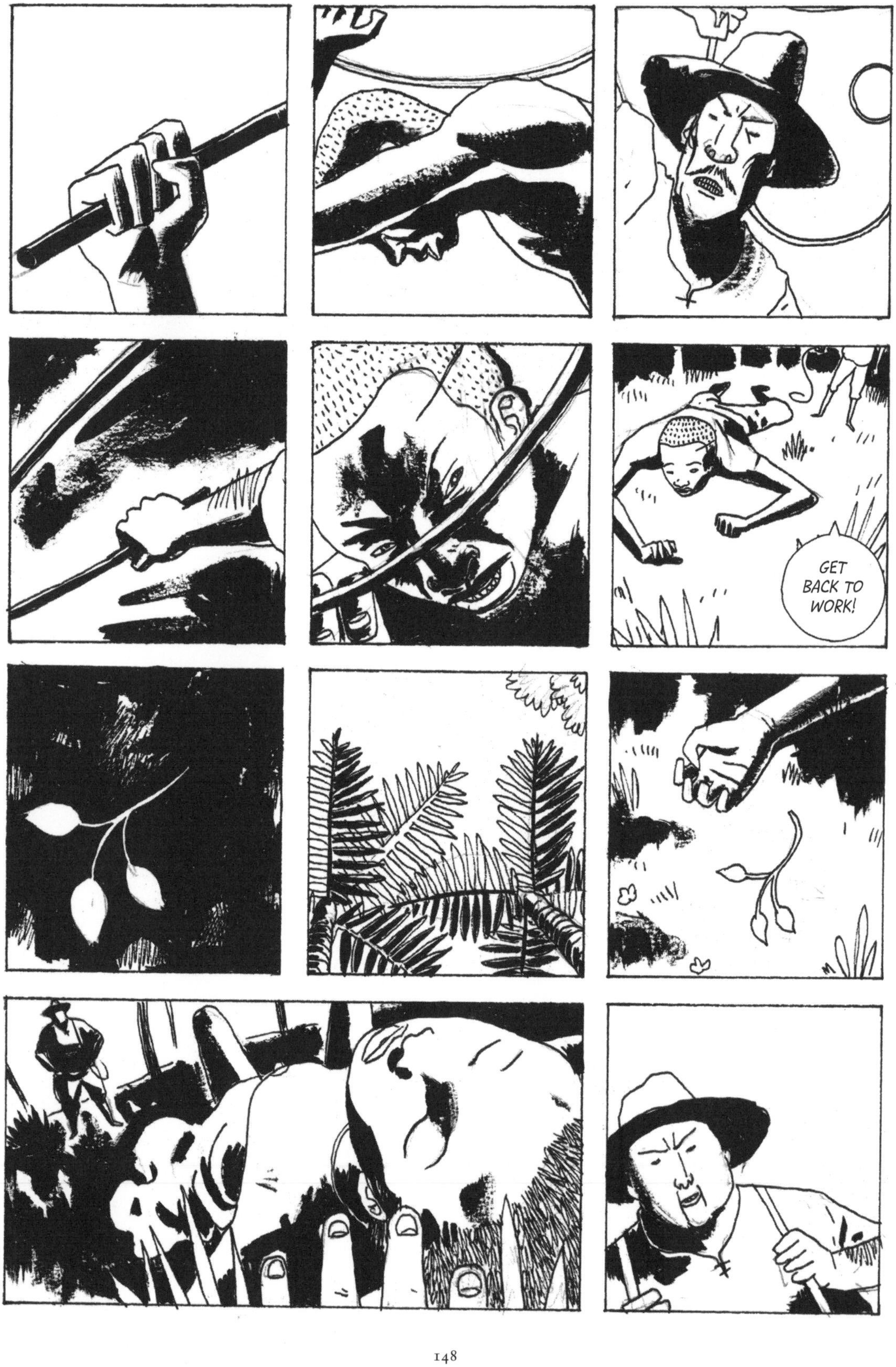
GET BACK TO WORK!

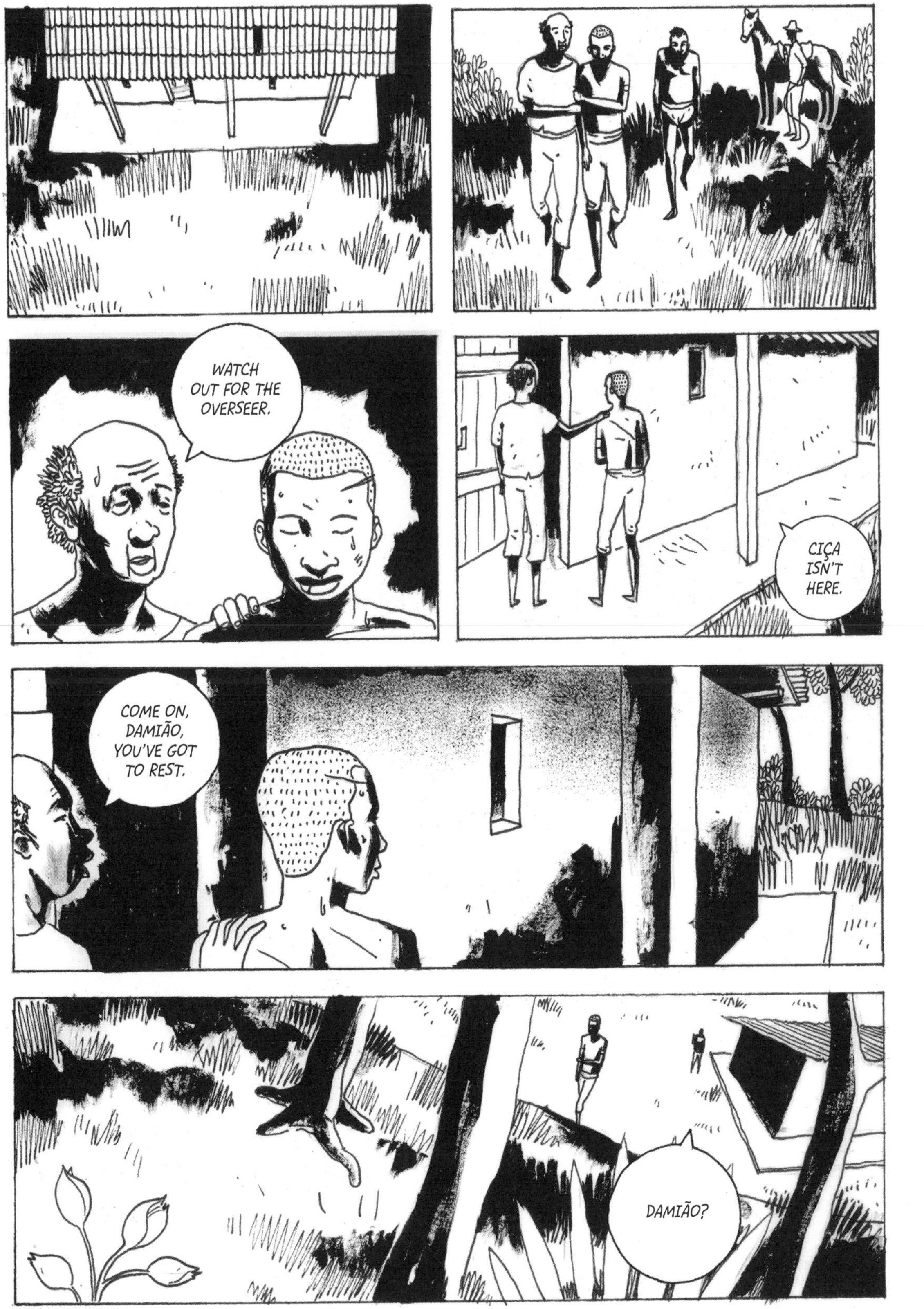
WATCH OUT FOR THE OVERSEER.
CIÇA ISN'T HERE.
COME ON, DAMIÃO, YOU'VE GOT TO REST.
DAMIÃO?

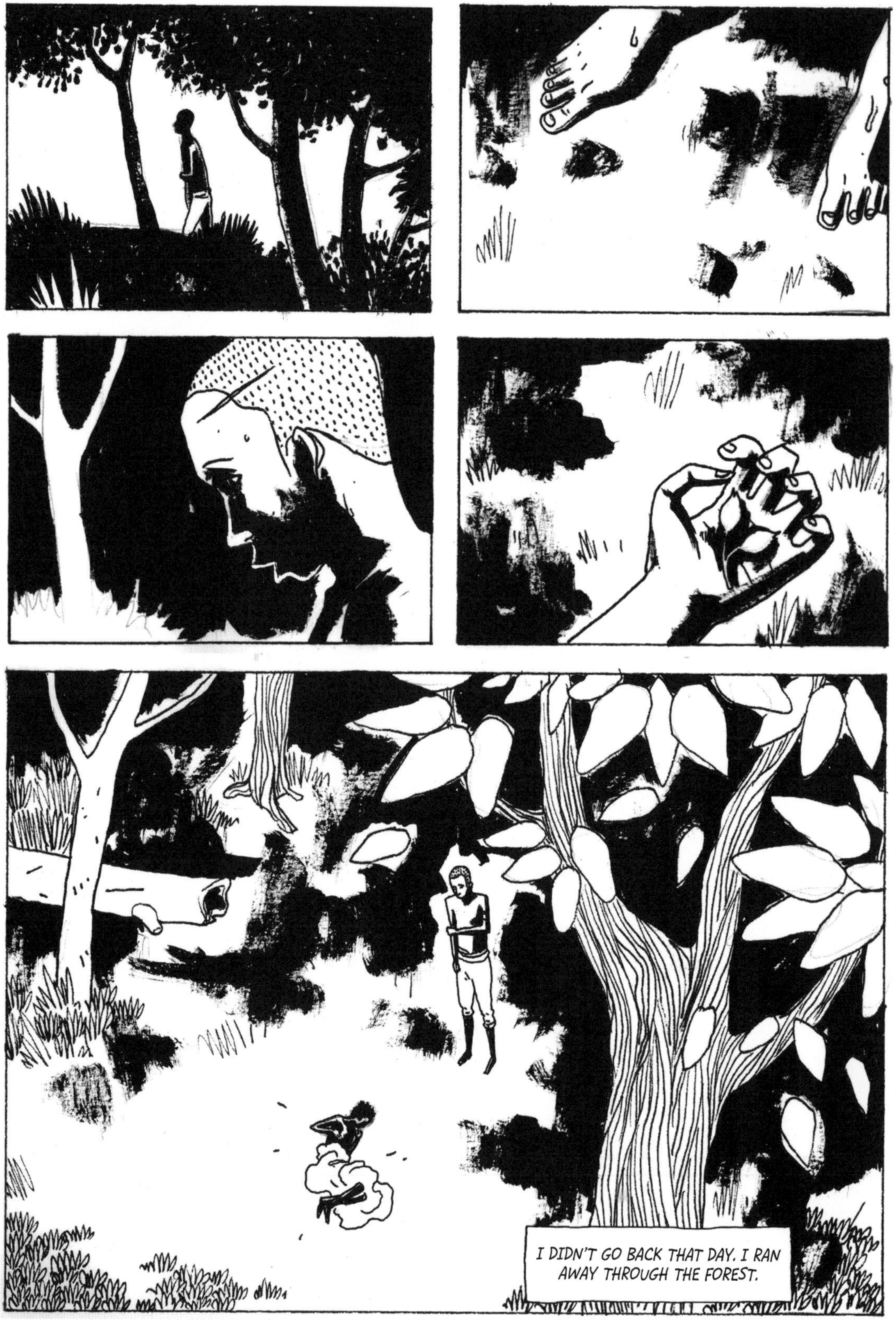
I DIDN'T GO BACK THAT DAY. I RAN AWAY THROUGH THE FOREST.

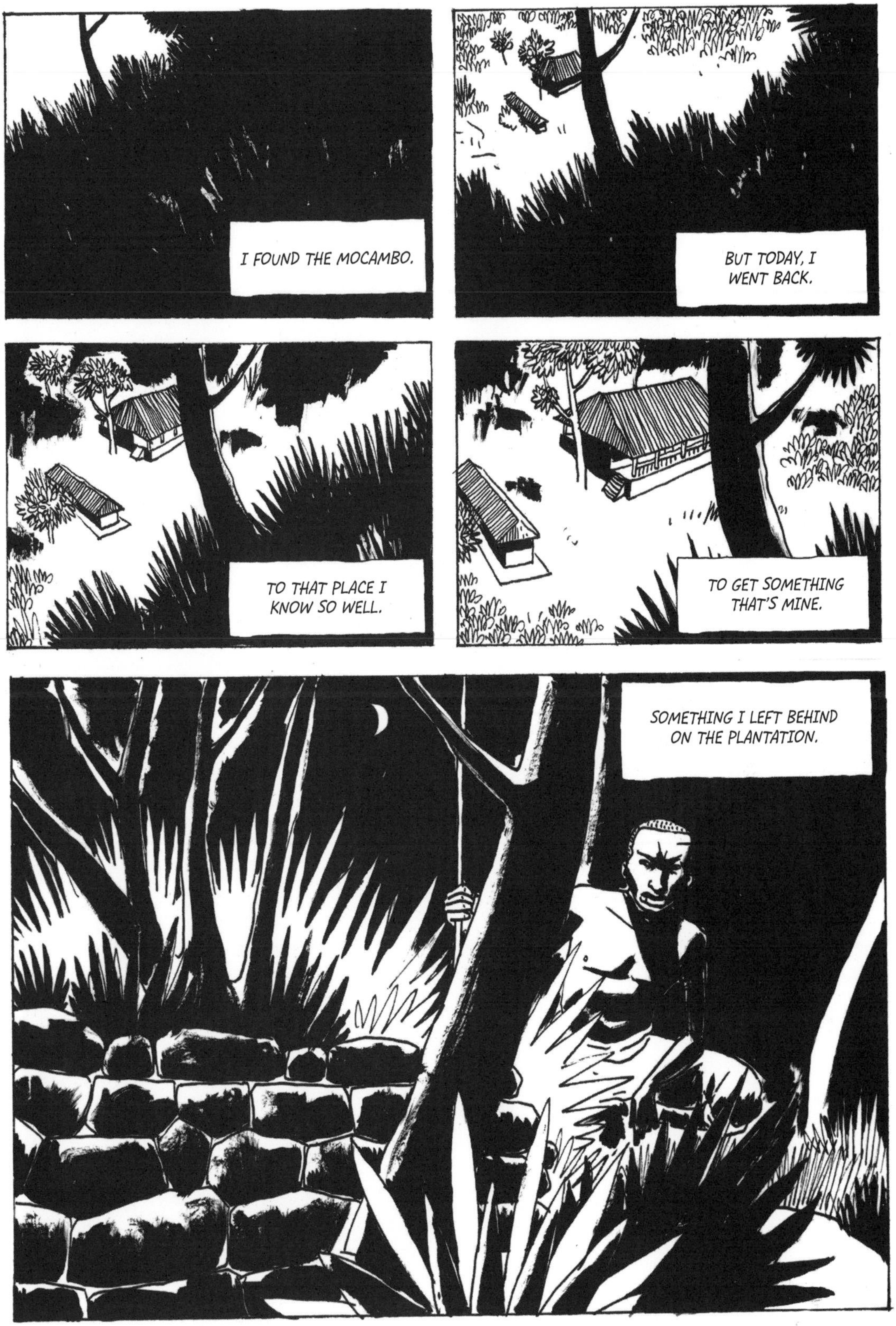
I FOUND THE MOCAMBO.
BUT TODAY, I WENT BACK.
TO THAT PLACE I KNOW SO WELL.
TO GET SOMETHING THAT'S MINE.
SOMETHING I LEFT BEHIND ON THE PLANTATION.

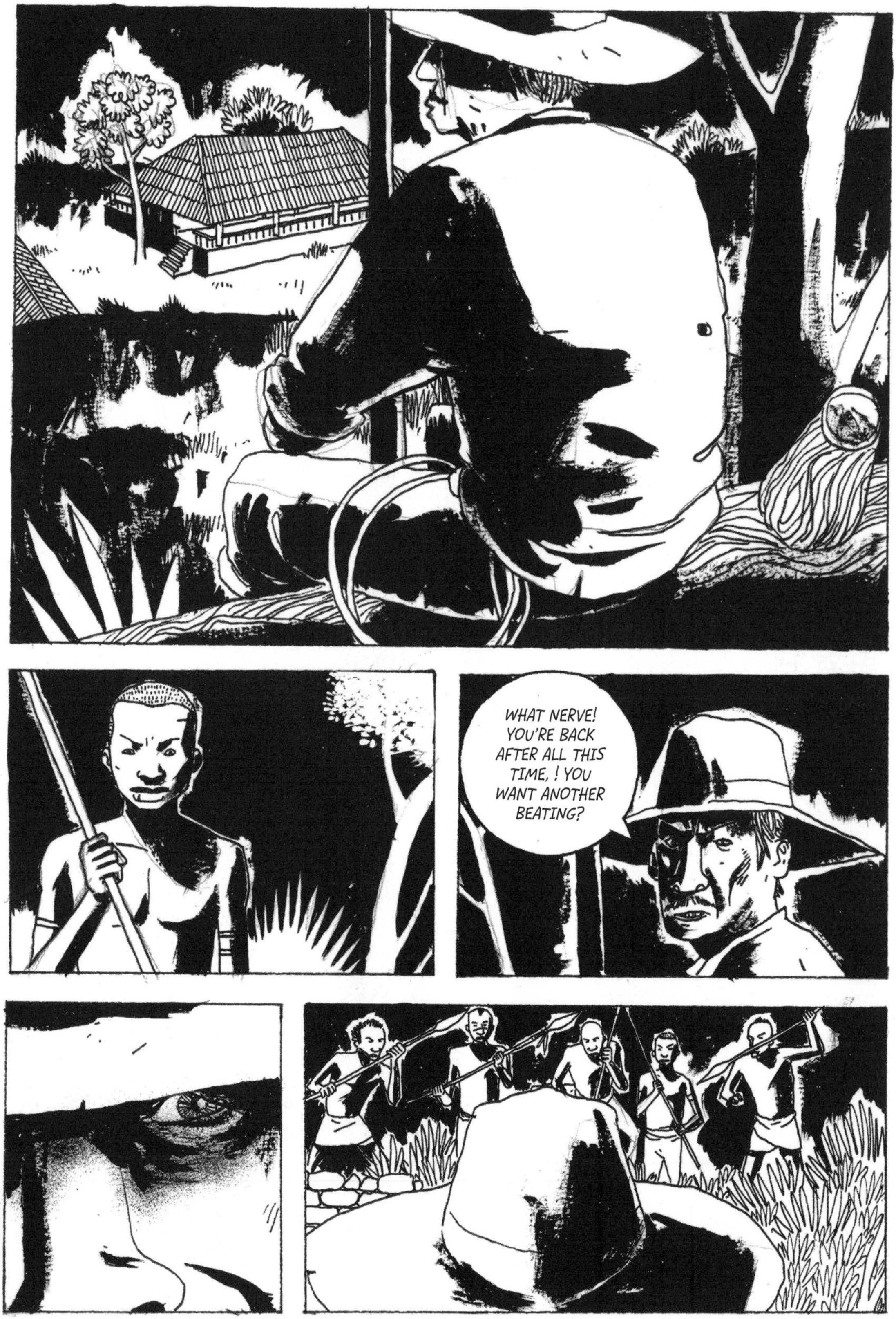
WHAT NERVE! YOU'RE BACK AFTER ALL THIS TIME, ! YOU WANT ANOTHER BEATING?

HE CAME BACK...

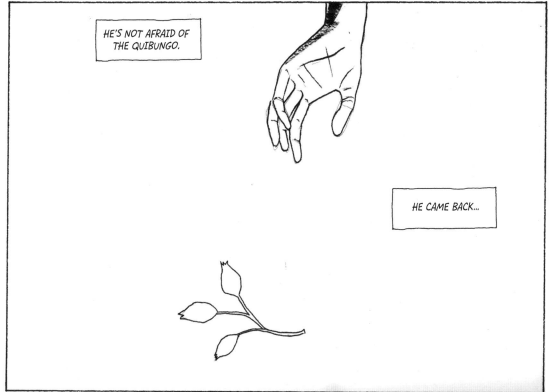

HE'S NOT AFRAID OF THE QUIBUNGO.

HE CAME BACK...

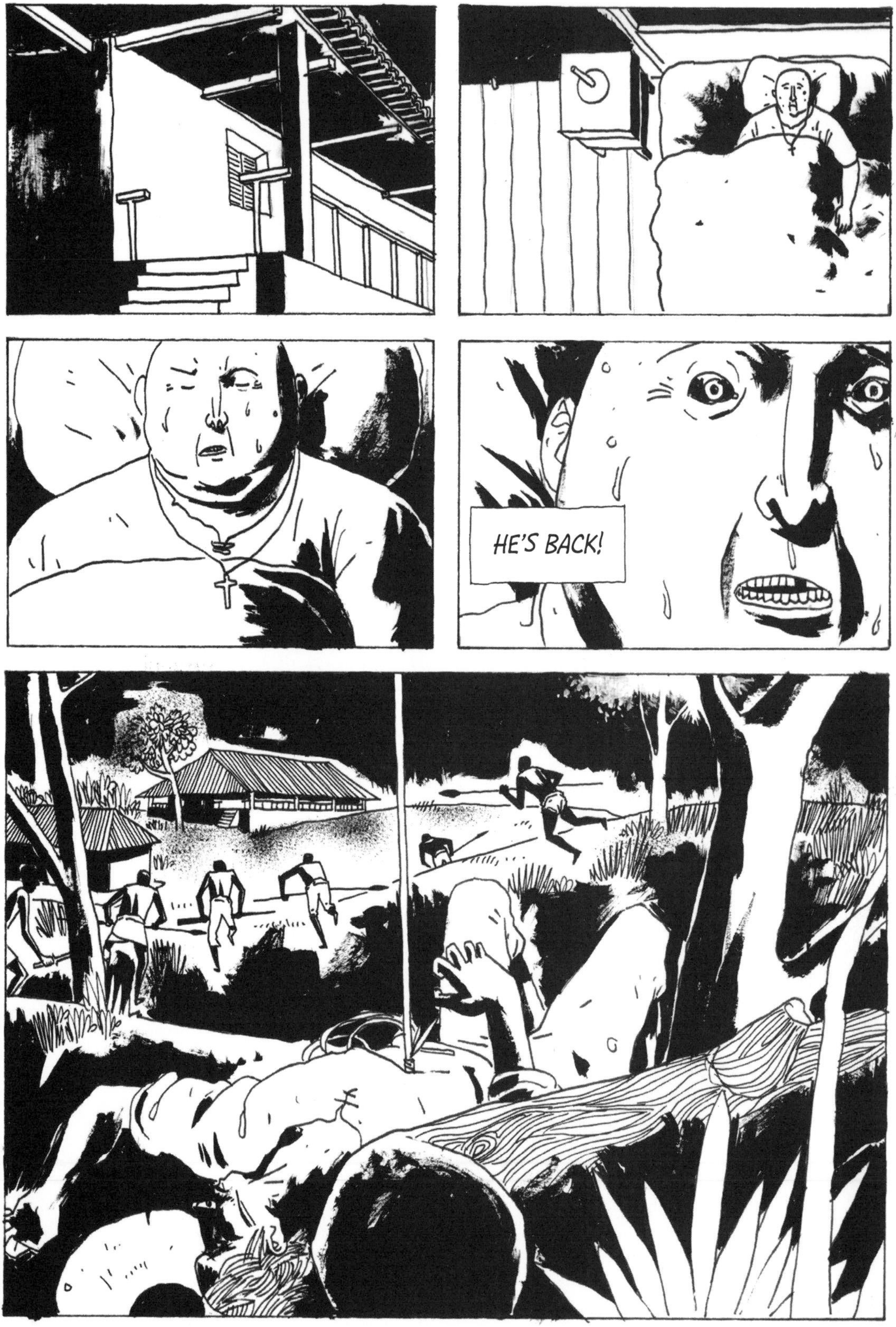
HE'S BACK!

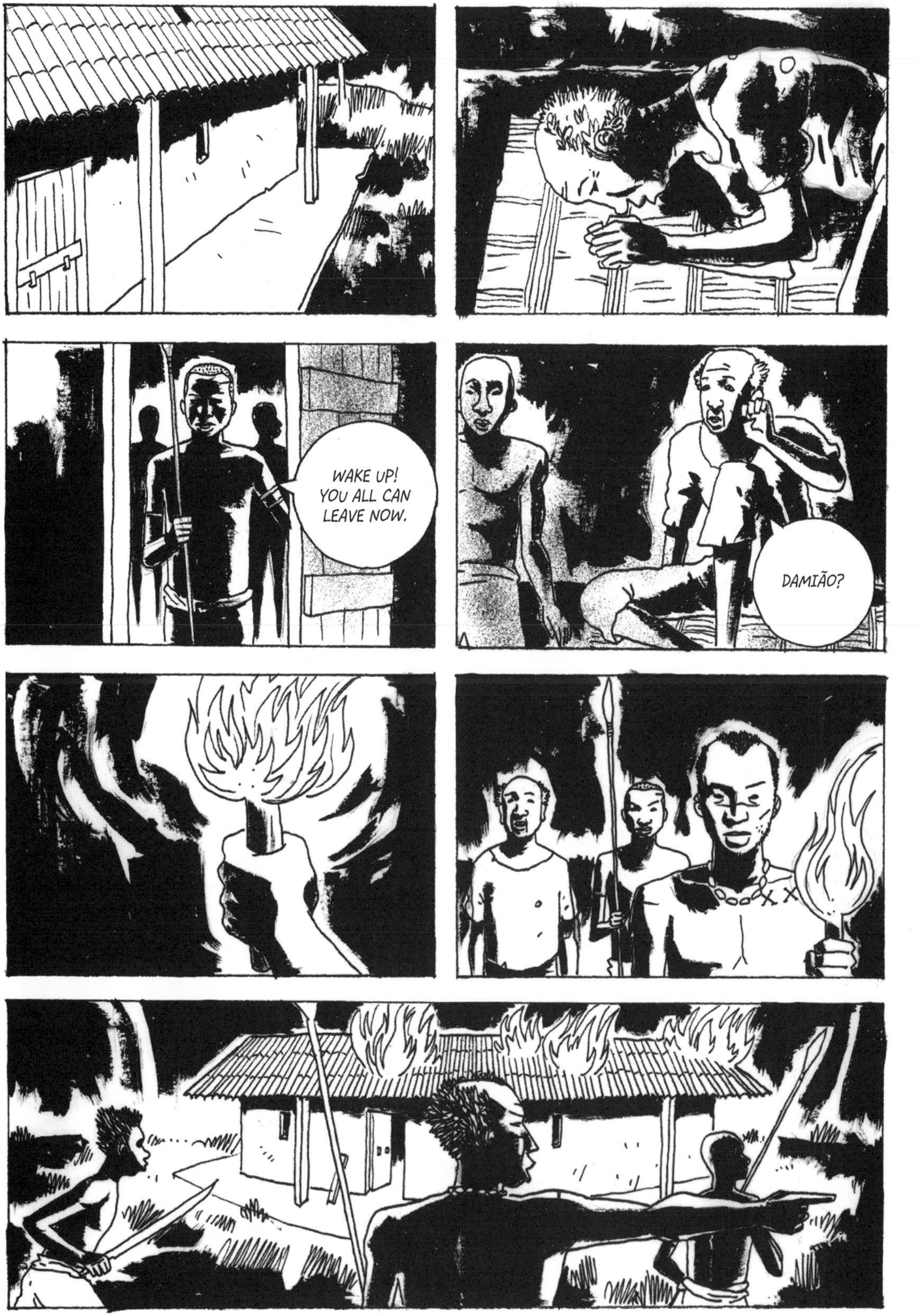
WAKE UP! YOU ALL CAN LEAVE NOW.
DAMIÃO?

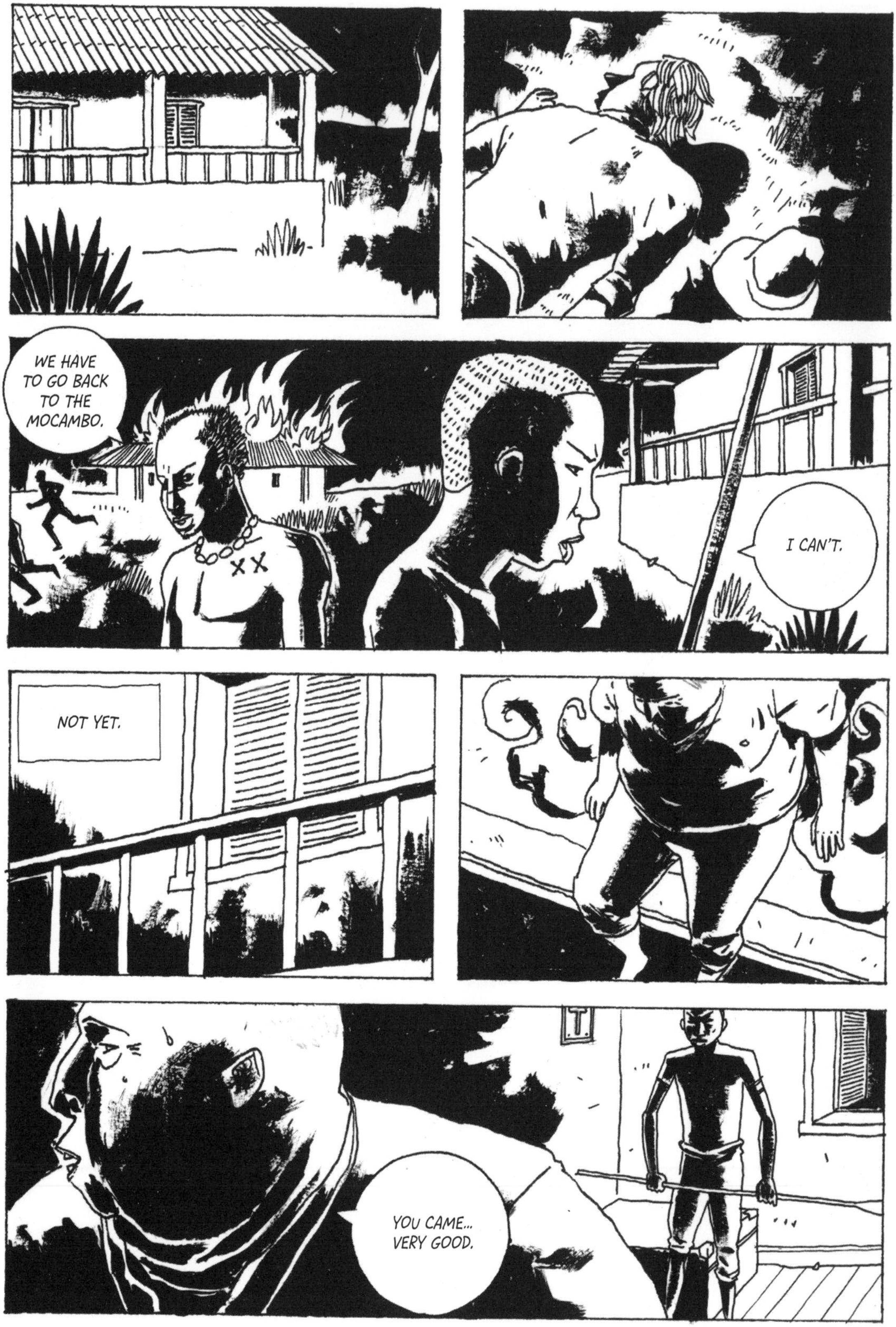
WE HAVE TO GO BACK TO THE MOCAMBO.
I CAN'T.
NOT YET.
YOU CAME... VERY GOOD.

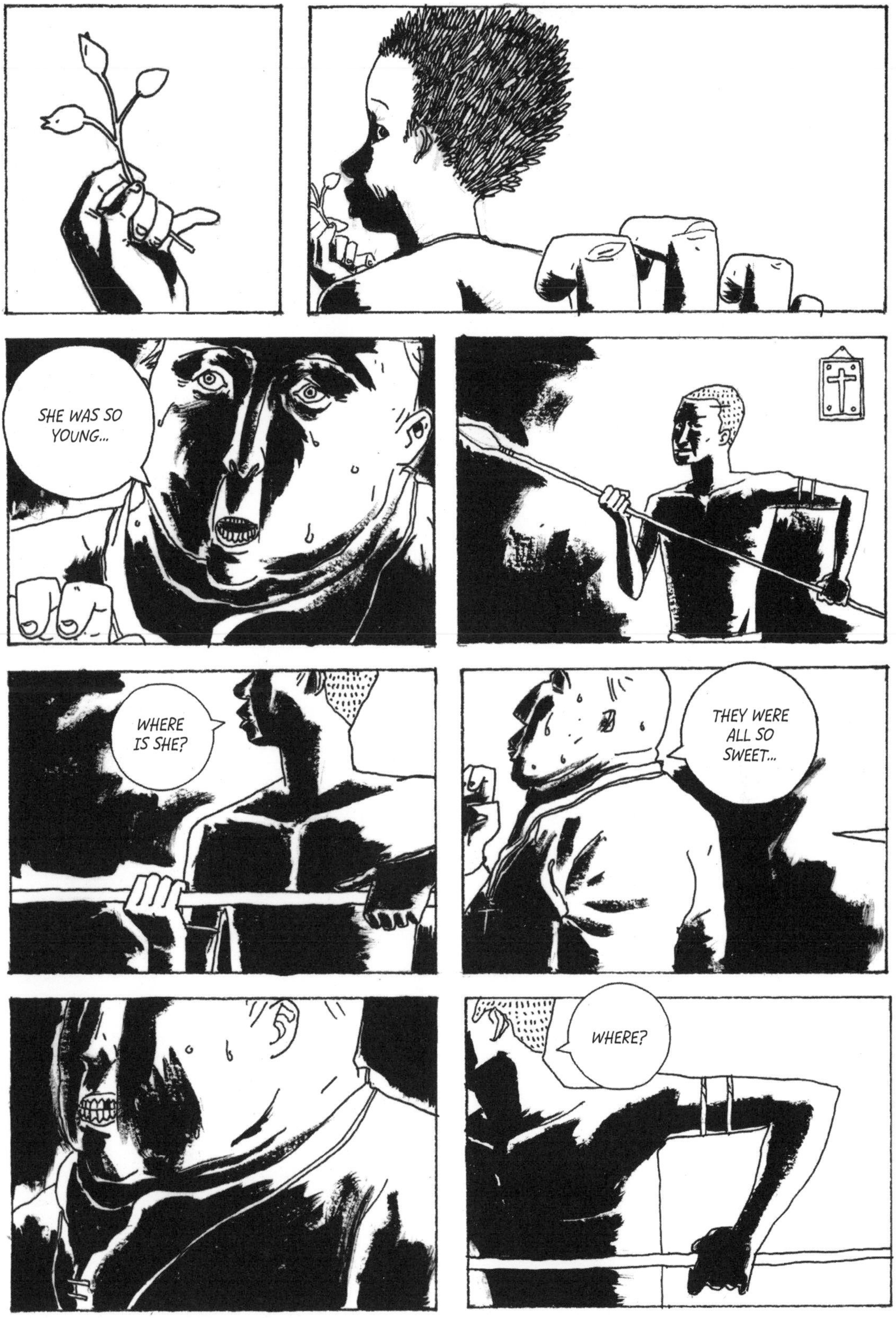
SHE WAS SO YOUNG...
WHERE IS SHE?
THEY WERE ALL SO SWEET...
WHERE?

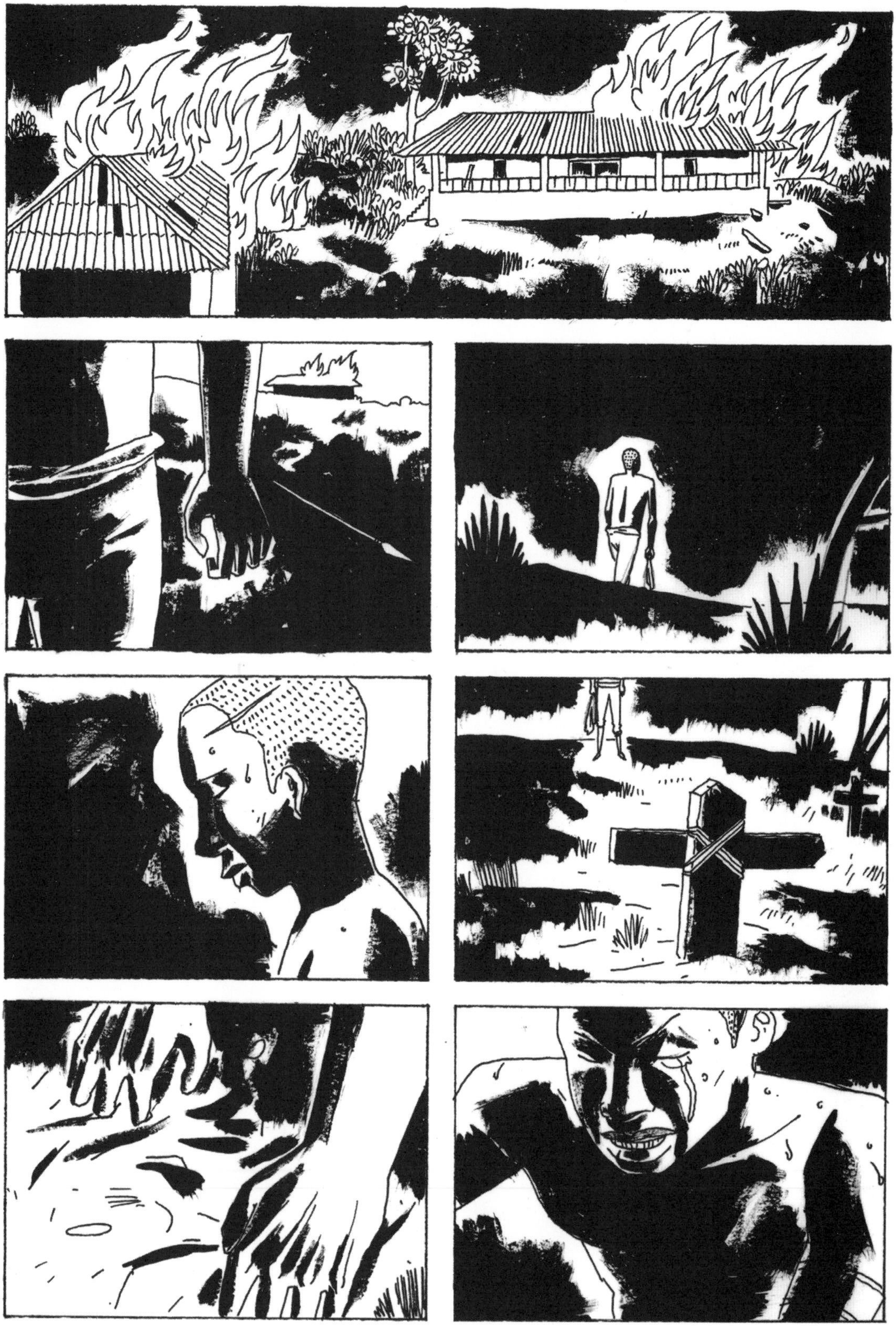

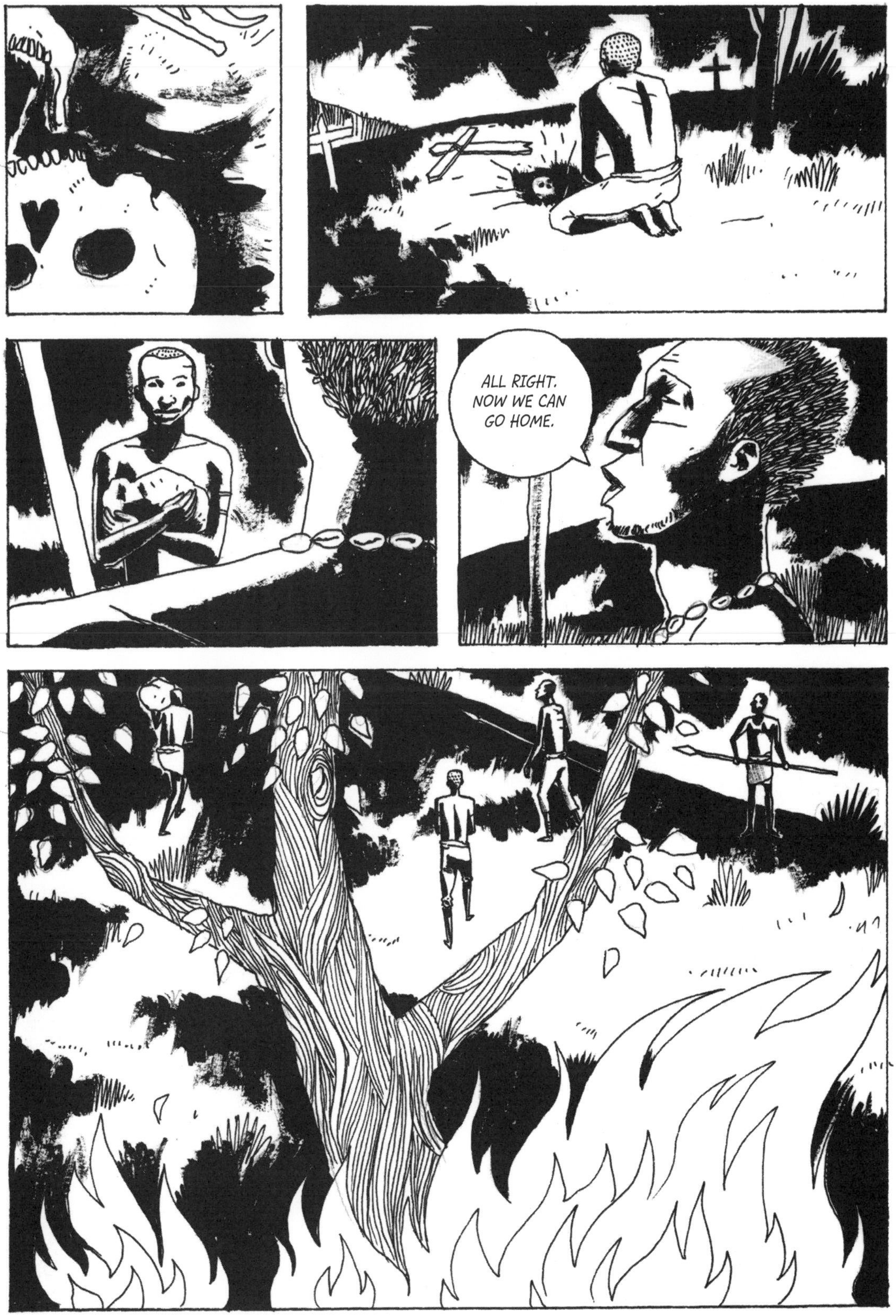
ALL RIGHT. NOW WE CAN GO HOME.

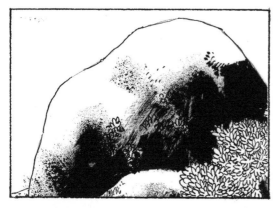

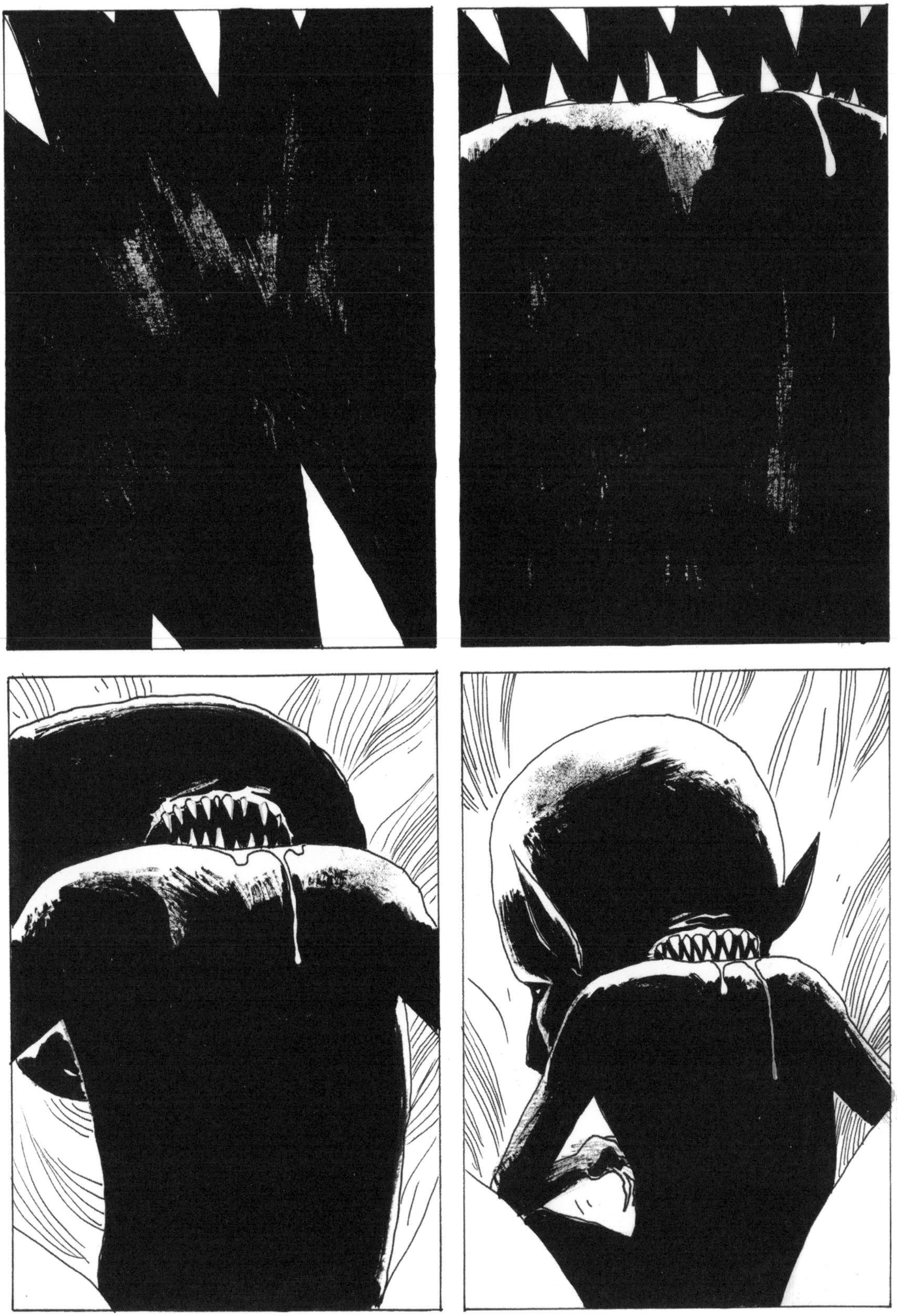

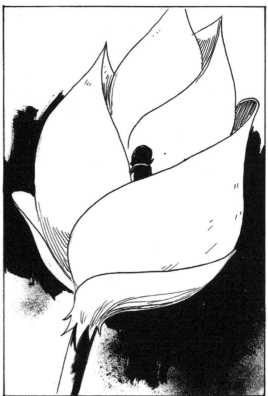

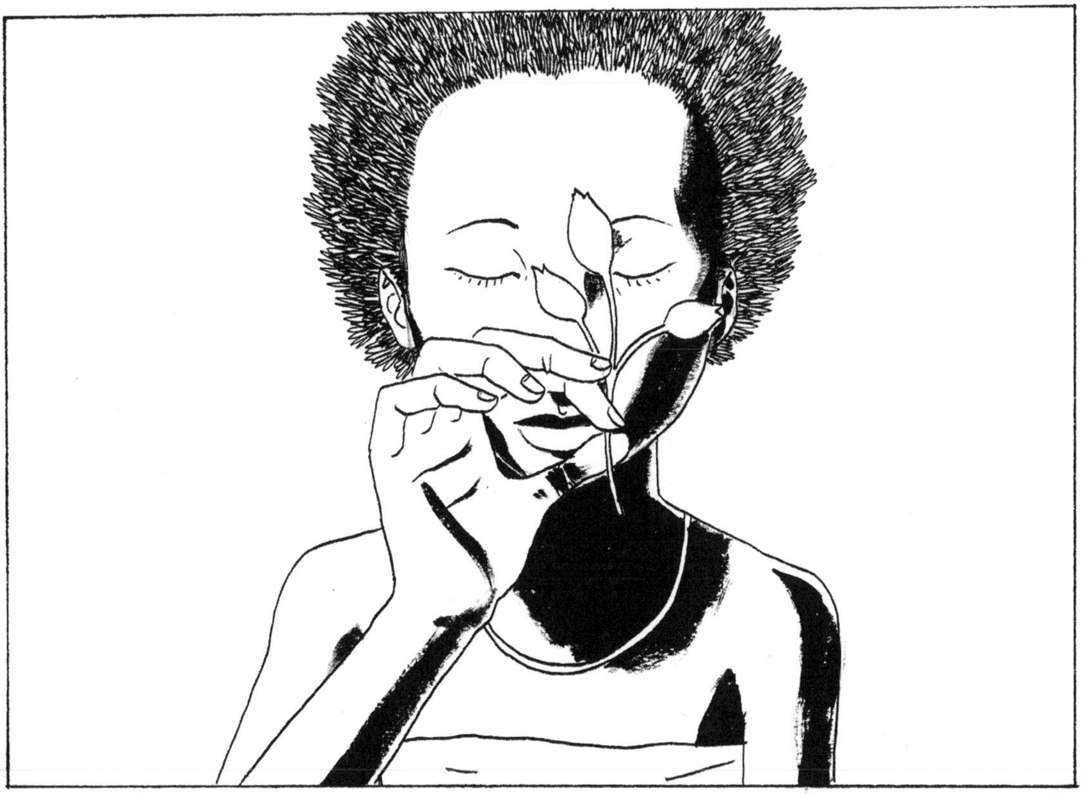

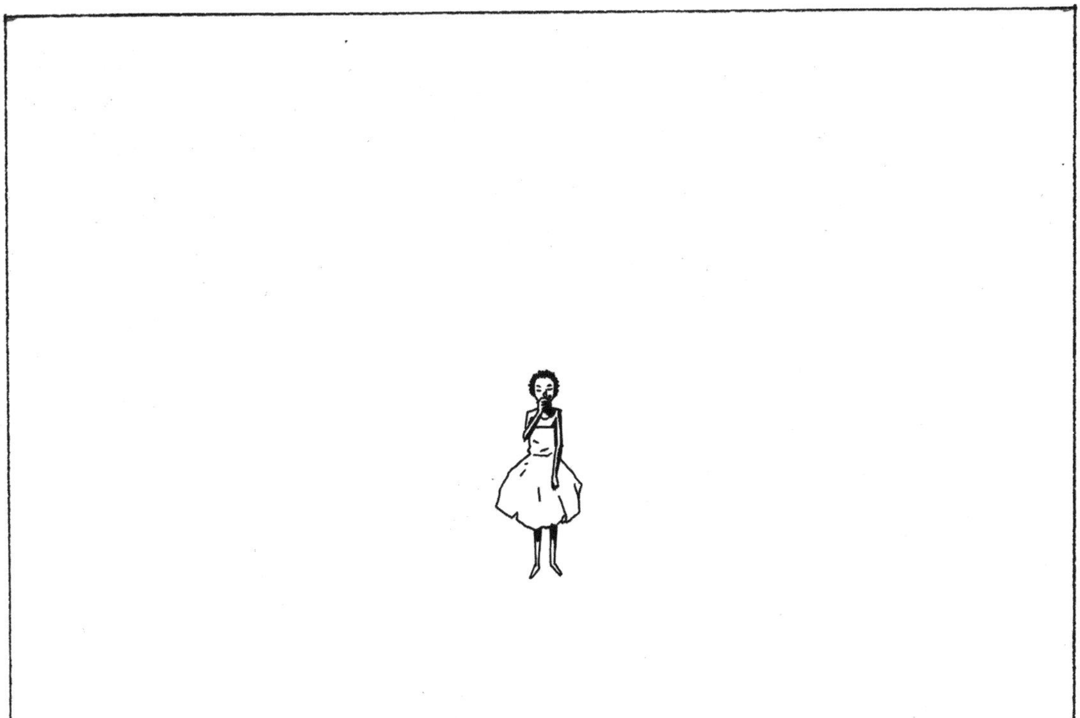

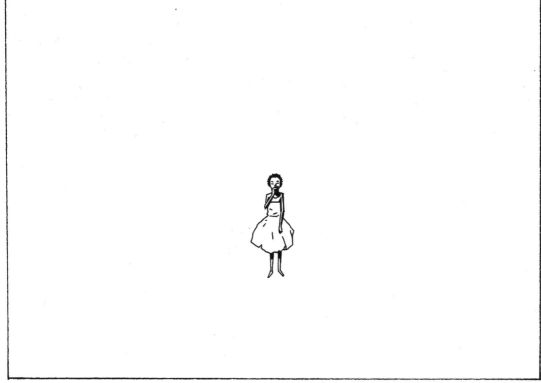

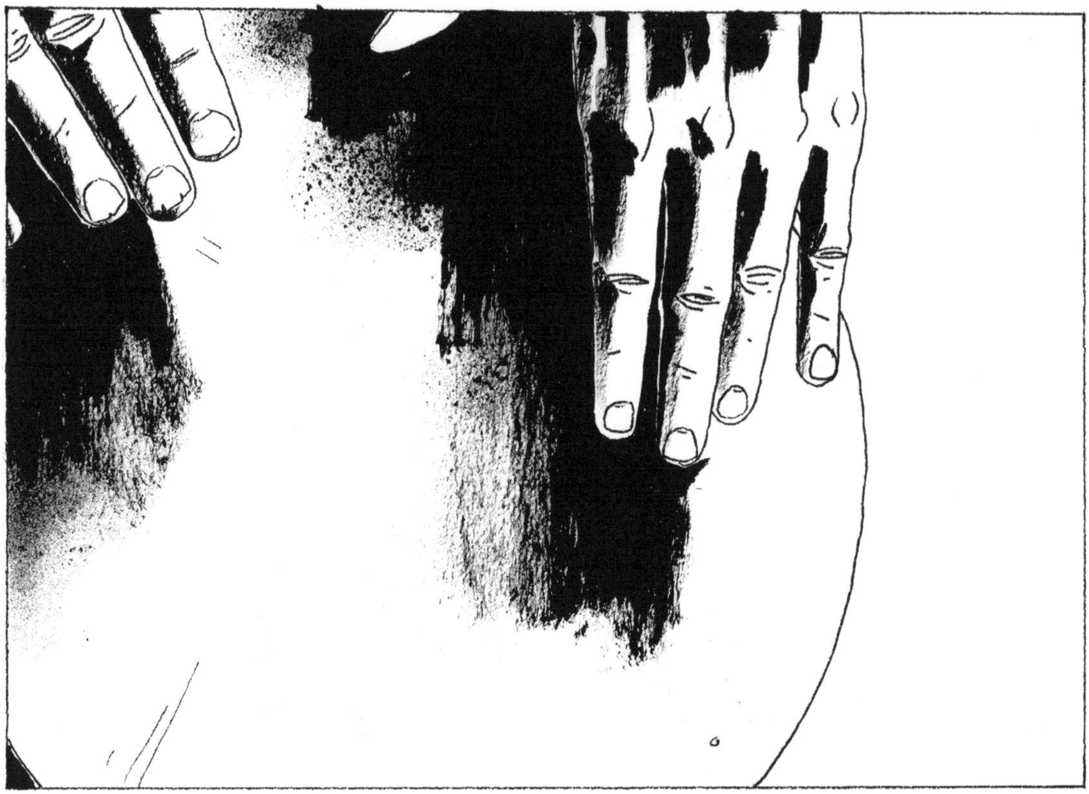
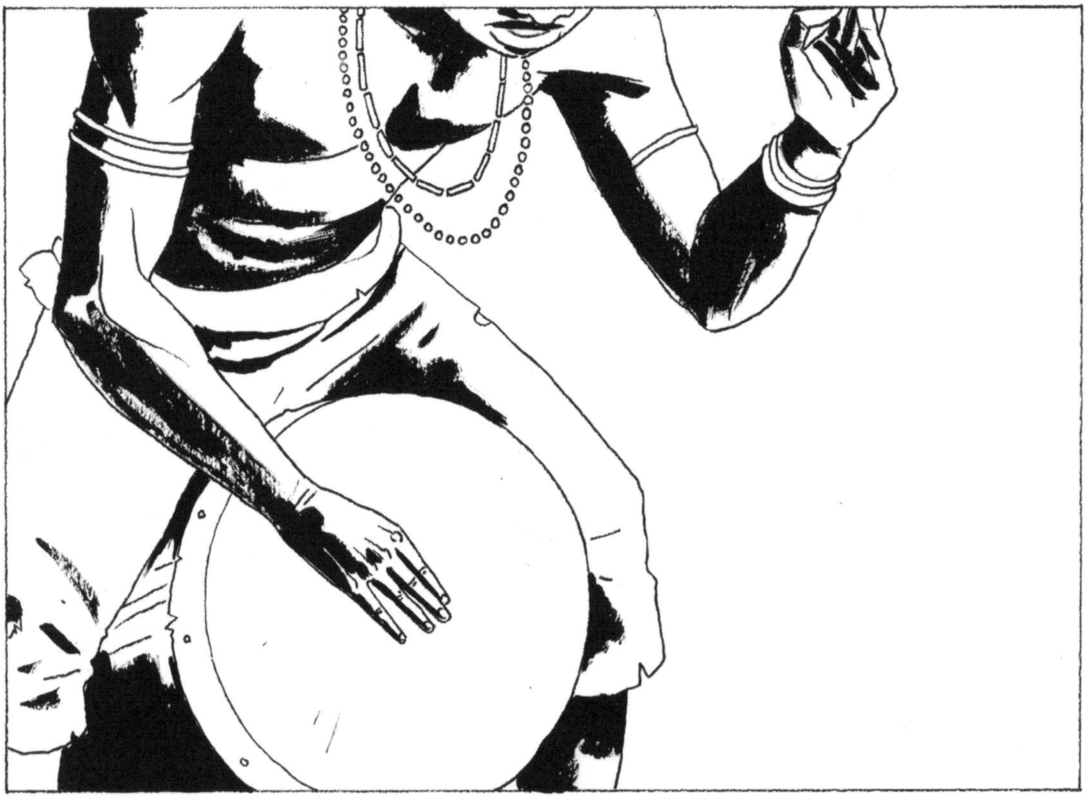

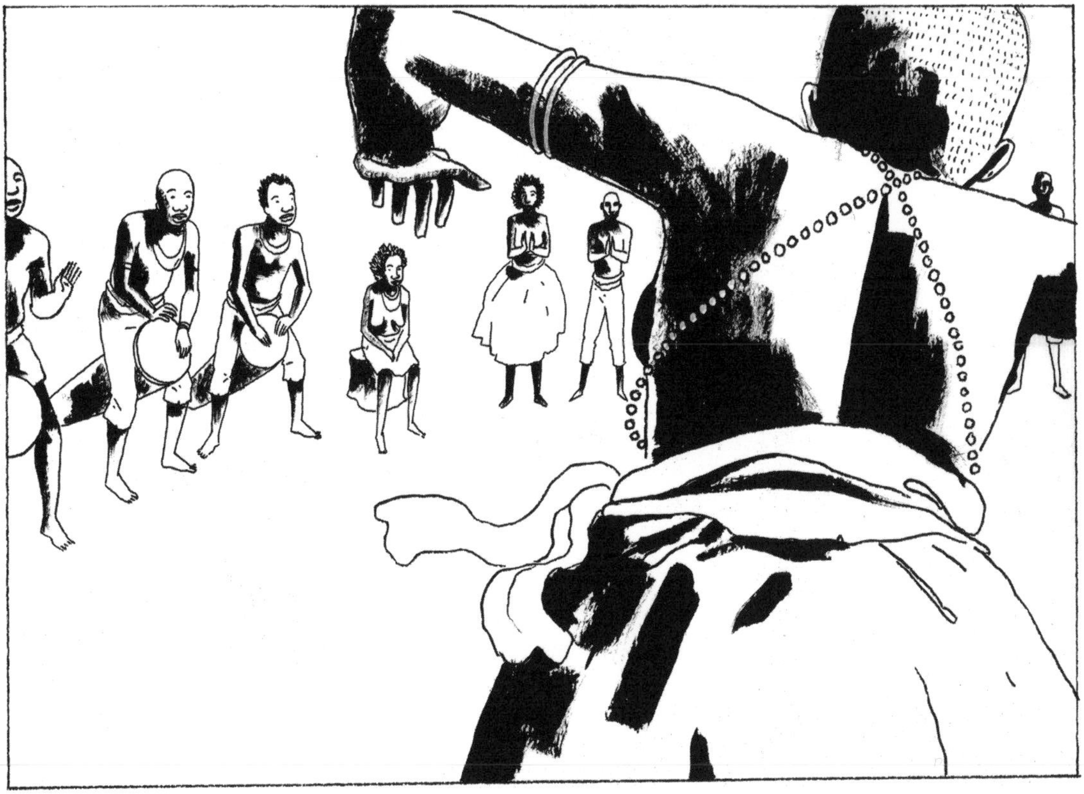

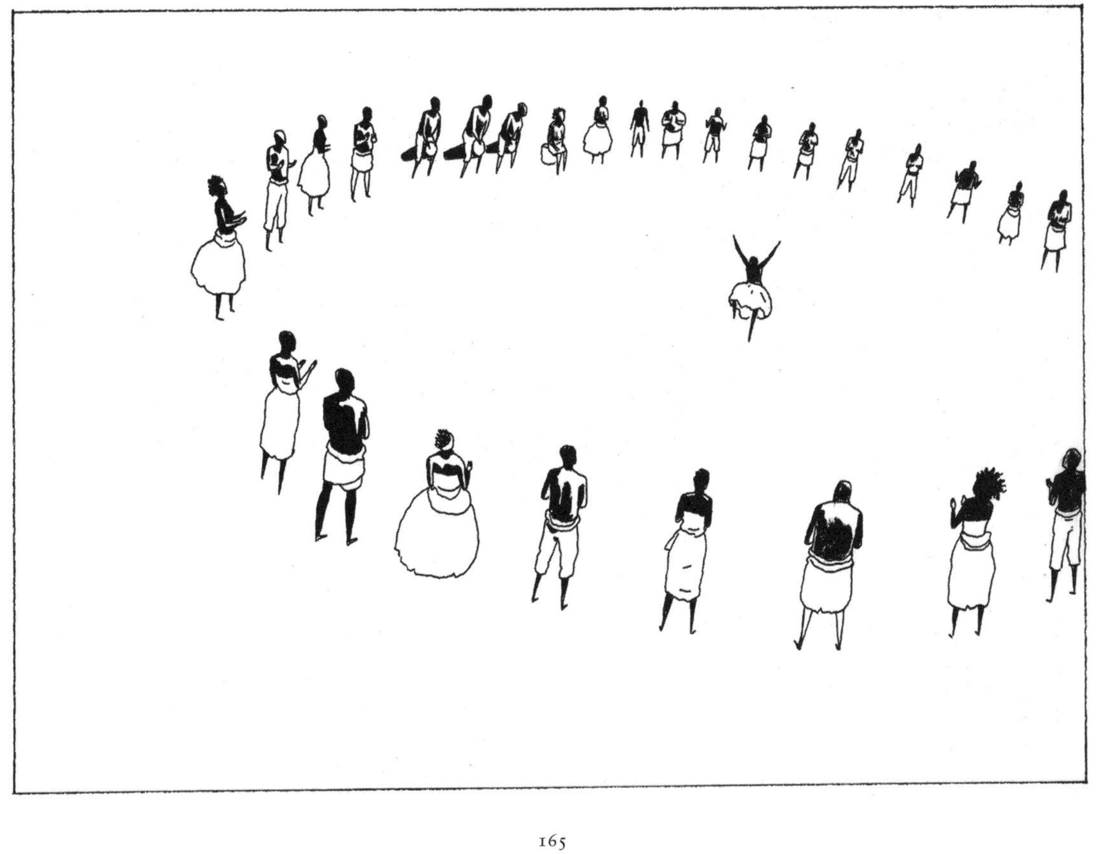

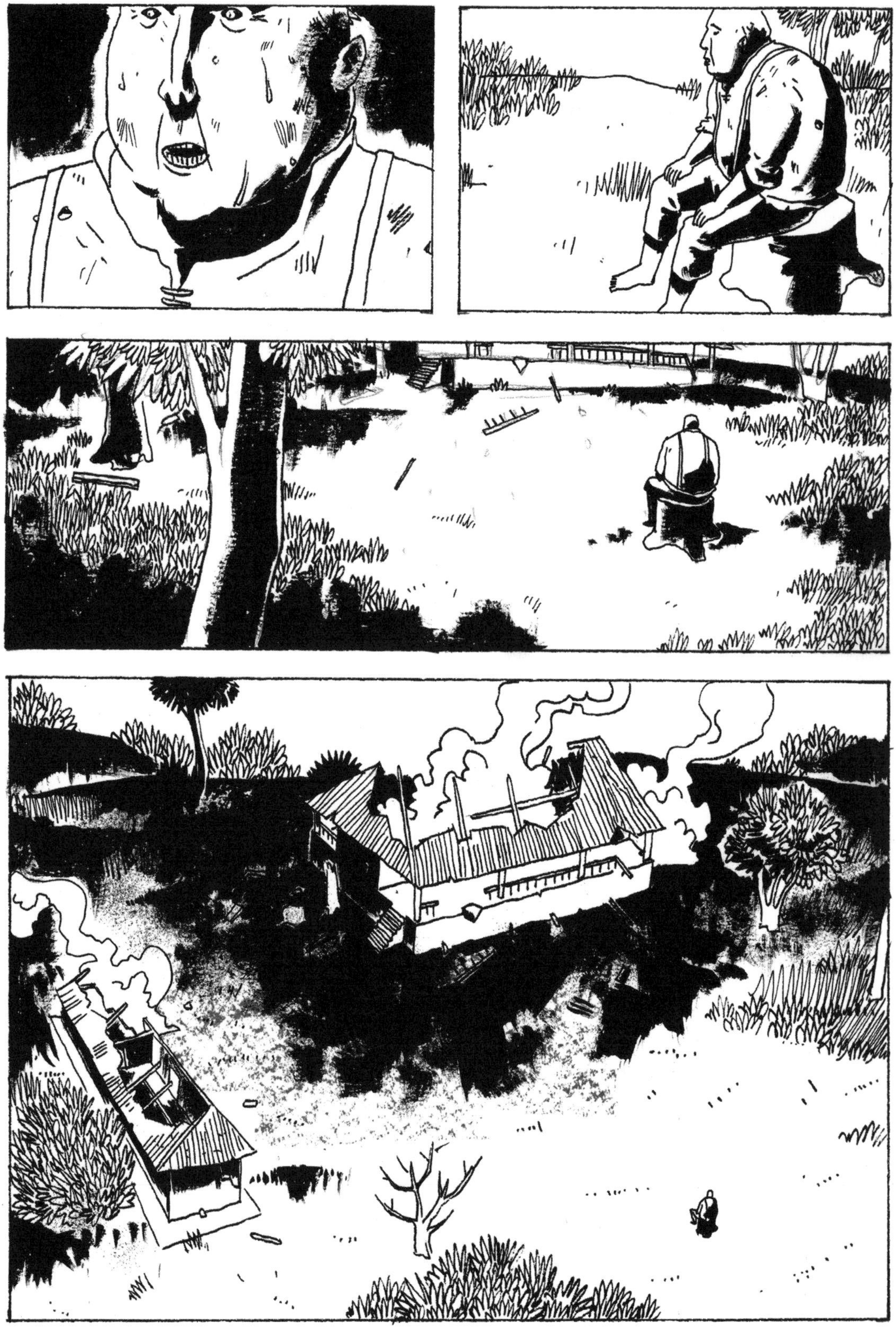

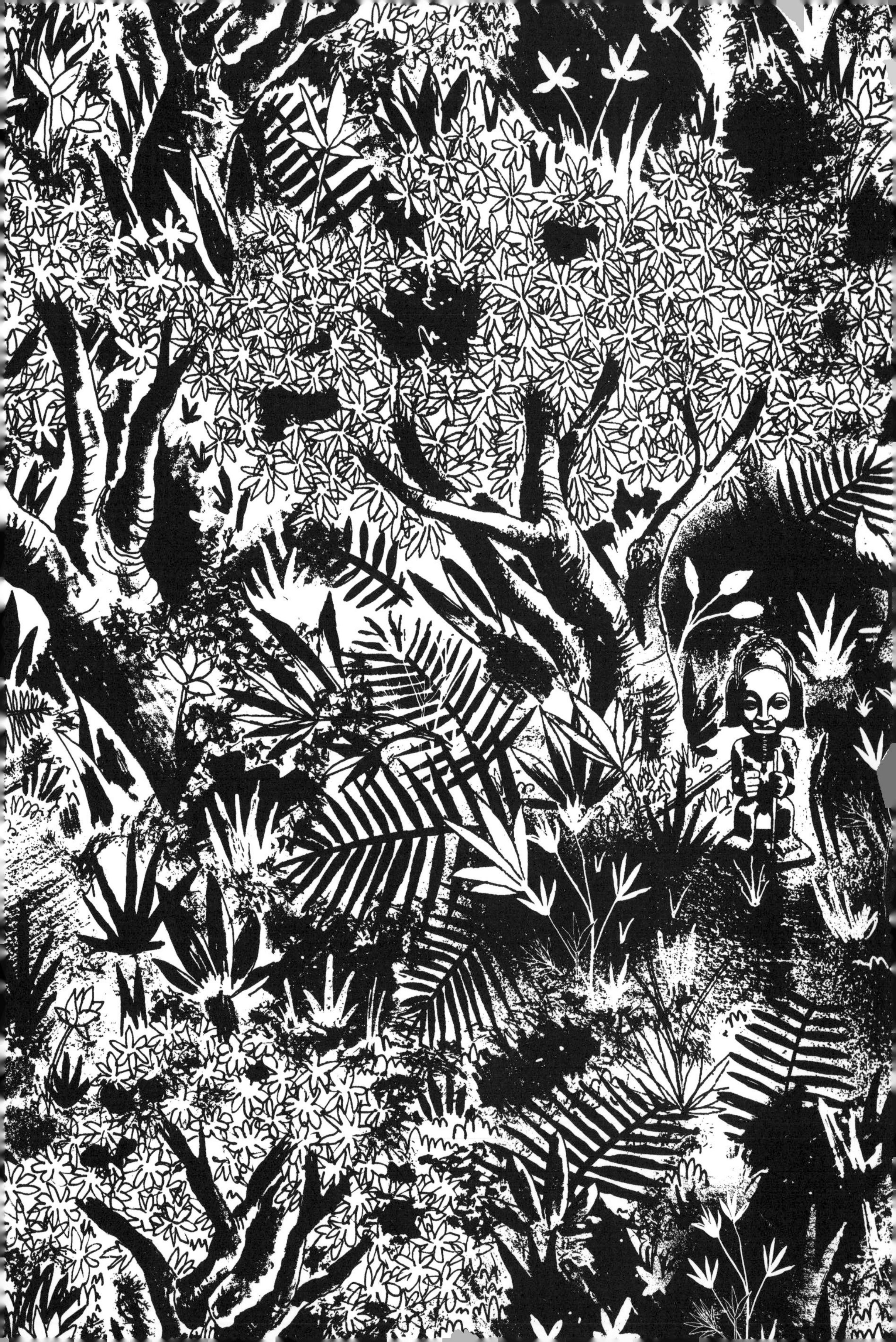

GLOSSARY

CABINDAN DESIGN (p. 91). The tortoise is a frequent subject of Cabindan art, with the patterns on its shell reproduced in woven mats and other objects. For the Cabindan people, it is an ancient symbol. It represents resistance because its shell, is an emblem of defense; and, as pioneering anthropologist José Redinha notes, independence and adaptability, because it's "carrying one's home, one's wife, with one, and seeking only what is necessary."

CHIBINDA ILUNGA (p. 106). The sculpture beside the old woman in "Cumbe" depicts Chibinda Ilunga, a mythical African king and hero. According to one legend, Chibinda (meaning "hunter") was captured by some warriors from the kingdom of Lunda when he was hunting in their realm. Though the members of the court voted to put the intruder to death, the beautiful queen Lueji (Lua) was charmed by the young man's beauty and asked that he be placed on her farm as a slave. In time, Lueji surprised the court by announcing her marriage to Chibinda Ilunga, shattering the taboo that prohibited vassals from marrying nobles. This led the royal family to revolt against the queen, but it also marked the beginning of the expansion of the Lunda kingdom, which became a great empire spanning territory that today belongs to Angola, Zambia, and Congo (see Peter Junge's *Arte da África* [*African Art*]).

CUMBE (p. 130). The word *cumbe*, a synonym of *quilombo*, is a term used in some Latin American countries to refer to settlements on the Brazilian hinterlands inhabited by people of African descent, primarily runaway slaves. In the Congo-Angola languages, it also means sun, day, fire, the force inherent in kings' power, and the way to sketch out and understand life and history (see Robert Slenes's *"Malungu, ngoma vem!": África coberta e descoberta do* Brasil [*"Malungu, ngoma vem": Africa hidden and discovered in Brazil*]). According to Nei Lopes, it comes from the Kimbundu word *kumbi*, which is related to the Umbundu *ekumbi* [*sun*].

KALUNGA (page 12). Nei Lopes, in his *Novo Dicionário Banto do Brasil* [*New Bantu Dictionary of Brazil*], lists various meanings for this Bantu word: a small doll, a mouse, a stick-figure drawing of a person, the doll in *maracatu* performances, death, a black man, and many other things. "The multilinguistic Bantu word *kalunga* encompasses the idea of grandness, immensity, referring to God, the sea, death." Maria Helena Figueiredo Lima, in her *Nação Ovambo* [*Ovambo Nation*], writes, "The word *kalunga* [God], from the verb *oku-lunga* [to be expert, intelligent], is found in the Ambo dialect and other neighboring groups. The prefix ka- appears here without its usual diminutive function. Instead, it affirms something that is important, large, valuable."

LUNDA-QUIOCO IDEOGRAM (p. 11). According to José Redinha, this Lunda-Quioco symbol represents a nest and two birds. It evokes sheltered expectancy and freedom from the outside world. Ideograms of this sort combine fables and riddles and set out the rules of mathematical games. From the Democratic Republic of the Congo to southern Luanda, these ideograms were drawn in the sand, on trees, on people's bodies, or on leather. For centuries, they were used during or before storytelling rituals, and they also teach values related to the shared economy and environment.

MALUNGO (p. 136). Companion. Specifically, it was the term used by slaves to address each other during their crossings on the slave ships. The word comes from the Bantu words for boat, such as *lungo* (Kikongo) and *ulungu* (Kimbundu). Antenor Nascentes, in his *Dicionário etimológico resumido* [*Abridged Etymological Dictionary*], identifies its origin as being *ma'luga*, a Kimbundu word for comrade, companion. But Renato Mendonça, in *his Influência africana no português do Brasil* [*African Influence in Brazilian Portuguese*], suggests that the word may come from *man'ugo* [neighbor].

MOCAMBO (p. 136). Antônio Geraldo da Cunha's *Dicionário etimológico da língua portuguesa* [*Etymological Dictionary of the Portuguese Language*] indicates that the word's origin is in the Kimbundu *mu'kamu* [hiding place]. But, according to Nei Lopes, it comes from the Kikongo *mukambu*, "rooftop, hut, in reference to the primary characteristic of this kind of dwelling: the thatched roof." Whatever the case, in Brazil, the word became, mainly among whites, another word (along with *cumbe* and *quilombo*) for a runaway slave community.

NSANGA (p. 29). A vital plant in the beliefs of the Bakongo and Umbundu peoples. It was used to reinvigorate political forces and support personnel, rebel leaders, and movements. According to Nei Lopes, it is a "medicinal plant used in ritual practices in Bantu candomblés—probably from the Kigongo term *nsánga*, a gourd with medicinal and magical potions." It was, claims Robert Slenes in *Nsanga: a árvore de nsanga transplantada* [*Nsanga: transplanting the nsanga tree*], an essential element in old cults of Kongo ethnicity in Brazil. *Nsanga* is also a war dance—in some places, the dance that is done after a battle in which no one was killed or injured. "While participation was a demonstration of group loyalty to the officiating ruler, individuals also exhibited their dexterity in their own *nsanga* solos against imaginary foes in attempts to outshine their rivals for the praise of the ruler," writes T. J. Desch-Obi in "Combat and the Crossing of the Kalunga" (in *Central Africans and Cultural Transformations in the American Diaspora*, edited by Linda M. Heywood). Cavazzi de Montecúccolo, in his *Descrição histórica dos três reinos do Congo, Matamba e Angola* [*Historical Description of the Three Kingdoms of the Congo, Matamba, and Angola*], says that, the meaning of *nsanga* "would be 'to have faith' or 'to exhibit faithfulness.'" *Nsanga* also means "sister" and "necklace" (hence the word *miçanga*, "glass bead").

QUIBUNGO (p. 142). In the Kimbundu language it means "wolf." In Brazil, it refers to a mythical creature that is half animal and half person, with a hole in the middle of its back where it keeps its captives. The hole opens when the *quibungo* lowers its head and closes when it raises it. According to Nei Lopes, the word comes from the Kimbundu language, from a cross between *kimbungu* [wolf] and *kibungu* [clever]. Several stories about the *quibungo* were collected by Nina Rodrigues in *Os africanos no Brasil* [*Africans in Brazil*].

SCARIFICATION (p. 107). Marks of initiation and belonging made on any part of the body, including the feet, face, back, and skull. Related to tattoos. The technique is not unique to Africa, but it is especially important for marking fraternities, exile, dedication, and membership in groups or associations, which are demonstrated through the use of intentional scarring on the faces and chests of slaves and *quilombo* residents.

SLAVE MARKET (p. 108). The first frame on this page depicts the Mercado da Ribeira in Olinda, Pernambuco. This market, built at the end of the seventeenth century, was a place for the buying and selling of enslaved Africans. The architecture reflects a number of characteristics typical of this kind of building, including windows reinforced with bars and a wide courtyard for displaying captives.

SUMIDOURO (p. 69). A deep well that was believed to be linked to an underground river. "Therefore, the term was used to refer to the place where rebellious slaves disappeared, as insurrection was punishable by death," says Clóvis Moura in his *Dicionário da escravidão negra no Brasil* [*Dictionary of black slavery in Brazil*]. Vicente Salles, in *O negro no Pará* [*Blacks in Pará*], discusses various *sumidouros* that existed in that state, including one inside the main church of the town of Vigia. The term also appears in the vissungo songs written down by Aires Machado Filho, and it was sung by Geraldo Filme in "O canto dos escravos" ["Slave Song"].

TATA (p. 12). In Bantu, it means "father." A term of respect, it indicates wisdom, life experience, knowledge of secrets. It is therefore used as an honorific for a father, grandfather, wise older man, or priest. Manoel Congo, a blacksmith and the leader of the nineteenth-century black revolt in Vassouras, in the province Rio de Janeiro, was also known as Tata.

VISSUNGO (p. 62). A work song with metaphorical lyrics, according to Clóvis Moura's *Dicionário da escravidão* [*Dictionary of Slavery*]. Often used by the blacks of Minas Gerais to communicate without being understood by whites. The lines "Ei oia lá/ô minino Mané no uandá..." were collected by Aires Machado Filho, and were sung to rock babies in one's arms. They mean, "The child Mané in the hammock, little Mané in the hammock."

ZAGAIA (p. 96). An African spear used in hunting, fishing, and war.

BIBLIOGRAPHY

ARAÚJO, Emanoel (curator). *Para nunca esquecer* (exhibition catalog). Museu Histórico Nacional, 2002.

FURTADO, Júnia Ferreira and Libby, Douglas C. *Trabalho livre, trabalho escravo: Brasil e Europa, século XVII e XIX.* Annablume, 2006.

HEYWOOD, Linda M. (ed.). *Central Africans and Cultural Transformations in the American Diaspora.* Cambridge University Press, 2002

JUNGE, Peter (curator). *Arte da África: obras primas do Museu Etnológico de Berlim* (exhibition catalog). Centro Cultural Banco do Brasil, 2003.

LONG, Carolyn Morrow. *Spiritual Merchants: Religion, Magic, and Commerce.* University of Tennessee Press, 2001.

LOPES, Nei. *Bantos, malês e identidade negra. Forense universitária,* 1988.
_____. *Enciclopédia brasileira da diáspora africana.* Selo Negro, 2004.
_____. *Novo dicionário banto do Brasil.* Pallas, 2006.

MACHADO, Aires da Mata. *O negro e o garimpo em Minas Gerais.* Itatiaia, 1985.

MONTECÚCCOLO, João Antonio Cavazzi de. *Descrição histórica dos três reinos do Congo, Matamba e Angola.* Junta de Investigações do Ultramar, 1965.

MOURA, Carlos Eugênio Marcondes. *A travessia da Kalunga Grande.* EDUSP, 2000.

MOURA, Clóvis. *Dicionário da escravidão negra no Brasil.* EDUSP, 2004.

OBI, Thomas J. Desch. *Fighting for Honor: The History of African Martial Art Traditions in the Atlantic World.* University of South Carolina Press, 2008.

QUEIRÓS, Suely Robles Reis. *Escravidão negra em São Paulo.* Livraria José Olímpio, 1977.

REDINHA, José. *Etnias e culturas de Angola.* Instituto de Investigação Científica de Angola, 1974.

RODRIGUES, Nina. *Os africanos no Brasil.* Editora Nacional, 1982.

SALLES, Vicente. *O negro no Pará.* Universidade Federal do Pará/Fundação Getúlio Vargas, 1971.

SLENES, Robert. *"Malungu, ngoma vem!" África coberta e descoberta do Brasil.* Revista USP, n. 12, December 1991.
_____. *Na senzala uma flor: esperanças e recordações da família escrava.* Nova Fronteira, 1999.

BIOGRAPHY

MARCELO D'SALETE IS an acclaimed Brazilian cartoonist, illustrator, and teacher. He has a master's degree in art history from the University of São Paulo.

Photo by Hudson Rodrigues.

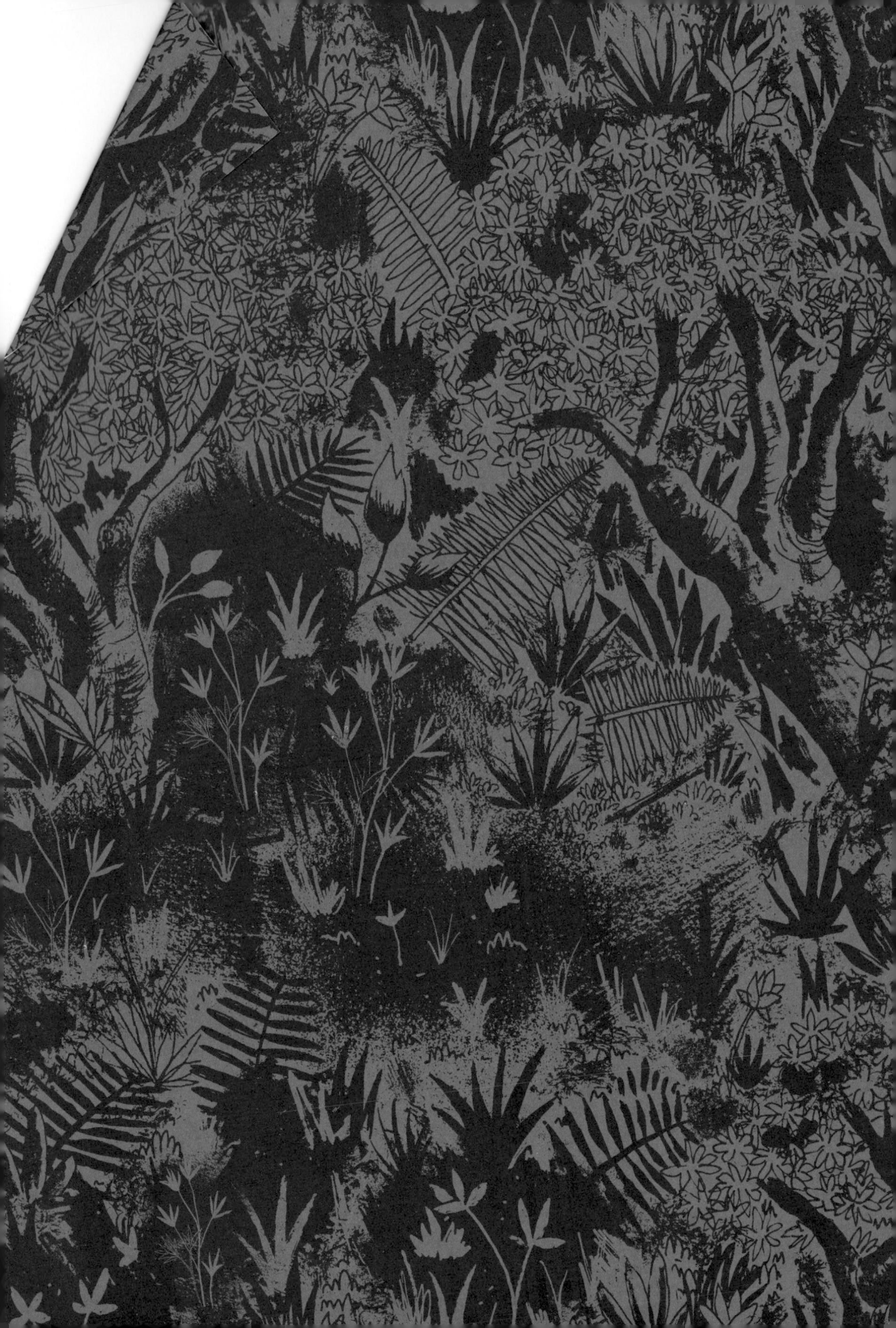